PERSON / PLANET

Other books by Theodore Roszak

Editor and contributor

THEODORE ROSZAK

PERSON / PLANET

THE CREATIVE DISINTEGRATION OF INDUSTRIAL SOCIETY

ANCHOR PRESS/DOUBLEDAY

GARDEN CITY, NEW YORK

1978

Lines from "The Second Coming" from *Collected Poems of William Butler Yeats* copyright © 1924 by Macmillan Publishing Company, Inc., renewed 1952 by Bertha Georgie Yeats. Used by permission of Macmillan Publishing Company, Inc., M. B. Yeats, Miss Anne Yeats and the Macmillan Company of Basingstoke and London.

Library of Congress Cataloging in Publication Data

Roszak, Theodore, 1933–
Person/planet: the creative disintegration of industrial society.

Includes bibliographical references and notes.
  1. Social history—20th century. 2. Social psychology. 3. Human ecology. 4. Individuality.
I. Title.
HN16.R63   301.1
ISBN: 0-385-00063-4
Library of Congress Catalog Card Number 75-6165

To Lewis Mumford

who taught me
my loyalty to the person and
the planet

Contents

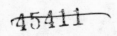

Each of us inevitable
Each of us limitless . . .
Each of us here as divinely as any is here

Walt Whitman

You and I . . .
we meet as strangers, each carrying a mystery within us. I
cannot say who you are; I may never know you completely. But
I trust that you are a person in your own right, possessed of a
beauty and value that are the Earth's richest treasures.

So I make this promise to you:
I will impose no identities upon you, but will invite you to become
yourself without shame or fear.
I will hold open a space for you in the world and defend your
right to fill it with an authentic vocation.
For as long as your search takes, you have my loyalty.

PERSON / PLANET

Introduction:
Things Fall Apart

Things fall apart; the center cannot hold;
Mere anarchy is loosed upon the world

So William Butler Yeats lamented in one of the more famous apocalyptic pronouncements of the twentieth century.

But sometimes societies fall apart in ways that release life-affirming energies. And what may look like anarchy from the viewpoint of the established cultural center may be the troubled birth of a new, more humanly becoming social order. There are creative, as well as destructive, forms of disintegration.

This book concerns itself with the point at which human psychology and natural ecology meet. My purpose is to suggest that the environmental anguish of the Earth has entered our lives as a radical transformation of human identity. The needs of the planet and the needs of the person have become one, and together they have begun to act upon the central institutions of our society with a force that is profoundly subversive, but which carries within it the promise of cultural renewal.

In following this line of argument, I will be expanding an investigation of contemporary social dissent that I began with the writing of *The Making of a Counter Culture* somewhere in the mid-sixties. In that work, I found myself siding with those who saw the disruptions that were then unsettling American society as, on balance, a welcome liberation of moral passion and imaginative vitality. It seemed that what was falling apart—or at least being roughly shaken—was an ominous, world-wide technocratic system which the governing elites of the advanced industrial societies had been assiduously rigging up since the end of World War II. I may have pressed the analysis further than others by observing that the ris-

ing forces of dissent, in their search for the root causes of our public ills, were probing well beyond the immediate issues of war and
social justice; they seemed intent upon subjecting many of our
most closely guarded psychological commitments and subliminal
cultural orthodoxies to critical examination. All about us, the popular art and music of the young were flirting with notions of consciousness expansion, therapeutic madness, alternative realities. No
question but that these were bizarre and dangerous forces to invoke, but there was sufficient reason why social dissent should run
to such extremes.

In a technocratic society—so I suggested—political authority is
based upon a mystique of scientific expertise. That is what supposedly guarantees the competence of the state and private corporations to keep an intricate industrial economy functioning. If people are to acquiesce in that mystique, they must pledge their deep
psychic allegiance to the world view of modern science and the industrial disciplines that support the myth of progress. Since this
demands a severe distortion of human nature (it is the essential
act of alienation), I identified it as a serious internal contradiction
of the urban-industrial system. But it is not a contradiction that
can easily be translated into any of the traditional ideologies of
protest, because those who refuse to submit to that distortion must
do more than challenge the integrity of their society's politics; they
must call into question the going standard of sanity, the established criteria of knowledge, our collective state of soul. At
their hands, the whole human personality, body, soul, and spirit,
must be brought into the arena of dissent as a critical counterpoise
to the diminished range of experience to which urban-industrialism
limits our awareness. In brief, they must create a politics of consciousness.

Since that book was published in 1969, I cannot remember a
year that has passed when the same inevitable question has not
come up a score of times, at public lectures and in private conver-
sations: "Whatever became of the counter culture?" One news-
weekly magazine began asking me that within three months of the
book's appearance, and then phoned regularly over the next five
years every time there was a lull on the college campuses—as if

perhaps I might be keeping the fever chart of late adolescent protest in America. Usually, those who asked the question were working from the book title and pure hearsay, which led them to assume that I had written a piece of reportage on the agitational
turmoil, the fads and fashions that preoccupied the college-aged
young of the later sixties. In reality, after its first chapter or so,
The Making of a Counter Culture had little to do with the young,
with campus matters, or even with the pressing political issues of
that period. Rather, it was primarily a study of more far-reaching
cultural transformations which focused on the campuses of
America only insofar as they had become the sounding board for
some highly heretical ideas about nature, knowledge, and human
needs. Whatever busy journalists and hasty phrasemongers have
seen fit to make of the term since it has left my hands (and I have
often cringed at the misuses), my specific characterization of the
counter culture was to present it as an episode in the history of
consciousness that unfolds in two stages. First, there is the almost
instinctive impulse to disaffiliate from technocratic politics and
from the scientific style of consciousness on which the technocracy draws to legitimize its power. Second, there is the search—
at once both desperate and gleeful—for a new reality principle to
replace the waning authority of science and industrial necessity.

"Whatever became of the counter culture?" If simple and spontaneous disaffiliation is what we have in mind when we ask the
question, then, to a significant degree, the counter culture has become less visible over the past decade only because it has dissolved
into its surrounding social medium. As a prevailing mood of disgust and discontent, it has spread well beyond the campus consti-
uency where it first announced its presence and has infiltrated
American society, if not Western society as a whole—though in
ways that are still mostly bewildered and embittered. This is what
underlies the commonplace skepticism that opinion makers and
the general public now openly voice toward the institutions, the
leadership, the basic premises and promises of their society. The
vile accusations that young protestors once had to run shouting in
the streets to make known now hover routinely over the news of
the day as a dominant, often paralytic atmosphere of negativity

and distrust. It is as if the dissenting outsiders of a decade ago served as the Distant Early Warning System for what Vietnam, Watergate, the revelations of officially sanctioned FBI and CIA criminality, the scandals of corporate fraud and corruption, the energy crisis, incurable inflation and unemployment, chronic economic dislocation, the deterioration of our cities, the relentless degradation of the environment have finally proved to everyone. Namely: that you can't trust the power structure, that the experts are knaves and fakers, that the promise of unlimited material progress and universal affluence is a lie, that the economy is an inhuman machinery operated by rogues and blunderers, that the system is running out of control. Cynicism, especially toward those in positions of corporate power and official authority, was one of the grim and angry lessons of counter cultural protest; now it has so swiftly pervaded the public temperament that its very omnipresence may make it difficult for many to register that fact as a victory—if a sad victory—for the social dissent of the sixties.

There are a few observers, however, who have discerned how the campuses served to disseminate a new spirit of skepticism and distrust. Daniel Yankelovich and his research associates, one of the more reliable polling organizations, were convinced at the end of the sixties that it would take "decades and perhaps generations" for the counter cultural values of the "forerunner college group" to work their way into the general mass of the population, if they would ever do so at all. But, as of the mid-seventies, Yankelovich and his pollsters were forced to revise their conclusion and to admit that "we are amazed by the rapidity with which this process is now taking place, by its complexity, and by the problems of adaption it poses to the institutions of the society." All their indicators showed that the unorthodox values "formerly confined to a minority of college youth"—values that represent a sharp decline in patriotic allegiance, political trust, careerist ambition—had achieved "an astonishingly swift transmission" to noncollege youth and had "now spread throughout the generation." "The enduring heritage of the 1960s," Yankelovich suggests, "is the new social values that grew on the nation's campuses during that same fateful period and now have grown stronger and more powerful."

But cynicism and disaffection are only half the story of the counter culture—the first half, the initial act of outraged and desperate rejection. Beyond the "no" there has been a "yes" emerging, the affirmation of a vision of life that belongs to a continuing, subterranean current of unorthodox thought and art which reaches back in Western society at least to the Romantic movement, if not into far older traditions. That is why *The Making of a Counter Culture* and its sequel, *Where the Wasteland Ends,* have so much to do with religious tradition and the psychology of science, with rhapsodic poetry and nature mysticism. My interest and conviction have been with those dissenting elements who have climbed aboard William Blake's chariot of fire to join his "mental fight" against the total secularization and scientization of modern culture. For theirs is the struggle to expand our conception of human personhood beyond anything that industrial necessity can tolerate or scientific intellect comprehend.

If we grant that counter cultural disaffiliation carries over into the search for a new image of nature and human identity by which to guide our lives, then we can see its more creative, ongoing repercussions in the many "New Age" religions, in the human potential and personal growth therapies, and in the various "consciousness movements" that have proliferated over the past ten years—as well as in the widespread search for a humanly scaled economics which has taken up the slogan "small is beautiful" and which may yet lead us to an ecologically intelligent, if not reverent, relationship with the natural environment. Here, again, these positive values have been scattered like seeds beyond the former college-aged minority into the culture at large. As Hans Dreitzel observes, in speaking of the "search for identity and authenticity on the personal level,"

such values are gradually becoming optional for a much larger part of the population in regard to *the organization of their private, everyday lives.* . . . Today the youth movement of the sixties has initiated a general search for a new integration of the moral, religious, and aesthetic dimensions of life which threatens the psychological credibility of the industrial system. And it is by no means sure that the political structure will, in the long run, be able to integrate the emerging new values via their devaluation as cultural products on an inflationary market.

I call this insistent quest for personal growth and spiritual fulfillment "positive"—but I do so advisedly, in full recognition of the mindless and meretricious nonsense one can find mixed throughout this burgeoning range of religious and therapeutic experimentation, as well as in the funky chic merchandise and life styles that seek to present themselves as "simple living." But I find myself far more concerned by the indiscriminate hostility that has been voiced against even the finest of these efforts in academic and intellectual circles by critics (often scandalously misinformed critics) who seem determined to see nothing new under the sun that is not folly and fraudulence.

I will comment on this backlash from the intellectual mainstream later in this work. Here, I will only mention the rule of thumb which I used in a recent study (*Unfinished Animal*) that surveyed the new religions, the humanistic and transpersonal therapies, and consciousness research generally, for it expresses the spirit that guides me still. I insisted that one must discriminate between the authenticity of the needs people express and the inadequacy of the material that may be offered to meet those needs. For to use the sins of charlatans as an excuse to mock the spiritual and moral needs of people is no better than to despise hungry people for eating the adulterated food that scoundrels have sold them. This is a cruel and senseless line of criticism—one that I suspect could only be taken by those whose real intention is to enforce an even tighter censorship upon our personal and transcendent longings. Otherwise, obviously, the duty of those who would criticize is not simply to denigrate the vices they see, but to offer something better and wiser to take their place.

What I see in these psychospiritual explorations that deserves to be regarded as positive is their protest against the human underdevelopment that has for so long characterized urban-industrial society, for all its world-beating claims to progress and cultural supremacy. In that protest, there is a yearning for growth, for authenticity, for largeness of experience which finds itself thwarted by the cultural orthodoxies that have shaped us all into this diminished and nervously compulsive being called modern man. It is that yearning I wish to focus upon in this book, as I attempt to give the counter cultural sensibility a broader and more pervasive place in the history of our time than can be contained in any one group or movement or political episode. I want to talk about that sensibility as I believe it most generally and consequentially enters the daily experience of people in their homes, their schools, their jobs, in all their transactions with official authority and corporate power. And this is not in some fully conscious and articulate way, as they might learn about "alienation in the modern world" in a university classroom or social movement or therapeutic session. Rather, it comes to them as a deeply unsettling encounter with *false identity* . . . as a sense of being cramped into some pre-existing social slot which simply will not adapt to their shape.

Essentially, before it inspired any political formulations, this is the experience that ignited the campus rebellions of the sixties —though (students being students, and their teachers being teachers) it was often quickly translated into heavy social analysis and issued to the world in manifestos. But the root of the matter was that a generation of peculiarly sensitive young people (or pampered and spoiled kids, if you prefer) found themselves being subtly maneuvered into careers and social roles, into tastes and values, into an all-encompassing sense of reality which had been prefabricated for them by the commanding powers of a high industrial economy. They discovered that they were being systematically processed and adapted—*used* by faceless forces, insensitive institutions which did not know who they were and did not care to know. Something was being stolen from them . . . what to call it? Their souls . . . their selves . . . their right to do their own thing. And to this, despite the rewards for compliance, they (or enough of them) said "No!" in a loud, public way—in fact, every bit as riotously as the black young in the ghettos of America were rising up in rebellion against the false racial identity which white society had prefabricated for them.

The style and directness of the coercion which these two insurgent groups confronted was widely different—different enough to place them on two distinct political horizons. The blacks and other nonwhite minorities were up against familiar, obviously brutal forms of social domination and police oppression; white middle-class college youth were up against something new. They were faced with highly refined forms of technocratic manipulation that played upon subliminal levels of acquiescence by way of well-disguised bribes and threats, images of authority and expertise, intangible kinds of psychological pressure and leverage. But the two populations had this much in common: Here were people who had drawn a line and at last insisted on their right to determine their own identities. They were demanding that the big, busy world slow down and wait for them to make that determination, and they seriously expected that, once they had, their society would make a generously comfortable space for them in all their unabashed angularity. They would live, love, dress, speak, work (or not work) as they chose. They would make their own music, dance to their own rhythm. They would become gypsies, mendicants, savages, witch doctors, rebels, clowns, freaks, and they would do so openly, in the streets and parks, asking nobody's permission, making no apologies.

Grant the obvious: that some of this rebellious self-advertisement weakened toward *culte de moi* bohemianism, and that there were those who too gullibly allowed their gestures of defiance to be exploited and cheapened by the media. Were not such false starts only to be expected, once the passion for authenticity became something bigger than an esoteric anguish of great artists and gifted philosophers, once it was brought out of the closet of high academic culture and into the streets as a public issue? Let "ordinary" people once get wind of the importance of self-knowledge and personal autonomy, and they are all too likely to think that idea has something to do with taking themselves very seriously, brooding over their tastes and motivations, delving into their experience, rebelliously asserting their peculiarities—in short,

becoming, in one degree or another, what others will then de-
nounce as "egocentric," "narcissistic," "self-absorbed." Just as,
once people are taught that there are howling injustices in their society, they may (if they are young and impressionable) conclude
that this has something to do with protesting, making trouble, raising hell—which will then expose them to the charge of being dis-
courteous. Contretemps of this kind were all the more likely
to occur on the part of a war-distressed younger generation when
it turned out that what many of their teachers meant by the pursuit
of self-knowledge was an upper-division course in Cartesian epistemology, and what they had in mind in the way of social justice
was a well-researched term paper on the civil rights movement.

So, in these early public gestures of self-determination, there
was a brashness, a vulgarity, a youthful impetuosity that proved
widely offensive. Even so, there was enough honesty and imagination to the effort—above all there was enough moral substance to
the issue—to have a historical effect. A fissure had been opened in
the great stone wall of the technocracy, and through it an image of
personal autonomy slipped out into the surrounding society that
rapidly heightened everybody's awareness of the false identities
that have been imposed upon our lives. And then the questions
began to mount—questions for which no social leadership has yet
found answers that will still the insistent public doubt: "Who has
the right to define the meaning of black or white, masculine or
feminine, old or young, sane or mad? By what authority are these
roles assigned to us? Whose purpose does it serve that we should
act out these prepared scripts? When do our lives become our own
to make and live as we decide?"

Here, then, if we view the matter in its most general manifes-
tation, is where the drama of contemporary disaffiliation begins:
with just this painfully intense experience of *being a person* in a
world that despises our personhood, a world whose policy is to
grind personhood down into rubble, and then to remold the pieces
into obedient, efficient, and, of course, cheerful personnel. It is the
experience of being shown what we are told is our image in a mirror society holds up to us, and then discovering that this is no mirror at all, but a crude, mass-produced composite photograph bear-

ing our name . . . or perhaps our number. So we draw back and say, "No! That is not *me*. That is not who I am." With that gesture of refusal, even if it is only a passing moment of inner hesitation, the world begins to lose the energy and allegiance it must have of us if it is to continue being this urban-industrial colossus we now inhabit. We live in a time when the very private experience of having a personal identity to discover, a personal destiny to fulfill, has become a subversive political force of major proportions.

And that is how things fall apart for us. But the "anarchy" that threatens to ensue may offer a remarkable cultural possibility: that of a postindustrial society whose highest social value is the project of self-discovery, whose principal wealth is the richness of the autonomous personality. What sort of world would we have to create to defend that project, to cultivate that richness? It is hardly enough to say it must be smaller, less industrial and urban, more decentralized and participative—though all of this may be true enough. But the violations of personhood to which people have grown sensitive reach down to the most basic and universal institutions of all social life—to the family, the school, the workplace. That is what finally stands behind the problems we perceive statistically as the soaring rate of divorce, increasing truancy in the schools, rising absenteeism and turnover in the plants and factories. At bottom, these resolve themselves into the crisis of personal identity played out in the lives of millions of ordinary and anonymous people who will no longer tolerate being what ordinary and anonymous people have always been: children who will be what their parents and teachers tell them good children are supposed to be, men and women who grow up to become the husbands and fathers, wives and mothers they have been socially programmed to become, workers who will stick at forms of alienated labor that bore or burden them to death. There is a point at which the need for self-discovery, in search of maximum latitude, not only challenges the institutions of the urban-industrial technocracy but calls into question a collective authority over individual choice and conduct that has been jealously guarded by every society. Yet, we will follow this inquiry to that seemingly indispensable minimum of conformity, where even parental responsibility, sex roles, the so-cialization of the young, the division of labor, the demands of economic necessity are called upon to justify themselves before the rights of the person.

These, I hope, are the larger issues we can keep in view as we investigate a search for personal authenticity which has entered so deeply into our popular culture that it has already been widely exploited for commercial and manipulative purposes. Doubtless, any number of ephemeral fascinations could be assimilated to the thesis I develop here: the endless succession of self-examination manuals that appear in the drugstore bookstalls, "pop psych" weekend workshops in self-development, newspaper horoscopes, magazine personality inventories, the spate of mass-produced "personalized" commodities that fill every shopping center. The confessional musicals (*Chorus Line, Runaways, Working*) that are Broadway's current fashion are popular blossoms from the same personalist seed. Even an adolescent craze like punk rock, which trivializes originality into an inane hair style and outrageous bad manners, is a feeble gesture of rebellious self-expression; and so too the Citizen's Band radio fad, which allows people to improvise risk-free identity games in their own tiny theater of the air waves. In all this there is more than enough frivolity for the nastiest satirists to sharpen their cynical wits on, and I would be the last to undervalue the service they and other critics perform in helping us identify the hucksters and hokum that crowd the scene. If I spare little time taking these matters to task, it is not simply because they are such easy marks for ridicule, but also because I would not do more to draw attention from the fact that even symptoms like these can be related to larger, more consequential historical movements. It is always a problem in the study of popular culture to discriminate the running tides of change from the froth that rides the waves. I work from the conviction that the growing ethos of self-discovery is charged with all the moral power we find in such high ideals of the past as the rights of man, the assertion of human equality, the belief in worldly progress, the struggle for social justice. The secret of that power is the spontaneous conviction and wonder that self-discovery brings into the life of every human soul it touches. There is an irresistible fascination to the project of creating an original identity. Even after we learn that it is also a demanding labor of the spirit, there is still nothing that can be nearly as fascinating. And nobody will ever talk us out of the adventure once it takes hold.

But there is more to the matter than the inherent delight of becoming one's own person. Another more inscrutable force drives the ethos of self-discovery forward with a special urgency. I will be suggesting that there is a planetary dimension to the spreading personalist sensibility which links the search for an authentic identity to the well-being of the global environment. The scientific status of this connection between person and planet can only remain speculative in these pages; but I have little doubt that, within the next generation, there will emerge a well-developed body of ecological theory that illuminates this subtle interrelationship and gives it enough political force to displace the inherited ideologies of industrial society. We will begin to grasp the evolutionary continuities that relate mind to matter, human consciousness to the basic chemistry of life in ways that are augmentative rather than reductionistic. Perhaps even the hard sciences of the Western world will find their way to a personalist paradigm that unites the knower and the known in a vital reciprocity. Meanwhile, the most I can do is to sketch in the ecological context of the cultural transformation we are passing through. As succinctly as I can put it, my argument is that *the needs of the planet are the needs of the person.* And, therefore, *the rights of the person are the rights of the planet.* If a proper reverence for the sanctity of the Earth and the diversity of its people is the secret of peace and survival, then the adventure of self-discovery stands before us as the most practical of pleasures.

I

MANIFESTO OF THE PERSON

Chapter 1

The Rights of the Person

> *Every man is more than just himself; he also*
> *represents the unique, the very special and*
> *always significant and remarkable point at*
> *which the world's phenomena intersect, only*
> *once in this way and never again. That is why*
> *every man's story is important, eternal, sacred;*
> *that is why every man, as long as he lives and*
> *fulfills the will of nature, is wondrous and*
> *worthy of every consideration.*
> — *Hermann Hesse*

A Secret Manifesto

In our time, a secret manifesto is being written. It will not go
out to the world as print on the page. No mass movement will ever
raise it as a banner. Rather, its language is a longing we read in
one another's eyes—the longing to know our authentic vocation in
the world, to find the work and the way that belong uniquely to
each of us. And its authors, even if they should come to number
millions, will never care to know themselves as an army on the
march, but only as the few who can come together here and there
in true companionship.

I speak of the manifesto of the person, the declaration of our
sovereign right to self-discovery. I cannot say if those who have
answered its summons are indeed millions. But I know that its
influence moves significantly among us, a subterranean current of
our history that awakens in all those it touches an intoxicating
sense of how deep the roots of the self reach, and what strange
sources of power they embrace. A contemporary cliché tells us we
are passing through a "revolution of rising expectations." That is
surely true—truer than many of us may realize, especially the polit-

ical leaders of the world, who are usually among the last to detect a shift in the cultural weather. For it is not only bread, work, physical security people have come to expect of life. Behind these obvious and absolute necessities—but no less fierce in its demands —there stands an appetite for personal recognition, for the recognition of each of us as a special and significant event in the universe, a center of delicate sensibilities and radical originality. On a scale that has no historical precedent, we are becoming *interesting* to ourselves and to one another as beings who carry unexpected destinies into the world.

The manifesto of the person—spontaneously composed, subtly propagated—marks one of the great turning points in the human story. If it takes hold and works its promised change, we may find that neither "history" nor "society"—those great collective abstractions which have always defined the human condition—any longer possesses a compelling reality for us. They will seem like quaint old tales told of some extinct, pre-human being called "everybody in general." We may come to see that tribe, nation, class, social movement, revolutionary masses . . . that all these have, like shadows that eclipse the sun, gained their existence at the expense of something far brighter and more beautiful: our essential and still unexplored self. And, recognizing that truth, we may seek to replace these "higher" social allegiances with an astonishing ethical proposition—*that all people are created to be persons* and that persons come first, before all collective fictions.

Taken at its full value, what does such a proposition require of us but that we create a seemingly impossible social universe, one that has as many centers as there are awakened personalities among us? Can we even imagine such a polynuclear world of liberated personalities? Can there be any practical cohesion to a society whose every imperative and policy must yield to the demands of personal fulfillment?

Countless problems and reservations spring to mind. What becomes of all our collective disciplines in such a society—law and order, the national defense, social responsibility, cultural excellence? Could we expect people to stick at their assigned roles in life, to work conscientiously at jobs they may despise, to compete for approval and reward? How would we shame them into obedience and high achievement? Is this anything better than universal anarchy we are contemplating? Already, as the manifesto of the person spreads its influence among us, we hear ominous warnings from political leaders and social critics who discern in the rising personalist style nothing better than a license for unruly rebellion against civil duty and cultural quality: a sort of reckless, Whitmanesque democracy of free self-expression . . . a million, million Songs of Myself. Thus, Daniel Bell laments the growing "megalomania of self-infinitization." Christopher Lasch and Peter Marin bemoan the "pathological narcissism" of the times. And with them, many learned, sometime-liberal, now sternly conservative champions of public order and high culture step forward to defend the traditional sublimative virtues: self-restraint, dutiful citizenship, the work ethic, above all *deference*—deference to intellectual "excellence," social "hierarchy," and "the public interest."

In days to come, as it becomes ever more apparent how profoundly this new personalist sensibility challenges the orthodox culture, we are bound to hear many more patrician critics summoning us back to discipline and duty. Their counsel has its value; I hardly mean to dismiss it out of hand. In a later chapter, I want to look more closely at their concern. But I think, at last, such critics misread the new ethos of self-discovery, mistaking it for the old vice of self-aggrandizement. They confuse the sensitive quest for fulfillment with the riotous hedonism of our high consumption economy—which is to say, they fail to distinguish the legitimate human need for personal growth from the false need of the market place for material excess and individual advantage. Or they easily interpret the insurgent personalism of the day as a menacing "revolt of the masses" against all standards of excellence. And of course there *is* such a beast abroad in our times, a many-headed monster whose despair and resentment make it the ideal servant of totalitarian unreason. But within that revolt of the masses there is another movement that now presses forward for recognition: a revolt of people *against* massification in behalf of their embattled personhood. And to turn from that out of a too-fastidious care for cultural tone and intellectual etiquette is to lose sight of the creativity and true conviviality that we may yet discover through the liberation of the person.

The Experience of Personhood

I cannot know how many of you will recognize what I have to say in these pages about the rights of the person and the historical meaning of their present struggle to emerge. In what follows, I will take up some of the more prominent features of that emergence: a few impressionistic observations that may help landmark the contemporary transformation of identity. But before I do that, before I offer these generalizations about what others are up to in the world, let me call upon the witness of your own experience. Because it is not in prominent and public things that the sense of personhood most decisively unfolds, but in the intimate textures of your daily life, often so subtly that many of you may already share in this cultural transformation without knowing that you do so. Its presence in your life may be no more than an elusive impatience with all assigned roles and restrictive social routines. It may only be a certain nagging sense that the world you live in does not *fit*. The job you hold, the education you receive, the institutions that claim authority over you (the government, the corporations, the unions, the courts, the welfare system), all these may seem to have been crudely designed for everybody *in general,* but for nobody *in person*—least of all for you.

These may come and go as fleeting, private irritations. Nevertheless, they are signs that the great change I speak of is at work in your experience, nourishing a certain brash assurance in you that you have a *right* to be handled with care, a *right* to the employment, education, time and space you need to find your peculiar style, a *right* to participate directly in the decisions that shape your life even if exercising that right means endless delay and disruption.

But where do you think these "rights" come from? How long do you think they have existed? Which is really to ask, how long do you think *your* experience of uniqueness has existed in the world?

Perhaps you sense that such rights would have been seen as pre-posterous luxuries by your grandparents, perhaps even by your parents. But do you know they would have been regarded as ut-terly incomprehensible no more than a century ago—even as a kind of intolerable insanity? Would you be surprised to discover that this right you feel so certain is yours, this right to have your uniqueness respected, perhaps even cultivated, is not at all a sim-ple extension of traditional values like civil liberty, equality, social democracy—which is precisely why it must now pit itself against so many institutions that were created to further those familiar ideals —but that it springs independently from another, far more mysteri-ous source, one (as I will suggest in the chapter to follow) that reaches into the biological foundations of life?

When do you begin to become this strange, subversive thing called a "person"? It happens when you first feel yourself aching beneath the weight of all that wants to make you a characterless and interchangeable piece of the social system. When an irrepressi-ble rage first rises in you against those who would use you as an unfeeling raw material of their designs—bend you, break you, sac-rifice you for purposes and policies deemed more important than your fulfillment. When you first flinch at being known as a num-ber, at seeing bits and pieces of your life speckled across a com-puter printout, at finding your needs, your beliefs, your values boiled down to a bland statistical gruel for the benefit of remote agencies and bureaus. When you are first moved to demand of all those who act in the name of the state, the company, the people, the law, the movement, the cause, that they look you in the face and acknowledge that you are *here,* that you are *real,* that you *matter.*

In moments like these, moments of spontaneous outrage, you may have found yourself casting about like someone drowning, reaching out desperately for a spar or timber to keep you afloat. What was it you were looking for? It was for some solid evidence of this incommensurable uniqueness you feel, something that would make you more real than the statistical phantom which the mass processing machinery of our society insists you are. And perhaps that is when your desperation grew most severe:

when, under pressure of insult or abuse, you became fearfully aware of how little of that uniqueness you have managed to salvage, of how much life remains unlived in you . . . the unrealized powers, the languishing talents, the untried adventures of mind and spirit. And still, you know, with an instinctive conviction, that there *is* an essential *you* somewhere inside, behind all the world's imposed identities, a *you* that needs a meaning of your own making, a personal emblem to hold in the face of grief and before the advance of death.

Death . . . it is a matter we will touch upon more than a few times in these pages. For it is death which approaches most closely to the core of the personalist experience, a shadowed presence that throws our need for an authentic identity into bright and urgent prominence. Perhaps you have noticed the extraordinary popular attention—literary, medical, psychotherapeutic, philosophical— which death and dying have attracted in recent years: an attention not at all morbid or morose, but intelligently curious and candid. It is sometimes called "thanatology" in our hospitals, but the concern is far more than a professional specialization. It is an effort to create what was once called an "art of dying," to take death "out of the closet" and into our lives as a stage of growth within our total human being. This is one of the foremost aspects of the new sense of personhood—this bravely inquisitive search into that most solitary, unique, and inward moment where our identity finds its decisive punctuation. It is also the aspect that lends a deep spiritual significance to the quest for self-discovery, reminding us again that inwardness is a religious direction.

If what I speak of here has been your experience, then you have taken into the moral and emotional fiber of your life what sociologists of twenty years ago identified academically as "the problem of conformity," "the problem of the lonely crowd." You have felt in your marrowbone the issue that political theorists currently call "the crisis of legitimation," "the disintegration of public authority." You have even found your way in sympathetic need beyond the boundaries of your own society and have reached out to join forces with those dissenting voices in the socialist countries who speak out against party elites and bureaucratic centralism in behalf of a Marxism that wears "a human face." And with that realization, you have confronted one of the hardest political truths of the modern world: that there is no more shelter to be found for the person in revolutionary mass movements and People's Republics than in the capitalist societies they struggle to overthrow.

In the street jargon of the day, you may speak of your longing for personhood as "doing your own thing." And perhaps you have not yet found more of "your thing" to do than to decorate your desk at the office or the bumper of your car with the slogan, *"I am a human being. Do not fold, mutilate, or spindle."* Even if your gesture is no more than this, you are in some measure part of a historical force that is eroding the institutional stability of urban-industrial society. Because the recognition you crave is more than the institutions of that society can give, more than its ideals sanction. You have seen your face among the faceless millions whose lives have been squeezed into dispiriting mass and class identities, as much by the revolutions that promised them liberation as by the class-ridden societies that still violate their personal dignity. And you know how desperately we need a new politics that will speak for these millions—one by one by one.

To give a face to the faceless, a voice to the voiceless—and to *each* person the *one* face, the *one* voice that is uniquely theirs . . . that is the meaning of personhood. But the politics of the person has yet to be invented.

Toward a Culture of the Person

Some signs of the times. I choose only three, one (the situational network) that is changing our perception of social reality; another (the new therapies) that is changing our standard of sanity; and the last (the new "helping professions") which have become a major conduit spreading the need for personal recognition. Taken together, they will serve to show us some of the more deliberate and dramatic ways in which people have learned or set about asserting the rights of the person—often with no idea whatever how radically they are revising the historical script of our age.

1. *The Situational Network*

Over the past decade, those along the dissenting fringe of American society have talked often—always vaguely, always wishfully—about "the movement." But in truth there has been no "movement." There have been fits and starts of agitation, brief and sometimes heroic campaigns, impassioned displays of protest powerful enough at their most persistent to bring down a presidential administration or to end a major war. Yet, for all the promise of its victories, the dissenting temper has achieved no enduring coalition of forces, no organizational momentum that lasts, grows, and rolls single-mindedly toward power.

Instead, the radical energy of the time fritters away into a fine, blowing dust of disaffiliation. Organizations disintegrate after a few, sometimes highly effective, efforts. Leaders turn out to be more the invention of the media than real wielders of power; again and again they vanish after a few spectacular moments in the limelight, leaving the media to ask, "What ever happened to . . . ?" For more than a decade now, within a few months of every major demonstration or mobilization, the press and the pundits have had the chance to replay their weary obituaries for dissent in America. That is what everybody sees, laments, and scorns in the revolutionary pretensions of the day: a surface of failed beginnings, the aborted designs of a radicalism that has never seemed to be wholly serious about politics.

Granted, some of this organizational mitosis is nothing more interesting than that Ol' Devil Factionalism up to his usual tricks among the left-wing militants. But ideological hairsplitting has been a minor theme of our politics. Except along the terrorist fringe, there has been little taste for such doctrinal abstractions. The rock that has far more effectively shattered the ground swell of dissent has been a stubborn concern for personal recognition and personal sanctity that can never submerge itself for long in the collective identity of any cause.

This is what many (especially in the media, which never look more than skin deep) have failed to see. The dissenting energy of this generation has been distracted by the appearance of a new, still prepolitical (or perhaps I should say transpolitical) entity in our cultural awareness: the human personality, in all its mystery and angularity. An unprecedented respect for personal autonomy has again and again asserted its priority over the disciplined pursuit of political power. That is the hidden issue, the latent cause that has underlain all others. Yes, it has made a chaos of every campaign for social change, but only because it has so fiercely resisted all efforts to impose the conventional identities of mass and class upon people, as if perhaps the pressures of organizational necessity might be as great an evil as any social injustice we seek to expunge. So we have had a style of dissent that has been fiercely determined to *particularize* people. Let us call it a *situational* sense of society, a principled effort to express what it is to be *this* person, and *this* person, and *this* person with a fidelity to biographical detail that more resembles art than politics.

Over the past ten years, the raw materials for building a big, unified political movement have been abundantly at hand—the numbers, the grievances, the cunning, the pregnant moments of crisis, even a few reasonably promising leaders. But clearly that is not the way enough people have wanted to go in expressing their disaffiliation. Rather, they have feared and have actively shunned bigness; they have been suspicious of large-scale organizational unities; they have mistrusted power. And at last they have opted to join small bands of kindred spirits, or to work at strictly local involvements and *ad hoc* projects. Or they have dropped out (periodically or once and for all) to explore their own private path . . . an interlude among the "new religions," an experiment in one of the handicraft livelihoods, a sampling of the personal growth therapies.

So instead of a movement, we have had a *mosaic*—a mosaic of shifting issues, causes, episodes, groups. And what is the picture this mosaic makes up? A landscape of individuated and universal liberation, and beyond that, the prospect of a world where people may freely assert the diversity and autonomy of their ethnicity, age group, sex, social deviance, life style. It is the vision of a Utopian garden where our species may blossom like a billion flowers, no two alike. In less than a generation's time, every conceivable form of situational belonging has been brought out of the closet and has forced its grievances and its right to exist upon the public consciousness. We suddenly discover how many of us have been one another's victims or oppressors, how many of us have been hiding an identity or an aspiration the world around us makes unwelcome.

How do people come together in contemporary America to work out their liberation? Not as a mass, not as a class, not as a party, a united front, a movement—but as blacks, Latinos, Native Americans, women, kids, students, old folks, dope addicts, convicts, homosexuals, transsexuals, mental patients . . . the variety multiplies indefinitely. Look closely and even the more familiar "movements" on the scene are not the well-defined unities the media take them to be. In the United States, women's liberation may have found its most prominent voice in the National Organization for Women, but that is, after all, a very white, very middle-class operation. The ongoing, daily reality of feminism resides in a congeries of local and finely discriminated groupings: third world women, divorced and widowed women, rape victims, battered wives, Gray Panther women, inorgasmic women, country women (living in rural communes), hookers, women athletes, gay women, bisexual women, radical lesbians, lesbian mothers, "chemically dependent" lesbians, unwed mothers, displaced home makers, women in the arts, women in-and-just-out-of prison. . . . There even exists in New York City a militant "Jewish Lesbian Gang." The groups may be small, but their binding loyalties can be all-consuming. And the secret of that bond is the specificity of the group's identity, the intimacy of its connection with each member's life.

The situational spectrum shades off into some very subtle hues indeed: obese people, ugly people, homosexual Native Americans, college athletes in search of "jocks liberation," the crippled and handicapped (who are in themselves a small universe of special causes and problems), impotent men, menopausal men, unwed fathers, women married to homosexuals. There is Parents Anonymous, an organization of chronic child-beating families which has rapidly become a nationwide organization in the United States only since the mid-seventies. There is the Non-Parents Organization, married couples organized to resist the stereotype that all marriages must produce children. There are new therapeutic groups that bring together people afflicted by strange, incapacitating phobias: fears of heights, of out-of-doors, of closed-in spaces, of flying, of dirt and vermin. There is a national organization of former cancer patients, seeking to break down the discriminatory barriers that surround those who have suffered the disease and may bear its scars. Currently, the terminally ill have been finding their way to an outspoken social identity, demanding their rights and dignities of doctors, hospitals, and families. In London, there is Gaycare, an organization of elderly and handicapped gays, and Gemma, a group for disabled lesbians. I have even come across an Aquarian Anti-Defamation League which has attempted to organize and defend the neopagans, witches, and warlocks among us from religious discrimination. Does that perhaps seem frivolous . . . something hardly to be taken seriously? But *that* is exactly why the group exists, and must exist. Because it deals in a condition of life whose injustices and hardships *you* cannot grasp or spare time for, an issue that cannot find a place in your political agenda, perhaps a cry for help you cannot even hear, even as whites once could not take seriously the plight of blacks, or men hear the anguished appeal of women. How easy it is to believe that nobody's grief matters but our own.

Clearly, there is no single ideological formulation that can corral such a rich and often tragic variety of human experience. That is why the catalogue and the "resource guide" have emerged as the distinctive political genres of the day. What the manifesto and the party platform were for the class struggle of yesterday, the catalogue is for the situational groups of today. Open any of the *People's Yellow Pages* directories that now appear in our major cities, and what do you find? The very pages are a typographical mosaic of disaffiliation, a picture of social turmoil made up of nitty-gritty bits and pieces of advice, guidance, resource groups, shared experience, books, periodicals. How else to put it all together and yet preserve the independence and authenticity of everyman's (and everywoman's and everykid's and everybisexual's) protest?

In times past, radical politics made do with the one brutally blockish social category of "class"; the only consciousness the old ideologies sought to "raise" was *class* consciousness, the self-interest of a vast, undifferentiated Many pitted against a privileged Few. We now see that this was primitive sociology indeed, and potentially the basis for a new generation of injustices on the other side of the revolution. A successful labor movement may only turn out to be a movement of *white male* workers; Black Power may at last become power for black *men* only. The victory of something called "the working class" may leave the sufferings of women, children, sexual deviants, old people, convicts, dope fiends wholly untouched. And how cruelly remote from that suffering a revolutionary leadership or a party bureaucracy may become if it cannot acknowledge any human identity smaller than "the proletariat," if it cannot give flesh and blood particularity to "the people."

Contemporary dissent has applied the microscope of a new sensibility—a personalist sensibility—to the old class category and has found within it a fine structure of amazing delicacy and diversity. It searches out the nuances of victimization, the secret wounds that only fellow sufferers can recognize. It attends sympathetically to the persecuted "deviations" which are often a committed life style for those who bear their stamp. It listens to hear the whispered anguish that has never been given a voice in the political arena. And, at last, in the place of "class" a personalist politics substitutes "the network"—a loosely structured awareness of grievances and concerns among autonomous, situational groups.

Is the network a practical political instrument? If by "practical" one means, will it soon be able to seize power and reorganize society, the answer is no. Certainly not in the foreseeable future. The network is very nearly predicated on the assumption that gaining power in that sense is wrong. I understand and have often shared the impatience of those whose organizational labors have been thwarted by this situational diffusion of protest. For example, an angry reader complains to one of the *People's Yellow Pages* directories:

Instead of uniting the people behind ONE cause of socialism that will benefit ALL, [your magazine] sends us scurrying off in 101 different directions which are conflicting and contradictory.

Organizing for socialism has nothing to do with religion, lesbians, or feminism, all of which can exist very nicely in capitalism. . . . Do you really think *working men* will go for something called "feminist socialism"?

The Marxist historian Russell Jacoby puts the point even more bitterly:

The reduction of the Marxist theory of alienation to a subjective condition by liberal sociologists has its counterpart in the left in the reduction of oppression to a whim of the individual. . . . What counts is the immediate, and here an economism-turned-feminism is promoted as if the blind endorsement of what every worker did or thought is improved when it is as blindly applied to women. Social analysis decays into group loyalty. The jealousy with which the oppression of women, children, homosexuals, and so on, is defended as a private preserve, off-limits to others, expresses an urge to corner the market of oppression.

The complaints have their validity. Nevertheless, of this much I feel certain: that the situational network is the only way we now have of bringing people together in our society for significant change, and that there will be no change that is significant or practical in any sense that does not, from this point on, *begin* with the network and do justice to its variety.

What is it that draws so many people to this unwieldy and fragile style of dissent? Ultimately, we must face the question, *why* the situational group? *Why* the network?

The answer is: Those who go this route are not simply responding to a political need. *They are using the situational group as a vehicle of self-discovery.* That is its special charm. It provides its members with the therapeutic companionship of those in whom they can see themselves, those with whom they can most securely *be* themselves. The role of the situational group is not only mutual defense and vindication; it is also (often primarily) confessional freedom and open self-expression. It is the little world of friends where we may each sing our own song. And that, as much as anything politically practical, is what people want desperately to find.

Here and now, they want to be recognized and affirmed, without waiting for the far-off success of the movement or the verdict of history. That need presses in upon us all with the force and alarm of an emergency. So we turn to the company of those who share our most intimate and forbidden identity. And there, we begin to find ourselves as persons.

2. The New Therapies

The situational network possesses both a public and a private face. In a public direction, it looks toward the political style we have come to call "participative democracy." The self-possession and independence of spirit that make people want a say-so in the issues and institutions that touch their lives flow in large part from situational companionship. People burdened by shame and timidity will never stand up for themselves in the world. But in the self-revelation and sharing of the situational encounter, they lose their sense of freakishness; they contact their buried rage, take command of their crippling fears. Above all, they fight their way free of the mystifications which others have piled upon them, and so gain the strength that can only come of knowing oneself and being oneself.

But the network also faces inward; it is the political offspring of therapeutic exploration. Both in structure and in dynamics, the "consciousness-raising" and the "rap sessions" to which victimized people turn for self-expression overlap the new personal growth therapies. Their methods draw heavily on group work like encounter, Gestalt, psychodrama. One could even argue that the Synanon Game—a highly structured form of aggressive encounter developed in the late 1950s to rehabilitate drug addicts and give them a new social force in society—represents a situational group that has contributed more to the new therapies than it has borrowed. The interplay between personal therapy and political consciousness-raising has become nearly impossible to sort out. In which category does one place the recently created Radical Therapy, for example? Here is a form of psychiatry which insists on treating its troubled clients exclusively as part of persecuted groups, with the strict intention of organizing them for political action against the social interests that have driven them into "madness." With RT, the public and private have become wholly congruent.

Or take another example—one reported to me from the midsixties, the early days of Black Power.

During a rap session, a group of black students who are planning a demonstration happen upon the question of hair-straightening. Some members of the group are wearing their hair straight; others are wearing their hair natural. Between them, an argument breaks out and within minutes it grows painfully heated—precisely because it is so sharply focused on a personal taste that is in practice here and now . . . or rather on a taste some have adopted and believe to be personal. The exchange soon broadens to cover sexual preferences generally. Do blacks *really* think "black is beautiful"? Do they honestly experience themselves that way? Is the love they profess—men for women, women for men—as real as they like to believe? Is their image of beauty their own or the imprint of white media and white advertising? Why (at least in the early stages of Black Power) did so many black male leaders take up with white women? Is Black Power simply the black version of male chauvinism? Will its result be a new put-down for the black woman? Have any of those present overcome "shade prejudice" within their own community of friends and lovers? How many of white society's standards have gotten inside their heads, inside their sexual responses?

Rarely did political action in the past intrude so deeply into the guarded quarters of the personality, rarely did it ask so great a measure of risky self-revelation. Impertinently personal, highly combustible questions like these were seldom treated as political material. Yet, we now recognize how seriously they may affect the solidarity of the group, the impact of the cause. That is the insight rap sessions bring to bear; they carry into social affairs all that our psychiatry has taught us about the elusiveness and self-deception of human motivations. The very word "black" as used by American blacks is in itself an indication of how psychologically sophisticated our politics has become; it plants the whole, ugly, explosive question of color right in the middle of the race issue. In that one word, we have all the emotional dynamite, all the essential madness of race hatred. By its presence, blacks and whites alike are forced to confront the psychotic overtones that make color prejudice far more than a matter of deliberate class oppression. Racism *is* that; but it is class oppression laced through with twisted sexual fantasies, with fears as dark as the grave and as dreadful as the demons of hell. Somewhere at the bottom of our assigned racial identities we come upon the symbolic transformations of blackness—blackness as evil, as death, as chaos . . . blackness as the primitive, the bestial, the untamed erotic . . . blackness as the diabolical . . . blackness as the archetype of the imprisoned unconscious itself, the entire threatening realm of forbidden experience. None of this emerges for purification as long as we pretend that color is merely a mask for class struggle.

It takes a therapeutic sense of politics to excavate the irrational anxieties which white society has branded into black flesh. Until the festering dread of death and the demonic has been purged, no black person can be a person, can wear the color of his or her skin with pride and courage, knowing that *their* blackness is not *that* blackness. Nor can white society discover its personhood until it admits who the nigger in its own psychic woodpile really is. In brief, a politics that faces the madness at the core of our lives has taken self-knowledge as its ultimate ground.

This same psychological sensitivity moves through all the liberation politics of our day, forcing victims and oppressors alike to deal with the ugly phantoms of the unconscious mind. How better to characterize the style of these efforts than to see in them the point at which the political and the psychic intersect and become the occasion for self-analysis? In politics as in all else, ours is the Age of Therapy, a time when "ordinary" people tire of the verbal surfaces and cover stories that cloud our lives, and begin to demand an introspective honesty which only the great souls of the past have known.

But there is something more to these therapeutic explorations than psychiatric business-as-usual. There is a dramatic change of psychological key which raises us above Freud's minimal sanity of catharsis and purgation. The important new therapies that have gained the largest followings, especially as part of group practice, are based upon an optimistic, forward-looking psychology of growth. They borrow heavily from sources like Jung's concept of "individuation" and Abraham Maslow's approach to "self-actualization." They invite open self-expression and the exercise of higher creative powers. They are also marvelously eclectic, willing to draw upon any device or technique that the person seems to need—almost as if we might expect one day to have a unique therapeutic mix for each client. Above all, there is the very practice of regarding people as "clients," rather than "patients," an approach that deliberately avoids assigning them to a negative and dependent category. Instead, they are summoned forward toward possibilities of growth that are considered their normal condition of health.

Through group work and play, and an expanding repertory of yogas domestic and imported, the new therapies work to liberate body, mind, and spirit. They draw freely upon exotic and ancient teachings, as well as upon modern science, assembling before us a rich inventory of unfulfilled potentialities. And steadily, steadily, the word gets round—through growth centers, university extensions, workshops sponsored by churches, social groups, professional organizations, through the expanding humanistic psychology network—that there is vastly *more* to each of us than the going fashion in normality will acknowledge. Maslow asked the key question in posing self-actualization as the proper objective of therapy: Why do we set our standard of sanity so cautiously low? Can we imagine no better model than the dutiful consumer, the well-adjusted breadwinner? Why not the saint, the sage, the artist? Why not all that is highest and finest in our species?

Here, I believe, is the spell psychotherapy has cast over the contemporary mind. Not simply that it brings us self-knowledge; more importantly, in pursuing Maslow's ideal, it invents a self that constantly outgrows our knowledge, drawing our imagination toward an expanding universe of human possibilities. And we are a curious animal, one that longs to know its true dimensions. That is why, even where we deal with hard political issues—victimization, persecution, injustice—personality comes to be the center of attraction, the paramount value at stake.

3. Helpers, Enablers, Facilitators, Counselors

Finally, we must take note of the strategic, if still ambiguous, role that has come to be played in most industrial societies over the past decade and a half by the so-called human services—the welfare workers, the psychiatric nurses and social workers, the legal aid advisers, the counselors of all descriptions who (especially in America) can now be found somewhere in the bureaucratic blood stream of every major institution: schools, child-care facilities, mental hospitals, prisons, shelters for delinquent children and abandoned mothers, halfway houses, retirement homes, crisis-intervention centers. Here, among these overworked professionals, we have one of the main conduits for bringing the insights of the situational network and the techniques of the new therapies into the lives of our worst social casualties.

Those in the human services describe themselves in a number of jargonistic ways. They are the "helping professions"; they are "enablers" and "facilitators." In effect, they are the shock absorbers of a ramshackle urban-industrial system. Or, to move the metaphor a bit closer to the unpleasant reality of the matter, they are in charge of collecting and disposing of our society's human refuse: the castoffs, the rejects, the downs-and-outs who cannot measure up to the demands of the economy. For the most part, their endless cleanup operation is supposed to be done on mean and shrinking budgets which are the first to feel the pinch whenever the taxpaying public decides it can no longer afford to pamper its misfit millions. For, from a hard-nosed conservative viewpoint, that is what the human services amount to. They are the worst excess of bleeding-heart liberalism and fiscal irresponsibility whose only result is to reward social incompetence. But, in fact, the helping professions are there as an open confession of advanced industrial breakdown, and the only alternatives to their presence would be riot (if not revolution) in the streets, or the astronomical costs of paramilitary police force in every city.

From a more radical perspective, it could be argued that the helping professions are performing a morally dubious function. *Whom* are they really "helping," after all—the dominant forces in our social system or its victims? In a sense, they are the lubricant in a social machinery that would otherwise freeze up; and might that not be for the best? The criticism can be extended with even greater validity to the enormous number of cheaply licensed, free-lance counseling activities that have thickly and opportunistically grown up around the officially funded human services. In America we have developed a veritable subculture of private and special-ized counseling to deal with every least problem or pseudo-problem in life: family-marriage-divorce, disease-death-dying, sex and intimacy, careers and money management, anxiety and the crises of middle life, the dilemmas of creative leisure, exercise and physical fitness, travel and entertainment. Much of this is apt to be trivial and self-indulgent in the extreme; very little of it can offer any evidence of social value beyond what it does temporarily to distract or palliate. One can easily imagine how, in some futuristic anti-Utopia rather like Huxley's Brave New World, such services might spread through their society, treacherously coating the chronic desperation of people with just enough relief to avoid so-cial disruption or psychic disintegration.

But there is another role that *some* members of the helping pro-fessions have come to play, especially those who have been human-istically educated and who bring some idealism to their work. When counselors of this stripe must meet the human wreck-age of our society face to face, day after day, they sometimes develop strong personalist instincts and radical values. They be-gin to regard their case loads, not as so many burdensome so-cial statistics, but as unique human beings who deserve a tender, loving care, if not an obvious justice that the system refuses to give. And, in turn, they may well become the one face, the one human presence to which the distressed and destitute can turn for personal recognition. There is no reason to doubt that many coun-selors *do* "pamper" and "spoil" their clients, at least to the extent of providing them, for a few hours a week, with a tiny enclave where they can feel human again. Perhaps they introduce their cli-ents to some form of self-help through a situational network or bring them the best benefits of one of the new therapies. They may even finally succeed in awakening some of the victims before them to their rights as persons—though in many cases this may lead to expectations that will be cruelly betrayed.

In my own experience, I have met few professional counselors who were not at least struggling toward a personalist ethic that would allow them to maintain a clear sense of the human reality of their clients. The one emotion I have most often heard them express is outrage for the demoralized mob they are expected to confront each day with never enough time or money. And I have met some who have finally been "burned out" by frustration and failure, and forced to quit. They could not continue to sweep the social debris out of sight. They leave their profession, but their experience is still with us in the world, along with whatever aspirations they may have encouraged in their clients.

There are obviously many things to criticize about the human services. How could it be otherwise with anything as big, official, and overburdened? Certainly, they can grow top-heavy with jargon and methodology and bureaucratic paper work. And no doubt they sometimes sponge up revenues that might better go directly to the victims down below. The charge has also been raised that there are counselors who "pathologize" everyone they deal with, driving people toward a still greater dependence on state support and professional care. That may be so. But the reason such a vice exists in the first place is because there simply *is* so much social pathology in urban-industrial society. After a time, perhaps one gets into the habit of automatically treating people as victims.

For better or worse, the helping professions are the furthest our society has gone in seeking to give official and professional structure to the crying need for personal recognition. Ultimately, I believe the effort can only prove to be a hopeless contradiction. What the victims of our urban-industrial economy need is compassion and a measure of justice that amounts to social revolution. Compassion cannot be professionalized; social revolution will not be licensed by the state. But, in the meanwhile, until all their principled and idealistic talent has been driven out or beaten into submission, the helping professions are still another force that feeds the appetite for personhood, if only on crumbs.

Odysseys of Identity

No more than two generations ago, the struggle for personal identity was the cultural monopoly of an elite few, a psychological delicacy reserved for the creative minority. It was a theme that one expected to encounter only in the high philosophy and literature of our society where artists and intellectuals might hint elusively at the authentic personality that lay beyond the boundaries of prescribed social roles. I think, for example, of a literary landmark of the early twentieth century like André Gide's *The Immoralist*. What was it that made Gide's immoralist so "immoral"? It was his impatience with the propriety of assigned identities, a restiveness that does not even mature into a clear act of rebellion in the book. Only the sentiment of resistance is there, a mere tantalizing and tormenting dream of greater possibilities which the novel's hero broods upon and treasures in his heart. Speaking of the conventionally moral man, the novel's chief spokesman for self-realization (he is cast in the role of diabolical tempter) laments,

> If there's one thing each of them claims not to resemble it's himself. Instead he sets up a model, then imitates it; he doesn't even choose the model—he accepts it ready-made. Yet I'm sure there's something more to be read in a man. People dare not—they dare not turn the page. The laws of mimicry—I call them the laws of fear. People are afraid to find themselves alone, and don't find themselves at all. . . . What seems different in yourself: that's the one rare thing you possess, the one thing that gives each of us his worth; and that's just what we try to suppress. We imitate. And we claim to love life.

When they were written (in 1901, at the same time Nietzsche's final work, *The Will to Power,* was in preparation), the words were a battle cry for creative self-expression. But when, at last, Gide's autobiographical hero Michel dares to confront his true self, what is the secret longing he discovers he has been so dutifully hiding from the world? A mild homosexual propensity, only cautiously admitted at the close of the book.

Today, when homosexual characters take center stage on prime-time television shows and when gay liberators run for public office or parade in celebration of Gay Pride week, how tame this seems, and how insubstantial a material on which to rest serious literature. The banner of shameless self-revelation has taken to the streets, inevitably losing its exquisite subtlety in the transition. But then nothing gains historical force without paying the price of becoming coarse, blatant, heavy-handed—and perhaps thereby taking on a certain commendable candor that helps set a more valid standard. There is, after all, an inflated preciousness about a character like Michel who finally has very little to hide or to reveal—certainly nothing that requires the license of artistic eloquence to win public admission.

Now, the search for the self, the craving for authenticity, has become commonplace. At least since Jack Kerouac's *On the Road* was published and Hermann Hesse's *Journey to the East* became a paperback best seller, we have had a growing army of adventurers in our society—young, old, middle-aged—literally or figuratively traveling the roads of the world, sampling identities here and there, in exotic places or in books, films, encounter sessions, leaving behind homes, marriages, careers, commitments, taking up new names, costumes, diets, creeds, life styles—and willing, at the least invitation, to recite their odysseys of identity to all who will listen. Over the past several years, the books I have written have drawn a remarkable number of people to me eager to tell the story of their journey through dope, divorce, rock music, social protest, psychiatric upheaval, extraterrestrial encounters, nirvana. Hardly a month goes by without someone seeking me out in person, on the phone, through the mail—too often with a heavy manuscript in need of my immediate attention. Even when these accounts find their way into publisher's ink—in the form of memoirs, diaries, premature autobiographies—not much of what one comes upon stands a chance of becoming immortal literature. And as intimate conversation or confessional outpouring, what people have to say about their broken marriages, their escape from parental tyranny, their abandoned relationships, their transient experience with gurus, therapists, situational partners can become painfully tedious. Even rebellion, rebirth, and transformation can fall into ruts of their own, as filled with jargon and clichés as the old conformities. After one has heard a dozen reports of how people faced up to their homosexuality, or broke free of some domestic entrapment, or found God in the wilderness, the experiences lose freshness— just as, for that matter, we can tire of hearing still another intrepid climber tell of his "conquest of Everest" or another astronaut tell how he explored the lunar landscape. Moreover, it is not often the case that these courageous escapes from the world's assigned identities lead to some wise and graceful new stance in life; they may be a jail break into personal chaos, a liberation that brings no integration. As Gide put it in telling his own story, "the capacity to get free is nothing; the capacity to *be* free—*that* is the task."

But the critical remarks I make here are really very much beside the point, for none of them alters the personal value or the historical significance of such experiences. Our evaluation of these experiments in self-discovery ultimately depends upon how we interpret the moral and spiritual need that underlies them. If that need is seen as essentially healthy and necessary, if we can recognize in it the emergence of a popular appetite for the self-knowledge that has always been the prerequisite for a wise and humane community, then perhaps we can forgive these early personalist gestures their awkwardness and repetitiousness. After all, we deal here with an experience that must be undergone in each person's life: a story many times to be repeated, and inevitably by many who can only stammer. After a fashion which nobody could have foreseen, the situational groups, the new therapies and religions, the counseling encounters are the Socratic spirit of philosophy carried into the streets and the market place—of course, with too few masters like Socrates himself to guide the inquiry, with too many profiteering sophists ready to move in on the demand. But nothing will do more to reduce this historical movement to a mere passing fad than the crushing intolerance of intellectuals who will hear nothing less from their fellow human beings than literary glories, or the fickle attention of journalists for whom self-discovery (like Black

Power, women's liberation, ecology, and a score of causes before it) must soon become yesterday's news. A journalist's ink, we must remember, is nine parts embalming fluid.

A rough historical comparison comes to mind. In seventeenth-century England there occurred an astonishing eruption of millenarian sects and enthusiast preachers, especially among the subordinate social classes: Shakers, Quakers, Diggers, Ranters, Pilgrims, Fifth Monarchists, Levellers. . . . From the viewpoint of the privileged classes and educated orders of the day, the beliefs of these groups were offensively vulgar, brazenly heretical. Their theology looked like an incoherent hodgepodge of amateurish biblical exegesis, untutored folklore, personal revelation, and pure hysteria. And, in truth, not much in the way of enduring thought or elegant literature ever emerged from these sects. Yet, among these God-intoxicated groups of artisans, farmers, laborers, housewives, and ranting preachers, there moved a fiercely independent spirit of egalitarian politics. In their Bible readings and strange ecstasies, they discovered a historically pertinent question:

> When Adam delved and Eve span,
> Who was then the gentleman?

In ways the sectarians could not have predicted—nor any of their critics—their libertarian convictions were destined to flow into the great age of democratic revolution that followed a century later, where their ideals would find other, intellectually richer formulations.

I suggest that the ethos of self-discovery is now passing through a similar, early stage of development, filtering into the popular consciousness along many crude and crooked channels that also offend cultivated tastes. But riding this turbulent wave is a deepening sense of personhood which is apt to become the politics of the postindustrial revolution, the crisis that awaits us beyond the withering away of megalopolis and its ecocidal economics.

"I Matter. I'm Special."

The ideals that change the course of history are rare combinations of the simple, the universal, and the profound. On the surface, at the level of slogans and symbols, they must burn with an invincible self-evidence that can spread across the parochial boundaries of the world, setting the most untutored minds afire with impassioned conviction. The ideal of self-discovery gives every indication of being just that irresistibly contagious. It is, in this respect, like the ideal of equality which has now carried the cause of democratic revolution around the globe. The man or woman who has learned to say, "I am the equal of kings and priests, I deserve to enjoy the full rights of the community," will never surrender the dignity those words bring into their lives. They may be terrorized or beaten into silence; but, no matter the social upheaval that must result, they will not give up their claim to equality once it has been made. They cannot, because it has utterly transformed their image of themselves. They would lose their identity with the ideal.

The same is true of the experience of personhood. It has the same uncanny feeling of a truth always known, but only now called up to remembrance. Those who have awakened to the summons of self-discovery, who have found their way to the point of saying, "*I matter,* I am *special,* there is something *more* in me waiting to be discovered, named, liberated," will never take back the words. Under the pressure of that declaration of uniqueness, the most venerable institutions may be shaken to their foundations, the worthiest political movements may collapse as they are deserted by people whose sense of personhood will not allow them to follow and obey as part of an organized mass. Learned critics and responsible leaders may wag their heads and darkly warn of the social chaos that is sure to come of seeking to grant every person his or her right to free growth. They will be right in what they say. But theirs will be a small, cautious fact pitted against a mighty and inspiring truth. And whenever it takes hold, that truth will win out against their resistance. It will, at last, perhaps win over its opponents who will come to see that they too are persons, unique, special, filled with creative promise.

"I matter. I'm special. There is more in me to be discovered." These are mighty words. To speak them is to assert the luxuriant potentiality of human nature, our capacity for unpredictable growth and originality. And learning that, people will persevere in the adventure of self-discovery, even in the face of the most grueling forms of self-examination. They will do so because we are, irrepressibly, a meaning-seeking species, creatures who must have a purposeful identity in the universe as urgently as we must have air to breathe, food to eat. If, then, our inherited identity has once been shaken, if a more vivid experience of authenticity presses itself upon us, we have no choice but to reach out, cling fast, and ride it where it carries us—even if it is a wild horse of an ideal. Many forces make history. But none makes more history than that which underlies and energizes all other human motivations—the hunger for meaning. For that, people will kill and die, build and destroy. They will even face their own bad dreams and brave the terrors of rebirth.

At the same time, simple and contagious ideals can have a profundity that allows them to mature and grow complex, as we have seen happen with the ideal of equality in our time. Every great moral truth has such a mysterious capacity to take on a life of its own. Gradually, as history wears away the surface simplicity, a richness of controversy is revealed beneath, issues and conundrums that give later generations far more to puzzle over, to explore and elaborate than was ever seen in the original statement. Already, we can see something of this hidden complexity emerging in the ideal of self-discovery. The Eastern religions especially are teaching us to scrutinize with great critical care the "self" that we expect to discover beneath all our assigned identities. Is this perhaps also a disguise of the ego, a pose and a role, as it clearly has been for so many Bohemian rebels? Is there, finally, a constant and continuous "me" underlying all the roles I play? Or am "I" simply the peculiar style in which those roles are interpreted—a mask beneath a mask beneath a mask? Is the self something we seek to find, or something we seek to see through, searching for some deeper ground of being?

And there are many more questions:

How much of the self is inextricably bound up with family and community? How much is visited upon us out of our genetic heritage or invested in the body which is our lifelong vessel?

Can there be a "self-beyond-culture"—or do we only, finally realize our identity through the custom and community of our birth? What sort of culture would a self-beyond-culture create? What basis would it have for excellence and critical judgment? Could such a self achieve any sane integrity?

Are there levels of the personality that deserve to be treated as demonic and forbidden? Are there forms of originality and self-expression that are pathological?

Can the free personality be a basis for conviviality and moral concern? What are its capacities for loving relationship? To what degree are duty and social conformity compatible with, or even essential to, inward growth? What place have the society-building energies of the ego in our sense of personhood?

How does personhood relate to the Christian conception of the soul as a specially created and eternal entity set radically apart from God and the other? And how does this traditional Western sense of identity relate to the Eastern teaching that psychic separateness is an illusion, that the human and the divine are One? At what point does the personal give over into the transpersonal—and where do we find the power to make that transition? Is it ours, or must it be given from beyond our resources?

Finally, and least palatable of all, there is the unsettling doubt: how easy, how rewarding, how gratifying do we think self-discovery is meant to be? Is there a tragic dimension to the project, a confrontation with vulnerabilities from which we are mercifully shielded by our assigned identities? What unknown aggravations of the spirit, what burdens of sacrifice wait for us along this path?

In the pages that follow, we will touch upon only a few of these weighty questions—mainly those that have to do with authority, conviviality, and excellence. I list them here merely to suggest the deeper implications of self-discovery, questions that have troubled my mind, problems I have found under discussion by those who are most closely in touch with the personalist currents of the day. I suspect that the wisest among them know that we have a daunting agenda ahead of us, one that is bound to leave us with many unresolvable philosophical issues—veritable *quaestiones,* as the old Schoolmen would call them. In truth, we do not, as yet, even possess a serviceable vocabulary in which to embody the issues. Here I am, for example, already heavily invested in this opening chapter in terms like "person," "self," "identity," "potentiality," "authenticity," in loose metaphors of "inwardness" and "depth," "growth" and "discovery"—as if I might expect these elusive words to carry uniform meanings to all who read them. Of course, they do not. They have all been manhandled out of clear shape by current overuse. But a writer must have words. If it can do no more, let the poor, blurred language I choose point a direction, sound a depth. The person is first of all a self—yourself, myself, and all too likely a very selfish, self-important, self-indulgent self. If there is another, finer self to be found within us—and of course there is—it will have to be brought to light by digging through the pride and desire of that lesser identity.

Chapter 2

The Rights of the Planet

And what is Earth's eye, tongue, or heart else, where
Else, but in dear and dogged man?
— *Gerard Manley Hopkins*

And why should it be happening now and among us—this eager
search for personal identity? Why should a need for self-discovery
that has always belonged to an outcast and eccentric few—sages
and saints, prophets and artists—now become one of the prominent
cultural currents of our time?

We are not apt to understand this strange episode in our history
if we try to see it as a simple extension of liberal or social democracy, the ideologies that dominate industrial society. We may be
dealing with a claim to *rights,* but the rights of the person raise us
to a qualitatively new level in the free expression of diversity. They
are predicated, not on the mere pragmatic toleration of difference,
but on a positive fascination with the human variety. In Chapter
Four I will return to examine this point more closely, suggesting
that the historical development of liberal and socialist values leads
to the antithesis of self-discovery. I will argue that these classic political ideals have taken us in very different directions—on the one
hand, toward an ethic of individualist self-interest that lacks all
personal depth, and, on the other, toward a militant class-con-
sciousness that would politicize the personality out of existence.
Thus, in their economic forms of capitalism and state socialism,
these ideological traditions have become the leading forces of industrial massification and class conformity, the very opposition
which our sense of personhood must now struggle against to defend its rights.

Where, then, does the contemporary longing for personhood
arise?

Add one more ingredient to the social dissent of our time, and perhaps the question is answered. At the same time that our sense of personality deepens, our sense of ecological responsibility increases. Just as we grow more acutely concerned for the sanctity of the person, so we grow more anxious for the well-being of the planetary environment. Which is hardly to say that ecological conscience has swept the field. But environmental concern, both as a matter of personal commitment and public action, has clearly established itself among us as a high ideal—a sharp focus of political action, a nucleus for ethical resolution. We are finally coming to recognize that the natural environment is the exploited proletariat, the downtrodden nigger of everybody's industrial system. Within less than a generation, thoughtful people around the world begin to see that nature must also have its natural rights: the rights of the planet to its life-sustaining integrity, its native dignity. Environmental consultation has become one of the strongest bases for international dialogue and cooperation. Not enough dialogue or cooperation perhaps, but vastly more than at any time in history. The rapidity with which this concern has taken hold is every bit as dramatic as the sudden unfolding of personal awareness in our popular culture. Ten years ago, few people had ever heard the word "ecology"—perhaps as few as had ever heard of "human potentiality" or "self-actualization." Today, we are fully accustomed to political programs that at least profess to include the interests of wild things, the enveloping seas and air and open spaces. At about the same pace at which we have seen T-Groups and personal counseling enter our major institutions, we have seen the environmental impact statement become part of our economic planning—though, in both cases, the use of the technique too often remains manipulative and meretricious.

Is it purely fortuitous that the dissenting temper of industrial society moves along these two fronts at once—to protect the person and the planet? Or is there a connection that unites the two movements?

The Common Enemy

I believe there is a connection, one that becomes visible when we realize that both person and planet are threatened by the same

enemy. *The bigness of things.* The bigness of industrial structures, world markets, financial networks, mass political organizations, public institutions, military establishments, cities, bureaucracies. It is the insensitive colossalism of these systems that
endangers the rights of the person and the rights of the planet.
The same inordinate scale of industrial enterprise that must grind
people into statistical grist for the market place and the work force
simultaneously shatters the biosphere in a thousand unforeseen
ways. Nor does this happen (as some radical social critics would
insist) because selfish, profiteering interests are at work. Sometimes that is so. But far more often the real culprit is the world industrial economy *as a whole* as it races toward global integration,
whether under private or socialized auspices. That is the paramount fact we must keep clearly in mind. Here we have an economic style whose dynamism is too great, too fast, too reckless
for the ecological systems that must absorb its impact. It makes
no difference to those systems if the oil spills, the pesticides, the
radioactive wastes, the industrial toxins they must cleanse are
socialist or capitalist in origin; the ecological damage is not mitigated in the least if it is perpetrated by a "good society" that
shares its wealth fairly and provides the finest welfare programs for its citizens. The problem the biosphere confronts is the
convergence of all urban-industrial economies as they thicken and
coagulate into a single planet-wide system everywhere devoted to
maximum productivity and the unbridled assertion of human dominance.

Consider only one recent, well-publicized example of our runaway industrial dynamism. A number of American, European, and
Japanese companies develop the fluorocarbon spray-can dispenser
—a commercial novelty of relatively minor economic significance to
the corporate interests of these societies. For nearly two decades,
the product is blithely mass-produced, advertised, and marketed
on a world-wide scale. It is in daily use everywhere before anybody can collect evidence of its environmental effects—or perhaps
even thinks of making such an investigation. Then, a few inquisitive scientists, acting on the basis of their own private research,
suggest the possibility that the fluorocarbons may be capable of
doing cataclysmic damage to the ozone layer. Their research is

disputed and a public debate ensues. Meanwhile, the fluorocarbons already released continue to rise skyward beyond retrieval, perhaps to rend the biosphere permanently and globally.

Obviously there are profiteering interests at work in the matter—interests whose own health and survival are as much at stake in the situation as anyone's. But the product itself might have been manufactured and distributed in any economic system. And if it had been invented in one of the planned and centralized socialist economies, there may not have been enough internal diversity, critical leverage, and access to publicity even to raise the dangers to public visibility. For it is notorious how little prominence and dissenting power environmentalist forces have in the socialist societies. Indeed, there simply are no independent, ecological movements or lobbies in the collectivist societies, where it is assumed that only capitalist evil can do harm to the people's environment. But in the case of the fluorocarbons, we deal with a problem that has resulted not from willful evil or greedy opportunism, but from simple ignorance. A potentially damaging product made its way into the market place before anybody could anticipate or measure its long-range impact. For that matter, once the danger was publicized—and even before a clear-cut hazard had been documented to everyone's satisfaction—many manufacturers voluntarily ceased production or came up with substitutes that are now smugly advertised as "the environmental formula."

But—and here is the crux of the matter—what if this change of course had not happened fast enough? What if vast and irreversible damage to the global ecology were already under way? What if that should be the case *now,* with any number of chemicals and toxic wastes that are infiltrating the environment and whose individual or combined effects we have not thought to monitor, or perhaps have no way to monitor? We are only now registering the problem of ecological lag with such elements as vinyl chloride, asbestos fiber products, food colorings, and agricultural additives whose impact may take generations to show up. And by then the products are everywhere, worked into the fabric of our daily lives, saturating soil and water, bone and tissue ever more deeply. Only a few years ago, the scare went up that the chlorination of drinking water—a nearly universal practice in the developed societies—might have a long-term carcinogenic effect. If that were so, has anyone any idea how the world would manage to change course and eliminate so pervasive a danger?

Within the past decade we have had a number of sobering conjectures raised by worried scientists about the potentially genocidal impact of industrial substances and practices upon the total biosphere—dangers as vast in scale as the threat which has been seen in the fluorocarbons. Specifically, we have been warned:

- —that the pollution of the seas by oil spills and chemical runoff may be annihilating the phytoplankton that renews much of the oxygen in the atmosphere
- —that deforestation and the massive use of fossil fuels might similarly decrease the global oxygen supply
- —that industrial pollutants in the atmosphere might either warm the planet sufficiently to melt the icecaps and desiccate vast land areas, or cool the planet sufficiently to bring on a new ice age
- —that the indiscriminate dumping of radioactive wastes by the developed societies might contaminate extensive areas of the land and seas, making them sterile zones
- —that overcultivation and the intensive use of petrochemical fertilizers might exhaust the topsoil, leaving the richest life-sustaining areas of the Earth barren
- —that research in recombinant DNA may create viral and bacterial mutants that, should they ever escape from the laboratory, could rapidly kill off whole species of plants and animals, including the human species, and so create ecological chaos.

All these horrors have been front-page news within the last several years; none has been proved or refuted; all are related to practices that continue or have increased. I recount them here to emphasize their most troubling common characteristic: They are vastly imponderable dangers of a nearly irreversible kind that result from the collective action of all the urban-industrial societies. And to them we may add one further and far less speculative risk: that of all-out thermonuclear war, which we might regard as instantaneous and total environmental collapse. The deterrence system of the major world powers is the biggest of all the big systems that menace the planet. And, in this case, the hair-trigger fragility of the war machine makes it possible that misjudgment or an act of political madness might bring about the massive devastation of life on Earth.

It should be clear that a system capable of damage on this scale would be a Frankenstein's monster even if it could be cleansed of all selfish motivations. Its sheer size and pace make it that: a blundering creation that can no more handle the environment with discriminating care than it can deal with its makers as unique persons.

The Problem of Scale

The person and the planet. Here is a connection—a political connection—which is a distinctive contemporary discovery, one that could only become apparent after our economic institutions had reached a certain size and complexity, a certain dizzy level of ambition and impersonal efficiency. Only now do we see that the *scale* of things can be an independent problem of our social life, a factor that may distort even the best intentions of policy. It has taken our unique modern experience with public and private bureaucracies, the mass market, state and corporate industrialism to teach us this lesson. We have learned that human beings can create systems that do not understand human beings and will not serve their needs. And at exactly the same time, we learn how easy it is for these industrial systems to shred the environmental fabric on which all life depends, perhaps even without our realizing what irreparable harm we do. We begin to see that it is not enough to have a worthy social purpose in view, nor even a noble one; we must know the scale of the enterprise which seeks to achieve that purpose. This is not a simple matter of quantitative size; at bottom, scale is a matter of quality, the quality of life and of human relations that results from our collective action in the world. Whatever dwarfs us into unbecoming dependence or diminishes our personal dignity is *too big*. And our sense that it is too big to suit our personal sensibilities is the best warning sign we have that the enterprise is also a hazard to the environment.

There are those who believe that the global environment can still be saved by some world-wide system of surveillance, planning, and administration that will finally stabilize world industrialism. I am thinking here of those like Buckminster Fuller and his "World Planners" or Alvin Toffler with his appeal for a "superindustrial futurism" whose designs are to be implemented by governments and multinational corporations. And of those, too, like the Club of Rome, independent intellectual watchdogs who have set themselves the task of monitoring the world industrial economy and issuing guidelines. It is difficult for me not to see such schemes as, prospectively, a sort of H. G. Wells "Wings over the World" benevolent dictatorship, the ultimate technocracy whose chief project is an ongoing, world-wide environmental impact report and resources inventory. In short, a still bigger system to police all the other big systems that have proved incompetent.

But there is another possibility, and that is the alternative I argue for here: to use the person/planet connection as our chief indicator of healthy economic and environmental policy. We begin from the insight that all systems and institutions that become large enough to inhibit our growth as persons endanger the planet as well. If, then, we work to deepen people's sense of personal worth, strengthen their natural instinct for spiritual growth, augment their citizenly need to participate in the institutions that govern their lives, then they will find within themselves the most delicate gauge of ecologically intelligent scale. *Perhaps this is even the subtle interaction which the Earth uses to defend against our depredations.* As the scale of the industrial system mounts, so also—at least along one important line of contemporary dissent in Western society—do our expectations for freedom and fulfillment, together with our intolerance for whatever denies us the right to achieve our unique being in the world. This, in turn, becomes an obstacle to the further growth and integration of that system; and, accordingly, it begins to *dis*-integrate, but for reasons that are essentially creative. Might we not say that the yearning of people to realize their full personal potentiality is in the nature of a feedback loop that works to restore the human scale of things? In seeking to save our personhood, we assert the human scale. In asserting the human scale, we subvert the regime of bigness. In subverting bigness, we save the planet.

Mother Gaia

> *I shall sing of Gaia, universal mother,*
> *firmly founded, the oldest of divinities.*
>
> Homer

Doubtless, for many of us in the modern West, this is an unfamiliar way to understand our relations with the planet. But I suspect there is very little in the idea which could not be given a sound, scientific interpretation by those who cared to do so. At that level of thought, it is simply a matter of extending the fundamental ecological doctrine that all things in nature are densely, subtly, and systematically interrelated until it includes ourselves, morally and mentally as well as physically. We take the idea as far as it will go, imagining the Earth at large, including ourselves and our culture, as a single, evolving system of life: the great mothering organism of organisms.

This would seem to be the image that the environmental scientists James Lovelock and Sidney Epton have developed in their Gaia hypothesis, an approach to global ecology that envisages the entire Earth as just such a unified entity, actively shaping the material conditions of the planet for the purpose of maximizing the survival and variety of living things. They put the idea like this:

It appeared to us that the Earth's biosphere was able to control at least the temperature of the Earth's surface and the composition of the atmosphere. . . . This led us to the formulation of the proposition that living matter, the air, the oceans, the land surfaces were parts of a giant system which was able to control temperature, the composition of the air and sea, the pH of the soil and so on, so as to be optimum for survival of the biosphere. The system seemed to exhibit the behavior of a single organism, even a living creature. One having such formidable powers deserved a name to match it; William Golding, the novelist, suggested Gaia—the name given by the ancient Greeks to their Earth goddess.

Now, Gaia, as Lovelock and Epton use the concept, is really only a charming metaphor designating their field of ecological study; and what follows from that metaphor is some highly technical chemical and geological analysis. As they admit, Gaia is a hypothesis, not a fact of experience. Still, there clings to the image something of an older and once universal natural philosophy that quite spontaneously experienced the Earth as a divine being animated by its own moods and intentions—the primordial Mother Earth who expected the reverent concern of her children and who was treated to a courteous reciprocity by them in the form of ritual, prayer, and sacrifice. It is striking that, when modern ecology searches for a way to think of the planet dynamically and wholistically, it gropes its way back to that classic act of personification. Mother Earth. Mother Nature. The White Goddess. The Queen of the herd and the harvest as old as human culture itself. And though they use the language of systems analysis, the ecologists finish on a note of urgent moral counsel which ancient Gaia would surely have appreciated.

One of the laws of system control is that, if a system is to maintain stability, it must possess adequate variety of response. . . . What is to be feared is that man-the-farmer and man-the-engineer are reducing the total variety of response open to Gaia. . . . Natural distribution of plants and animals is being changed, ecological systems destroyed, and whole species altered or deleted. . . . Long before the world population has grown so large that we consume the entire output from photosynthesizers, instabilities generated by lack of variety of response could intervene to put this level out of reach.

And there follows an appeal that might almost be a shaman's prayer: "Let us make peace with Gaia on her own terms and return to peaceful co-existence with our fellow creatures."

The Return of the Goddess

> *The women gather to invoke the Goddess.*
> *The women gather in a circle and speak*
> *Her name.*
> *The women call the Lady out of darkness and*
> *give to Her a shape they recognize.*
> *The women gather in a circle. With their*
> *words they give the Lady form.*
>
> (lines from a women's summer solstice ritual)

The Gaia hypothesis may never finally rate higher in biological circles than a minor, marginally useful paradigm in the still fledgling science of human ecology. But in other quarters of our society outside the perimeter of professional science, the image of the Earth as a living personality has sounded strong existential chords. There are, for example, the various neopagan cults that have sprung up in America since the mid-sixties as part of the current religious and mystical revival. At the hands of sensationalistic journalists, such groups have usually been indiscriminately lumped together with astrology, tarot cards, psychic readings, etc., and reported as an "occult explosion" that supposedly represents the worst excesses of irrationality. And, admittedly, there has been enough in this mixed and muddled scene to sensationalize and disparage; much that goes by the name of witchcraft and magic has been little more than childish fancy or mindless mumbo jumbo. But there are also those whose pagan sympathies stem from a serious desire to salvage the nature worship of the pre-Christian past and to adapt that lost sensibility to the needs of the time. There are neopagans who speak of having an "ecopsychic" mission and whose goal is to restore that vivid sense of dialogue between person and planet which represents the most significant meaning of magic. As Margot Adler, one of the most competent and critical students of the neopagan cults, observes:

they [the neopagans] are usually polytheists or animists or pantheists, or several of these things at once. They share a goal of living in attunement and harmony with nature and they tend to view humanity's "advancement" and separation from nature as the prime source of alienation. They see ritual as a tool to reunify human beings with nature and to end that alienation. . . . The story of the revival of Wicca is . . . the story of people who are searching among very powerful and archaic images of nature, of life and death, creation and destruction. Modern Wiccans are using these images to change their relationship to the world. The search for these images and their use must be seen as valid, no matter how limited and impoverished the outer forms of the Wiccan revival sometimes appear, and no matter how misreported this revival is in the press.

What the new pagans "revive" can sometimes look like an anthropological collage of myths and rituals that smacks more of research than religious experience, and which may owe more to modern interpreters like Robert Graves than to any more primitive source. But at the heart of the matter there is the significant insight that our environmental ills will not be healed by economic reform and aesthetic sensitivity alone. Underlying these, there must be a sense of ethical respect, if not of reverence, that can only exist between persons. As one modern witch interviewed by Adler put it, "paganism is the spirituality of the ecological movement."

Avowed neopagans are, of course, a minute minority of our society, and their cultural influence must not be exaggerated. (Adler estimates there cannot be more than between five and ten thousand people directly involved in the cults in this country, and even that figure includes many weekend witches and dilettante druids.) Their presence among us is more important as one marked symptom of a widespread restlessness with the ascetic objectivity of modern science and the compulsive productivity of industrial life. The materials and interests from which the neopagans have formulated their world view have found an audience that extends well beyond their own limited numbers. The best-selling popularity of Carlos Castaneda's Don Juan books, of Tolkien's sword and sorcery fantasies, of science fiction mysticism like Robert Heinlein's *Stranger in a Strange Land*—all these reveal an undiminished public appetite for the mystery and enchantment our science no longer yields. As does—along more morbid lines—the appeal of satanic and occult films like *The Exorcist*. To be sure, such sources, like all the sources on which popular culture draws, may be ersatz or highly doctored, distorted or sentimentalized, and their persistent popularity will be seen by some critical minds as a "failure of nerve," an incorrigible human weakness for superstition. But I believe, among all its follies and perversions, this fascination for the extraordinary participates, or ought to participate, in our authentic knowledge of the world; for it is what personalizes knowledge, lending it the force of metaphysical security and moral conviction. William C. Gray, a contemporary scholar of Western magic, is exactly right in his conclusion that

> the function of magic in our times lies largely with fulfillment of an almost desperate need for advancing individuals to maintain a sense of spiritual identity in the swelling seas of collectivism threatening to swallow all our souls. If entities are ever to evolve efficiently, they need to become exactly what they ought to be in and *as* the Selves they fundamentally are. . . . Some magical systems claim to awaken this spiritual Self-sense by processes often involving stress techniques and ritual psychodramatics. Be that as it may, the field of genuine magic in the West does afford unique scope for souls struggling to individuate in a modern world.

Thus far, the neopagan sense of living personality in nature has found its sharpest focus and what may be its greatest cultural force in the women's liberation movement, where a lively concern for "feminist spirituality" has inspired an outspoken commitment to witchcraft, geomancy, and ritual magic. This effort to re-create the ancient Mother Earth mythology and its women's mysteries brings together ideological and religious energies in ways that can sometimes confuse political principle, psychic need, and historical accuracy. But however much one may wish to question the scholarly and scientific credentials of feminist neopagans, theirs is a significant contemporary attempt to invent a new (or perhaps I should say to revive a very old) relationship to the Earth, one which grants the planet its personhood and its sacred rights. What we have here might be called an exercise in participative research that seeks the empowering truth behind the anthropological facts.

> Our bleak and holy Mother
> Carries our souls in Her gaunt
> Womb. And we, like tides, rise up to greet
> Our exiled selves in Her.

So runs, in part, an invocation to the Earth delivered at the first major festival devoted to women's spirituality; it was held in Boston in the spring of 1976. There, witches and would-be Amazons, priestesses and daughters of the moon assembled unashamedly to celebrate the Old Religion that lies (in Mary Daly's phrase) "beyond God the Father." It was called "a gynergenetic experience" and brought together an extraordinary variety of women from many backgrounds and political persuasions, of all ages and talents. From the outside, especially to any academically inclined men looking on, such a gathering must have seemed bizarre in the extreme. Deliberately intended to remain formless and fluid, the event respected none of the hierarchies and structures of male conferences. Its spirit was wholly one of participation and free imaginative invention. Rituals were shared, celebrations and rites improvised in a way that blended art with research. No doubt for that very reason the meeting brimmed with fresh insights and ideas: a fine example of what may come of the creative disintegration of established forms. And, if viewed with even a touch of supportive sympathy, it presented a compelling indictment of "masculinist and patriarchal" culture for its crimes against the person and the planet. Barbara Starret put the case with sensitive precision in the keynote address:

> The male society has made rape the prototypical expression of its patterns. Domination of the other by force: of nature and land and resources, of "inferior" nations and groups, of women, of money and markets and material goods. . . . Victim: that's an important word. It is the most descriptive noun we have to designate the role women (and homosexuals and the environ-

ment and nature and third world people, etc.) must play in order to act out the prevailing drama of the death pattern. . . . Take a look at male institutions. There is no way to function as a person within them. You are either the victim or the oppressor (most often both) in a vertical and sado-masochistic system. The system itself absorbs the responsibility and the guilt. . . . Value judgments, moral action, emotions and personal relationships are destroyed within the impersonal but internally consistent structure of the system's vertical lines of power.

But the festival did more than issue an indictment; it reasserted buried feminine values that will have a central role to play in saving the rights of the planet. Since Henry Adams wrote his famous essay on "the Dynamo and the Virgin" in the early part of this century, many sensitive minds have counseled us to welcome the traditionally feminine virtues back into our lives—the intuitive, the compassionate, the organically nurturing and trusting—as a life-giving discipline that will balance our society's technological excesses. The idea is one of the central insights of Jungian psychiatry and, along these lines, has flowed into much of the art, literature, and philosophy of our time. Now, in these bold, new celebrations of feminist spirituality that emerge from the women's movement, we see that insight becoming an experience, and the experience becoming a cause. There are women who want to do more than talk learnedly about repressed femininity. They want to *live* those virtues in ways that will give them a distinctive public expression, a healing cultural force. Does it matter very much if their ritual improvisations and mythological variations are often based on some shaky historical speculation? That is, at most, a minor pedantic objection, and once it has been spoken as a sort of cautionary footnote, it has nothing more to offer. It is to the present need of our culture that these neopagan revivalists are speaking, and I think, in doing so, they speak with a power greater than their own. They bring the militancy of personal urgency to what is otherwise no better than some plausible academic theories. Which is how ideas make history, if they ever do.

. . . the spirit of the Earth has roused herself again [so wrote one participant at the Boston festival] and, after yawning away centuries of sleep, has looked at the havoc man has wrought upon her. Slowly, slowly, she wakens, her rage begins to build! Slowly, slowly, as her rage builds, her daughters, remembering themselves as goddesses, Ancient Ones, feel her rage as One, and light the fires of change. And now we move. And now we burn again.

Clearly, there are those among us, at least in the women's movement, who recognize the ecological emergency of our time for the profound spiritual failure it is. They know we are not going to save ourselves with a quick technological fix and more efficient resource management. Rather, the Goddess is going to have to be reborn in our midst, not simply as a systems analyst's hypothesis, but as living culture. Where the movement for women's liberation reaches to that awareness, it becomes something far larger and stronger than another political cause. In the depths of their tormented personhood, women—*some* women—join forces with the life of the planet and become her peculiar voice.

The Bride of Frankenstein

These current explorations of feminist spirituality call to mind a scene in Mary Shelley's *Frankenstein,* a single, terrifying moment that foretells and diagnoses the ecological disaster of our time. I have always been impressed to find so brilliant an insight in so flawed a book, especially in this first, amateurish effort of a girl not yet out of her teens. It is evidence, I suppose, that great myths write themselves, carrying their human instruments beyond their own powers.

The incident comes immediately after the doctor, "the modern Prometheus," has brought his unnatural creation to life and has seen the hideous thing awaken. Horrified by what he has done, he rushes from his laboratory and locks himself in his bedroom.

At length lassitude succeeded to the tumult I had before endured; and I threw myself on the bed in my clothes, endeavoring to seek a few moments of forgetfulness. But it was in vain: I slept, indeed, but I was disturbed by the wildest dreams. I thought I saw Elizabeth [his fiancée] in the bloom of health, walking in the streets of Ingolstadt. Delighted and surprised, I embraced her; but as I imprinted the first kiss on her lips, they became livid with the hue of death; her features appeared to change, and I thought that I held the corpse of my dead mother in my arms; a shroud enveloped her form, and I saw the grave-worms crawling in the folds of the flannel. I started from my sleep with horror; a cold dew covered my forehead, my teeth chattered, and every limb was convulsed: when, by the dim and yellow light of the moon as it forced its way through the window shutters, I beheld the wretch—the miserable monster whom I had created. He held up the curtain of the bed; and his eyes, if eyes they may be called, were fixed on me. His jaws opened, and he muttered some inarticulate sounds, while a grin wrinkled his cheeks.

These are significant dreams that boil up in the great scientist's fevered brain. Elizabeth is the woman he is to marry. But he has put off the wedding and turned from her to pursue his unholy experiments. Instead of the child he might have brought into the world through her love, he has undertaken to create his own artificial offspring—a monstrous son who is no more than an animated cadaver. Methodically, maniacally, he has spent his days and nights in a dismal laboratory, stitching together the morbid remnants he has stolen from the graveyard. Now, regretting his deed, he reaches out in his dream to take back the love he might have had . . . but his bride becomes a corpse in his arms, and the corpse becomes his dead mother, crawling with worms. At that moment, he wakes to see the monster's face grinning down at him, blotting out the images of bride and mother. Later, on Frankenstein's wedding night, the monster will return to murder the doctor's bride.

Who is the mother that Frankenstein holds in his arms? Mother Nature . . . Mother Earth . . . killed by his ruthless, masculine claim to dominance. He would outdo her, strip her of her mysteries, replace her with his own scientific cunning. Therefore, she dies to him—dies *within* him. All that was womanly in his nature is blasted by his arrogant design, and he is left alone in a world terrorized by the soulless monstrosity he has created. Our habit is to give such images—whether we find them in a Gothic tale or in the old myths—a psychological translation. We take them to be "mere" symbols, ideas wholly generated from inside our own heads and therefore having no "real" or objective status. They are only fears or feelings, only so many fragments of mental furniture; we may make of them what we will, distort or ignore them. We do not experience them as a word addressed to us; we do not think they are "facts."

And there we have the furthest extreme that masculine dominance has reached in our technological culture. Obsessed with numbers, objects, property, physical force we have learned to deny the facts of our feeling, the reality of our intuitive powers. We split the "inside" from the "outside" and then denigrate the subjective, insisting that it is fantasy wholly of our own arbitrary invention. That is how we deafen ourselves to the voice of the sacred, to the language of the Earth. We turn from the truth of symbol, which is the language of the sacred within us. We do not hear the message of the Goddess because we say her language is without "objective reference." So we insist that myths, symbols, visions, rituals—all these that were the teachings of the Old Religion—have "only" a *personal* meaning. But what if personal meaning is where we find the planet's message? Where, after all, did Dr. Frankenstein discover the truth about himself and his work? In a dream . . . and then, too late.

What we know of ourselves "inside" is ultimately what we will allow ourselves to know of nature "outside," for nature is also *us*. It is all that has gone into our physical, mental, and moral identity, both as we might study and as we must experience these aspects of ourselves. We are intimately part of the pattern we try to understand when we investigate the world. When we "step back" to gain an objective perspective, nature steps back with us and is still there, the viewer as well as the viewed. The web of the universe threads its way through our art and dream and intellect. This is what it means to have an "organic" sense of the world—to know

things as we are part of things, rather than as if we were comput-
ing machines imported into an alien universe merely to measure
and classify its behavior. Thus, visions, myths, and rituals are a
way of knowing the world as our presence permeates that world;
they are a humanly participative science. This is the critical point
Noel Phyllis Birkby and Leslie Kanes Weisman raise when they
counsel women that,

> in our continuing search for origins and expressions of sexism,
> we must develop and project our own imagery and values into
> environmental forms. . . . We must begin by evaluating our
> *manmade* environment from a feminist perspective. Our physi-
> cal environment, whether it is buildings, communities or cities,
> reflects the nature of our institutions and the priorities of the de-
> cision makers. . . . We feel that this process will increase our
> awareness of the powerful nexus between fantasy and reality. In
> this way our dreams and visions can become tools for the crea-
> tion of actual change.

If there are now women among us who want to stop being part
of the "we," the collective, masculine "we" I have been so loosely
using here to refer to our scientized modern culture, that is the beginning of a remarkable historical departure. If they look to Wiccan tradition for pride and guidance, I think it is because they
have begun to hear a long-forgotten language. The planet is making herself heard through those who have suffered her own oppres-
sions. She catches at the edge of women's minds, re-*mind*ing them,
re-*mind*ing us. Wholeness is our goal; but just now, at this juncture in history, for all of us who are sunk in this Frankensteinian
culture of compulsive masculine dominance, the road to wholeness
leads through the feminine.

> The New Age will be the Age of the Female. [So Barbara Star-
> ret has put it.] We must consciously will the emergence of that
> age in ourselves, for it will be born of us. We must break out of
> and through the old, patriarchal programming, step by step, un-
> til this planet is truly free, truly loving, truly power-full. The
> strongest emotion is love. Can we begin to love each other, love

our visions, love ourselves, so intensely, so passionately, that the power of love is transformed into new realities? That is the meaning of alchemy. We are the new alchemists.

Science Beyond Reductionism

At this point, I realize I am a long way into what some may regard as feminist extremism and what others might see as some very tenuous mystical speculations. Yet, the living continuity of person and planet I discuss here happens to be a remarkably constant and ordinary part of my own experience and, I suspect, of many other people in their private moments. If the experience is "mystical," it is only in the sense that it has been censored in one odd culture for a few odd centuries at a certain narrow, but highly influential level of specialized, scientific intellect. We have, as a culture, been talked into the proposition that our security as a species depends upon our power over nature; and, in turn, we have been persuaded that our power over nature requires us to screen the personhood of nature out of our lives—even as a professional torturer must begin by denying the personhood of his victims in order to gain total control over them.

But now, that proposition turns out to be exactly wrong, and blatantly so. The power upon which it is predicated is rapidly proving to be illusory; the environment deteriorates in its supposed master's hand, and our promised security dwindles. How quickly can we expect a new cultural consensus to develop that respects the personhood of the Earth and summons us to live more trustfully within her life-sustaining disciplines? At first glance, everything about the natural philosophy of urban-industrial society may seem to thwart that possibility. In earlier books and articles, I have written at length, and with no little polemical heat, criticizing the "single vision" and "alienative dichotomy" of modern Western science—habits of mind which have sternly repressed the experience of vital reciprocity between ourselves and nature. But then, in the many encounters I have had with scientists over the past ten years, I have again and again met men and women who insist that this is *not* what science must be, that their own sensibilities have never surrendered to what I have called "the myth of objective consciousness." They have convinced me that this vast, many-sided adventure we call "science" is far from being a monolithic establishment. As much today as in the past there are unorthodox currents and eddies of resistance within the mainstream that flow toward divergent methodologies, alternative realities. It may well be that, under the pressure of crisis, these dissenting forces will carry us toward a sacramental vision of nature that is distinctly contemporary in style, and which does less violence to scientific fact than at first might seem necessary. It may only be a question of attention respectfully offered, properly directed—or, more accurately, attention liberated and allowed to respond to perceptions we have formed the habit of blocking. Let me mention only a few of the sources we can draw upon within the province of science itself in developing a new consensus on the nature of nature.

1. There are, to begin with, a number of informed critics, many of them trained scientists, who have raised challenging questions about the adequacy of scientific method and theory, not with a view to subverting science but with the intention of broadening its sensibilities and eliminating its reductionistic propensities. Where the critique is pursued far enough, it reaches beyond abstract epistemology; it becomes an inquiry into the psychology and metaphysics of scientific thought—its quality of experience, its capacity for critical, corrective self-awareness. Abraham Maslow has called the program that derives from such an approach "hierarchical integration," the graceful blending of scientific objectivity with the sensuous, intuitive, and visionary capacities of the mind. (Maslow's pioneering study *The Psychology of Science* is basic reading here. So too the work of Michael Polanyi, Arthur Koestler, Seyyed Hossein Nasr, Owen Barfield, Jacob Needleman. In this category as in those that follow, I make no effort to produce a complete list, but only to give representative names whose writing will introduce other readings. See the notes for this chapter for other authors and titles.)

2. There are the expanding fields of consciousness research and parapsychology, which, beginning as they do from the unexplored potentialities of mind, tend to choose paradigms of nature that are

mental rather than mechanical. Almost invariably, the methodologies of these fields assume transactional possibilities between mind and matter, the human and nonhuman. Thus, Charles Tart speaks of creating "state specific sciences" that pay as much attention to preparing the consciousness of the knower as to examining the physical properties of the known. (Tart, Lawrence LeShan, R. B. Thouless, Karl Pribram, Stanley Krippner, John White, Joseph Kamiya.)

3. There are the frontier theoretical physicists and mathematicians who deal in paradoxes of time, space, mass, and perception that often lead them back to insights derived from mystical and Oriental traditions, all of which propose images of nature that are spiritual-mental-organismic, rather than materialistic-mechanistic. For example, J. H. M. Whiteman contends that "physics itself has forced upon us a new world view, which corresponds in an astonishing way with what famous philosophers and mystics, from direct insight and experience, have been declaring over a period of two thousand years at least (Buddha, the Upanishads, Plato, Plotinus, Leibniz). We have today reached the point where all these currents of research have begun to merge." (David Bohm, John Wheeler, Fritjof Capra, Charles Musés, Werner Heisenberg, C. F. von Weizsäcker.)

4. There are the morphic and systems scientists who trace back to the school of German Romantic *Naturphilosophie*. This style of science deals in ideas of creative form, global variables, co-ordinative and hierarchical process, systematic integration, all of which suggest a conception of nature as purposive, finalistic, teleological. Once again, this brings us close to a vision of natural reality as mind or consciousness. (Alfred North Whitehead, Lancelot Law Whyte, Ludwig von Bertalanffy, Adolf Portmann.)

5. There are the wholistic and psychic-mental healers whose work in autogenics, biofeedback, theta training, voluntary self-regulation, etc., suggests a nonreductive mental-physical continuity which demands a greater place for organic and mental models in our understanding of nature. (Elmer and Alyce Green, Kenneth Pelletier, Gay Luce, Carl and Stephanie Simonton.) At its extreme, wholistic healing shades off into the transcendent body al-

chemy of Michael Murphy's Transformation Project, which hopes to unify Western science and a variety of yogic exercises for the purpose of achieving an etherealization of physical matter.

6. There is Sir Alister Hardy's Religious Experience Research Unit at Manchester College, Oxford, which is continuing the line of psychological investigation begun by William James and Edwin Starbuck in the early twentieth century. Hardy, coming to the field from a distinguished career in biology, works from the assumption that consciousness in nature transcends its physical-chemical apparatus, most fully revealing its autonomous powers in the form of ecstatic and visionary experience. The project has led Hardy into many unorthodox lines of speculation, including the possibility of telepathic influences in evolution. At this point, his work joins forces with a sizable body of dissenting biological thought which inclines to giving purpose and will a greater role in evolution than natural selection. (Pierre Le Comte du Noüy, Edmund Sinnott, C. L. Morgan, W. M. Wheeler.)

7. There are anthropologists and environmental scientists who have drawn upon primitive and folk cultures to develop a stronger sense of the values to be found in myth and ritual for the maintenance of healthy ecosystems. (I have already mentioned James Lovelock. Add the work of Ian McHarg, Dorothy Lee, Stanley Diamond. Among the ecologists who are cultivating a sense of moral rapport with the environment, we have Aldo Leopold, Paul Shepard, John Todd and his colleagues at the New Alchemy Institute.)

8. Moving further into the controversial fringes, we have scientists and philosophers who draw skillfully upon the insights of esoteric, occult, and alchemical tradition with a view to supplementing scientific knowledge. Whatever we borrow from these sources contributes to our capacity for a personalistic experience of nature. (Ernst Lehrs, Theodor Schwenk, Arthur Young.)

9. Finally, to step outside the boundaries of professional science, we have the rhapsodic pantheism of the Western nature mystics reaching back to St. Francis and down to Dylan Thomas, Gary Snyder, Wendell Berry, Allen Ginsberg. In our own time, this native strain of visionary art mixes freely with primitive and Oriental

influences, thus feeling its way back to what Snyder has called "the Great Tradition" and what I have referred to in other works as "the Old Gnosis": the ancient and original natural philosophy of our species. But why must this powerful and incisive body of work continue to stand apart from science? The experience of nature poets and landscape painters is no less studied and disciplined, no less empirical than that of scientists. It evidences the natural reality around us and within us as astutely as atomistic analysis or laboratory experimentation. This is the point that the chemist Thomas Blackburn has made in arguing for a "sensuous-intellectual complementarity in science":

> By relying lopsidedly on abstract quantification as a method of knowing, scientists have been looking at the world with one eye closed. There is other knowledge, and there are other ways of knowing besides reading the position of a pointer on a scale. The human mind and body process information with staggering sophistication and sensitivity by the direct sensuous experience of their surroundings.

Thus, when Wordsworth tells us that

> To every natural form, rock, fruit, or flower,
> Even the loose stones that cover the highway,
> I gave a moral life: I saw them feel,
> . . . and all
> That I beheld respired with inward meaning,

might we not regard his utterance as the sensuous and imaginative *inside* of the same objective continuities which modern science has taught us to see throughout nature? Scientific fact experienced from *within,* understood as we seek to understand the patterns of human conduct—by sharing their intentional meaning, their personal address.

The Vital Reciprocity

Once, so we have been taught by science textbooks since our school days, the Earth was barren rock and vapor. Then her lethargic chemicals were somehow touched with life, and, at last, the planet "peopled"—as spontaneously as a tree bears fruit in season. All this, the long natural history of the Earth, is treasured up in us. The salt of ancient seas can still be found in our blood. The rhythm of the moon is echoed in the cycles of the female body. The remembered shapes of our evolutionary ancestry are recapitulated in every human embryo. In some sense that blends science and myth, vision and history, we were mothered out of the substance of this planet. Her elements, her periodicities, her gravitational embrace, her subtle vibrations still mingle in our nature, worked a billion years down into the textures of life and mind. Even our queer, alienating consciousness rises out of some uncanny potentiality of her elemental stuff. Can a few generations of urbanization and a century or two of scientific skepticism really be enough to cut us off forever from the sense of vital reciprocity between ourselves and the planet that was once the universal knowledge of our race? I think none of us who have experienced even a glimmer of that living continuity should find it hard to accept that our destiny is tied to the need and the will of the Earth. Perhaps what we lack is only the courage to speak what we know.

How, then, could we now pass into an era of acute ecological emergency, as terrible an emergency as the planetary biosphere has ever known, and not feel the tug of that reciprocity upon us— a deep organic remembrance, a warning, *an instruction?* But how would we expect the Earth to issue such an instruction? Would we expect it to roll down from the skies—or be proclaimed to us by a goddess who rose from the sea? Surely, we know that the web of nature is spun more subtly than that. The instruction would come to us in the one language most capable of transforming our conduct: not as a command from above or beyond, but as a moral idea realized from within. Just as the planet thinks through us, so we, in our thinking, may draw upon themes and images as ancient as the planet's own star-burst birth. Again, to quote Lovelock and Epton:

We are sure that man needs Gaia, but could Gaia do without man? In man, Gaia has the equivalent of a central nervous system and an awareness of herself and the rest of the universe. Through man, she has a rudimentary capacity, capable of development, to anticipate and guard against threats to her existence. . . . Can it then be that in the course of man's evolution within Gaia, he has been acquiring the knowledge and skills necessary to ensure her survival?

Suppose, then, that we and the Earth who mothered us are indeed a single organic network, a pattern of life within which it is our special role to be the planet's risky experiment in self-conscious intelligence. Suppose the main purpose of that experiment has now been achieved: the creation of an interdependent world society that promises physical security for all and a world-cultural synthesis that will at last express the human oneness we see prefigured in the magnificent image of the Earth herself as she has been photographed from outer space. Finally, suppose—as is all too obvious—that the planet's prime need is now to moderate our technological and organizational excesses so that all her endangered children might live.

What, then, does the Earth do? She begins to speak to something in us—an ideal of life, a sense of identity—that has until now been harbored within only an eccentric and marginal few. She digs deep into our unexplored nature to draw forth a passion for self-knowledge and personal recognition that has lain slumbering in us like an unfertilized seed. And so, quite suddenly, in the very heartland of urban-industrial society, a generation appears that instinctively yearns for a quality of life wholly incompatible with the giganticism of our economic and technological structures. And the cry of personal pain which that generation utters is the planet's own cry for rescue, her protest against the bigness of things becoming one with ours. So we begin to look for alternatives to that person-and-planet-crushing colossalism. We search for ways to disintegrate the bigness—to disintegrate it *creatively* into humanly scaled, organically balanced communities and systems that free us from the deadly industrial compulsions of the past.

That the needs of the planet should be the needs of the person—

of course, the idea can be dismissed as fanciful conjecture. But not without risking the loss of a valuable scientific possibility. After all, the science that dominates our culture is pledged to the supposition of nature's unity. At one critical point, however, that supposition seems wholly unable to advance; that is where it confronts the human mind. Here, the only continuities that have been elucidated to the satisfaction of conventional science are essentially reductionistic efforts to assimilate mentality to the neurological behavior of the brain. But the brain clearly does not "explain" the mind. It may reveal how certain low-grade processes take place, or perhaps only *where* they take place, but it tells us nothing of the higher powers of consciousness—will, inspiration, creativity, intuition, humor, invention, moral choice. Neurology cannot even begin to cope with the way in which the mind constructs meaning —including the meanings that make neurology itself "meaningful." From what we know of the brain's electrochemistry, we could not predict the potentialities of the mind any more than the music of Chopin could ever have been predicted by an exhaustive physical analysis of the piano. The mind uses the brain just as the composer uses the piano—and, in both cases, creative imagination constantly and astonishingly expands the capacities of the instrument it employs.

Where, then, do we look to find intimations of mind in nature that are consonant with our experience of freedom, originality, and meaning? Or is mentality, the very origin and motivating force of science, to be left as an isolated anomaly in the universe, a radical disjuncture in the continuity of nature?

Perhaps the problem is that modern science, especially biology and psychology, continues to work from a physical-mechanistic model of nature and then, assuming this to be an accurate image of reality, seeks to account for everything, including the mind, in terms of that model—at most allowing its mechanistic metaphor to assume the sophistication of the latest data-processing technology. This may grant the brain and the biochemistry of the cell as much complexity as the computer, but that is still not enough to account for the inventive richness of self-conscious mentality as it expresses itself in language, art, visionary experience. And, in any case, the only mechanisms we know exist because they were created in the first place by intelligent organisms; that temporal sequence—organisms first, machines second—vitiates every effort to subsume life and mind under a materialistic-mechanistic explanation. Machines do not make themselves, and the only meaning that exists in matter is mind-imposed.

What, then, if the mechanistic model of reality is exactly the inverse of the truth? Suppose that mentality is the basic, irreducible continuum of the universe, in the sense that wholes, patterns, purposes, co-ordinated processes—all of which look as if they were modeled on ideas—are more fundamental than their constituent bits and pieces. It is a hypothesis that continues to haunt the borders of science, as the several kinds of scientific speculation mentioned in this chapter indicate. Sir James Jeans, extrapolating from the findings of modern physics a half century ago, surely exaggerated the willingness of scientists to relinquish their reductionistic habits; but his words embody what may yet become the guiding image of the next scientific revolution:

> Today there is a wide measure of agreement, which on the physical side of science approaches almost to unanimity, that the stream of knowledge is heading towards a non-mechanical reality; the universe begins to look more like a great thought than like a great machine.
>
> Mind no longer appears as an accidental intruder into the realm of matter; we are beginning to suspect that we ought rather to hail it as the creator and governor of the realm of matter.

Similarly, Sir Arthur Eddington, writing at about the same time, suggested that "the stuff of the world is mind-stuff."

If orthodox scientific thought has not yet come round to endorsing such ideas, it is because, in its impetuous search for power, modern science began its history with a hard, stubborn emphasis on the reductive, mechanistic aspect of nature. Only from such a vantage point could it gain its manipulative purchase on the natural forces it sought to control. Thus, physics came to be seen as the most "fundamental" science, because it studies nature at its deadest, most depersonalized level. If there is mentality to be found in nature—something that corresponds to and resonates with the powers of human thought—it could only emerge in a science that studies comprehensive, self-regulating natural wholes and purposeful patterns of interaction that include the human as well as the nonhuman. We call that science "ecology," the last science of all to assume professional status, and the one science that seeks to integrate mind and matter within some sensible paradigm.

Certainly, one paradigm that would suit the needs of ecology is that of personal communication: mind reaching out to mind, intention impinging upon intention. I cannot say how the ecologists might best envisage the notion that nature "speaks" to us; I doubt that any of the traditional, animistic world views we inherit from the past could be adopted directly. They come to us too much bound up with a lore and imagery we have grown away from; but the transactional sensibility on which these older natural philosophies were based is still within our experiential repertory waiting to be given a lively, contemporary translation.

Ecology is the one science that possesses the ability to recapture the experience of personality in nature. And it comes into its own as a profession at exactly the same time that an intense awareness of personhood enters our political life. We have begun to liberate the Earth from her false identity—the mechanistic-reductionistic image which has made nature into an object of unfeeling manipulation—just as we begin to fight our way free of the false identities which have made human beings the objects of social power.

In the two chapters that follow, we will enter more deeply into the psychology and history of the rising personalist ethos. We will discuss, first of all, the ways in which its attendant sense of innocence is working to subvert the culture of guilt from which industrial society draws its harsh ethical discipline. And secondly, we will trace personalist political philosophy back through a strange and ancient genealogy. As we pursue the discussion—both of inner experience and of historical development—let us keep in mind the planetary forces that may lie behind the cultural transition we are in. Perhaps what announces itself in our experience as political idea or moral ideal is first of all in the Earth as a mothering instinct, the natural will of this remarkable planet to shelter and perfect her cargo of life.

Chapter 3

Innocence and Anarchy: The Ethics of Personhood

The Boy Who Wasn't "Quite Right"

Not far from the house where I grew up in Chicago there lived a young man named Lester, or Les, as he preferred to call himself. Les had a special reputation in the neighborhood. He was known by everybody as the "funny-looking" boy . . . the one who wasn't "quite right." Looking back now, I suspect Les suffered from cerebral palsy, but no one in my neighborhood seemed to know the term then. I remember once or twice hearing him called "spastic" and at other times (in a considerate half-whisper) a "moron." But most often, people, including his parents, spoke of Les as "not quite right."

Les was crippled in one arm and one leg, and he had a nasty twist to his body. When he walked, he lurched along and dragged one foot with the toe pointed in. He was short and dumpy, and that helped make him "funny-looking." But when people said he wasn't "quite right," what they had in mind was his seeming retardation. His eyes goggled a little, and, when he talked, his voice came out hoarse and halting. Sometimes he stammered and drooled over his words, though he seldom said more to people he met on the street than "hello," "good-by," "yes, sir . . . no, sir," "yes, ma'am . . . no, ma'am." He also tended to squinch his nose over to one side and labored noticeably with his breathing; you could sometimes hear him snorting as he came by.

When I knew him, Les may have been in his mid-twenties, but he still liked to play with the boys on the block. He was surprisingly good at tossing a ball around and owned some deluxe athletic equipment he would let us borrow. Since he was old enough to buy cigarettes for the boys in the local shops, he became a popular companion. The fact is, we came to know Les the way no-body else did. When he was with us, he didn't show any signs of retardation or general incompetence. His speech became clear and confident and utterly intelligent. I remember he could talk baseball better than anybody in the neighborhood. Moreover, he had the gift of mechanical aptitude. He had built a fine model railway that filled most of the basement in his house, and which was the envy of us all.

Les didn't work. His mother "looked after" him all day, every day. He stayed home, read books, worked on his model trains . . . and simply got looked after. Les's mother had very definite ideas about looking after her boy. She kept him close to home at all times, reminded him not to dirty his clothes, watched to make sure he never exerted himself too much, chased the boys away if she heard any obscene language, and called Les in to take his nap every afternoon. When she called him in, she always called him "Lester." The name made Les scowl. He would stammer curses under his breath, and once I heard him mutter, "She could call me Les. She could do that." But he always obeyed and went in for his nap. Odd, now that I think of it, that he should have wanted to be called Les. "Less" was not what he wanted to be.

Three or four times each week and regularly every Sunday, Les and his parents would go for a walk through the neighborhood. Les's mother would dress her son up in a hat, tie, and freshly pressed suit, so that he might have the chance to "look like other people," as she put it—though there were not many people in our neighborhood who dressed that way. The family would have Les walk a few paces ahead, tipping his hat to everybody as he passed and saying "hello," "good-by," "yes, sir . . . no, sir," "yes, ma'am . . . no, ma'am." That was also odd. Nobody else went about tipping his hat or saying "sir" or "ma'am." But when Les came by, all the neighbors would say, "Don't they dress him up neat?" "Isn't he polite?"

Then, one day, Les began to carry a small bouquet of flowers on some of these peregrinations. Those, his mother explained as they stopped along the way, were for "Lester's girl friend." The girl friend was a second cousin who lived a few blocks away, out of the neighborhood. Les's mother described her as "a very nice, *normal* girl" whom Lester was "just visiting, you know." She said that with a look that showed she didn't want anybody to get the wrong idea. Lester was calling on a young lady, but it was only his cousin, so it wasn't *really* what you might think.

One day, the word got around that Les was gone. He had been taken away—by the police. The neighbors spoke about it in hushed and scandalized tones. I found out from the other boys what had happened. Les had gotten up in the dead of night, had taken his deluxe baseball bat, and had smashed everything in the house he could get at, including his railway trains and several windows. So the police had come and his parents had "put him away." The rumor was that Les had proposed to his cousin the day before the incident and had been rejected. In some reports, there were darker hints: that he had "made a pass" at the girl, or that he had tried to "*do* something, you know, something he oughtn't." I recall people saying, with great distaste, that he had no business trying anything like *that*. He was a very neat boy, and very polite, but he had no business "forcing himself" on a "normal" girl, because, after all, he wasn't "quite right." So of course he had been rejected. And that must have been why he "went off his head."

After that night, we never saw Les again, and a few months later, his parents moved away.

Identity Boxes

Les belongs to the world of a million years ago: the world of alienated identities and natural-born victims. It was a world that knew there were "right" and "not quite right" ways to be, and regarded those ways as eternal, indisputable, inexorable. They were fate—everybody's fate. That world is still with us. But almost by the day, it shows up in more people's eyes as a prehistoric landscape. Now, as I recount Les's story, I do so with every confidence that those who read it will recognize at once what I cannot recall anybody recognizing when it happened—that it is the story of a vi-

cious injustice, the injustice that results when human identity comes
to be seen as an assigned duty, rather than an open adventure.

In the America of the thirties and forties where I grew up, there
were only a finite few roles in life. Those roles were defined by parameters which stood like great stone walls across one's life: age,
race, sex, class, sometimes job and profession. There were just so
many ways to be rich or poor, old or young, male or female; so
many ways to look, act, dress, feel. The variations were tightly restricted. A woman ought to be married and at home, but she *could*
work; economic necessity demanded it of millions of women, especially during the war years. But if she did, she became Tillie the
Toiler in the office or Rosie the Riveter in the factory. Very sexy
in the former role, permissibly butch in the latter—and therefore,
by virtue of a special wartime dispensation, allowed to wear slacks
—but only on the job. Of course, everybody knew these roles
didn't fit "real life." That disjuncture was the stock in trade of
popular melodrama: people violating their assigned roles, experiencing well-justified shame, suffering the inevitable consequences. Where that happened we had "scandal," the rasp of
scorn on hypocrisy's lips. And where there was scandal, retribution was sure to follow.

As for race and ethnicity, these were parameters that were still
being guarded in my childhood by open violence and legalized big-
otry. Lynchings, race riots, police brutality in the ghettos were
commonplace practices. But alongside such institutionalized coercion, there was the relentless, pervasive ridicule that guarded the
boundaries of race and nationality: hatred with a grin on its
face. In the last few years, after a long period of fastidious censorship in the press and media, we have developed a permissive nos-
talgia for ethnic humor. We can get away with it again. We treat it
as quaint and innocent fun. On television, ethnic characters make
ethnic jokes about themselves. They laugh and we laugh; and we
laugh too at the Archie Bunkers who cling to the old racial stereotypes. But in my youth, ethnic humor was no laughing matter. It
was plain mean, and it covered the Earth with ugly contempt.
There were nigger jokes, greaser jokes, spick jokes, mick jokes, yid
jokes, pollack jokes, wop jokes, kraut jokes, chink jokes, jap jokes,

hunky jokes, limey jokes, dumb Swede jokes, cheap Scotch jokes. As I look back, I cannot recall ever hearing very many jokes that were not made at somebody's expense. *Hurting* was what humor was for. Nobody (except possibly 100 per cent WASP Americans) escaped this tyranny of vicious laughter. Moreover, the laughter defined real social roles to which people, grudgingly or obsequiously, accepted assignment. In the Chicago of my childhood, for example, I never came across a Chinese who wasn't at work in a laundry or a restaurant; I never saw a black who wasn't a menial worker, a street-corner hustler, a razzmatazz entertainer, or a loudmouthed preacher. If there were exceptions, they were so few that their visibility, especially for kids in a segregated city, was severely limited.

And then there were the jokes reserved for people like my friend Les—the "not quite right" types, the absolute untouchables whose major assignment in life was never to embarrass "normal" people by their very existence. Their duty was to hide and keep quiet. For them, there were moron jokes, booby jokes, freak jokes, spastic jokes, idiot jokes, jail-bird jokes, tramp jokes, dumb-and-ugly jokes, faggot jokes, pervert jokes, drunk jokes. Les was somewhere in the spastic-moron category—a stuttering cripple, a limping simpleton, probably the sort of person who has, since time out of mind, played the role of village idiot in society. But when he "went off his head," he fell into another category. He became dangerous-crazy. So he had to be "put away" by his parents. They committed him to Dunning, Chicago's version of old Bedlam. The booby hatch. The loony bin. The bughouse.

As kids, we used to play a game about Dunning. We would all "go crazy" and see who could be the most menacing, disgusting, or obscene. We imagined it was like that inside the madhouse: a wild and terrifying sort of hell. We were very likely right. Dunning was a great, grim set of decaying buildings surrounded by a rusty iron fence. The inmates were allowed to walk in the barren yard, which was a well-known human zoo in Chicago. I recall that people, out for a Sunday afternoon's amusement, would drive by the institution, hoping to catch sight of an entertaining imbecile or two. The first mad people I remember seeing were in the yard at Dunning on just such a drive. A crazy, toothless old man shouting obscenities and spitting through the bars. A crazy old woman who would lift up her skirt for the passing cars. A crazy young woman who stood against the wall giggling and scratching and chewing on a length of string.

Les wound up in Dunning because he forgot to be respectable in the only way a spastic moron could be respectable—which was to remain an innocent and obedient child, neatly dressed by his mother, and always very, very polite. Instead, Les asked a "nice, normal" girl to marry him, or perhaps even to make love with him. And when she refused, he "went off his head." That made him a public nuisance whose proper place was in the nut house. It was that sort of world. Its principal business was to squeeze people into identity boxes; and these were not merely metaphorical containers. They could be literal, physical prisons, walled-about and guarded, marking out one's few square miles or yards of legally allotted space in the world. For madmen, the madhouse. For lawbreakers, the jailhouse. For kids, the schoolhouse. For lonely old folks, the old folks' home. For the poor and black, the ghetto and the slum. For women, their father's or their husband's home.

Whatever happened to this world I grew up in? No, it has not passed away. But it has become recognized for what it always was, a place of grievous wrong and intolerable cruelty. How readily we now acknowledge that fact! How clearly we now see those who cling to the old identity boxes as pathetic throwbacks! I am continually astonished at how casually people now regard the rapid disintegration of that world, how smoothly its assumptions seem to slip from their lives. Today, it is not remarkable to hear people refer to the assigned roles of the past as . . . "roles," merely arbitrary "games," "programming," "scripts."

We see the transition markedly, but again casually, taking place in such a major social indicator as television entertainment. A generation ago, all situation comedies were based on well-defined types and roles; they were comedies of manners belonging to a genre that dates back to Molière. Today, the stock plot of situation comedy is identity crisis: people resisting a stereotype, an assigned status, a social restriction. There is a mother, a father, a husband, a wife, a boss who seeks to enforce the conventional role. But the women in the shows don't want to be ordinary housewives or sweethearts; the kids don't want to be conventional kids; the grandparents refuse to be what grandparents are supposed to be. The shows vie with one another to introduce bizarre and once-controversial types: free-lovers, interracial couples, unwed mothers, homosexuals, midgets, dwarfs, transvestites, ex-convicts, the mentally retarded, the physically handicapped. All of these appear and refuse to apologize for their way of being; all insist on their right to be themselves. So there are funny complications, and finally the rebel gets his or her way. And thirty or forty million viewers laugh along, sympathize, and approve.

After Equality—Specialness

Television programs, psychological programming. Television scripts, "life scripts." "All the world's a stage"—the idea must be as old as the theater. But it is only in our time that people—lots of people—begin to *live* the idea as a true insight, and so to live their way through and *out of* their assigned roles. In part, this remarkable shamelessness traces to some obvious sources. There has been the heroic struggle of the minorities against ethnic prejudice and the tyranny of racism. But that long campaign never called into question the essential validity of white middle-class society, as many radicals would have preferred; it never called into question the hierarchy of fixed roles and assigned identities on which our society and every society is founded. On the contrary, it affirmed those roles and identities; its demand was for admission and integration into the benefits of white America. From that struggle alone, we could never deduce so much more that has since happened—all the other "liberations" that nobody saw coming, even as recently as a decade ago. Women's lib, men's lib, gay lib, gray lib, kids' lib, mad lib, fat lib . . . even animal lib. We can now begin to see the struggle of the minorities as part of a much larger cultural movement, a shift of awareness that is more than a strictly political phenomenon. We are not dealing here with a mere extension of liberal-democratic ideals: equality, liberty, the traditional civil rights. In theory, such political and social enfranchisement is regarded as a universal possession belonging to the undifferentiated Party of Humanity. It is a goal pursued and won by mass political organization. Its champions have labored to inspire a binding class or racial solidarity; their principal weapon has been a disciplined rank and file, a nation of loyal cadres.

All this belongs to the politics of fleshless abstractions and faceless collectivities. It is just this propensity for massification that has led observers like De Tocqueville to see in the democratic ideal a serious danger of cultural homogenization, a world flattened into dull, despotic, egalitarian uniformity. The fear is amply justified. Democracy has made its way forward in history as a guarantee of basic human dignity, not as a call for deepening self-knowledge. It has nothing to do with cultivating one's own specialness or with enjoying the specialness of another. It is one thing —by now a traditional thing—for a black man or woman to demand the universal and color-blind recognition of equal rights. That was the ideal of the early civil rights movement. It is another thing entirely to tell the world that "Black is beautiful," that black has a right to its cultural style, to its language, its dress, its *consciousness*. To do that is to demand, not an equal space in the world, but a *special* space, one that opens the world to variety. The catch phrase we have for this phase of black politics is "black nationalism." But I think that is misleading, because it does not recognize the dynamic flow of contemporary awareness as it moves deeper and deeper into these provisional, victimized identities— ethnicity, femininity, homosexuality, old age—searching for the person that lies beyond. "Fat is beautiful," "Bald is beautiful," "Gay is beautiful," "Ugly is beautiful": all these—"mere" bumper-sticker slogans—are somebody's way of standing up unashamed in the world, reaching out righteously toward a peculiar destiny.

Again, to take the case of my childhood friend. Do we not see at once that Les is the sort of madman who has been *driven* mad, trapped in a crazy space and then labeled "crazy" by those who purport to love and befriend him? In his behalf, we not only ask for some due process of law to protect him from unjust confinement, but we must go further and say, "Who has the *right* to impose their definition of acceptable conduct on a physically handicapped person? Who has the *right* to label some people sane and some people crazy? Who has the *right* to define normality?"

These are no longer merely questions about civil rights and equal protection under law—though they may at times have to be translated into such legal terms. These are questions that challenge the conventional reality of the culture we live in. They go well beyond the political ideals we associate with Jefferson, Mill, Marx, and Mao. We can only ask them because of what we have learned about the variety and strangeness of human nature from Freud, Jung, Laing, Maslow, Szasz—from them and from several generations of artists who have forced us to confront the madness we find in our own inner life, and to *value* what that madness may tell us of our true nature. To raise questions of this kind is to make war upon the very concept of the identity box, as if we meant to have done with every kind of assigned and enforced being.

Les—spastic, moron, freak—was yesterday's victim, because the only defense he could find was an act of crazy violence. Today, there are still victims; but there are other, more effective defenses. Here, for example, is a poster whose language belongs to the manifesto of the person:

Listen to Radio Free Madness, sponsored by NAPA, the Network Against Psychiatric Assault, an organization of former psychiatric inmates working to protect the rights of people exposed to the current coercive psychiatric system.
MADNESS IS
a 9 to 5 job and a house in the suburbs
MADNESS IS
a step on the way to truth
MADNESS IS
a myth

Here is another: in the window of the Center for Independent Living in Berkeley, California, an organization of the handicapped to help the handicapped. A drawing of a person in a wheel chair, and under it the words *"You gave us your dimes. Now we want our rights."*

Rights. The word is among the brightest stars of the Western political tradition. But what rights are we speaking of here? The right to be mad . . . strange . . . *different?* The right *not* to be made ashamed? In what conventional sense of the word is it a violation of people's "rights" to make them feel guilty, inadequate, "not quite right"?

Even where the "not quite rights" of the world lose a battle—as homosexuals lately have in several elections and legal skirmishes around America—the issue is now joined in a very public, very outspoken way. The old, oppressive prejudices are still there; but what they confront is no longer guilty reticence and evasion, no longer a minimal demand for "toleration." Instead, they are faced with proud and open defiance, even a passionate determination to make one's story known, one's life style visible. They encounter the manifesto of the person as it is being written word by living word, often by people who have no idea how radically they are altering the historical script of our age.

"This is the way the world ends . . ."

And this (perhaps) is the way the industrial world comes to an end—if not (so let us hope) with the bang of its nuclear bombs, then in a noisy celebration of social deviance and personal defiance. It ends by a disintegration that begins within the sensibilities of its subjects and victims, its masses and classes as, one by one—man, woman, and child, old and young, straight and gay, mad and handicapped—they desert the identity boxes on which every civilization has rested its authority and expectations.

It is a prospect that can only, finally, be perceived as a lethal threat by all the forces of government and the economy that have institutional interests to defend. Institutions, after all, presuppose some finite number of assigned and reliable identities which they were designed to manage—so many predictable human patterns of taste, conduct, response. But now, as the personalist ethos makes its way forward in our industrial societies, people begin to flirt with the extraordinary possibility that the age-old relationship of person to institution can be *reversed,* that institutions might actually be cut to *our* size—yours, mine, his, hers. Perhaps we can have a world that is infinitely plastic, limitlessly adaptable to personal need and style. Alvin Toffler, for example, imagines the future as an "adhocracy" of neatly disposable institutional arrangements: nothing stable, permanent, absolute, but everything filled with exceptions and special indulgences . . . and yet somehow, so Toffler hopes, still compatible with the demands of high industrial efficiency.

Custom-tailored institutions: It is, of course, another name for anarchy, which can never serve as a social base for the urban-industrial dominance. Yet, there is currently a deal of blithe and optimistic talk about the possibility, and even some marginal experimentation. "Open marriage" contracts that allow partners of any sex and in any number to specify what sorts of husbands, wives, or occasional housemates they will agree to be. "Individualized instruction" and independent study programs in the schools—usually merchandised as part of a computerized teaching machine package. "Flextime" and "job enrichment" in the workplace. Volunteer armies whose enlistees are permitted to choose their own hair styles, room decor, and social schedule. Corporation T-Groups where all the personal frustrations of the day can be vented. A battalion of personnel technicians in every major industry to soothe away everybody's special grievance. And somewhere in every big bureaucracy, professional "client-centered" counseling services to usher people through every crisis and turning point in life.

For the most part, these are trivial and grudging concessions. Often, the spirit behind them is mere public relations legerdemain. Such manipulative intentions show up plainly in the advertising that shrewdly tries to capitalize on personalist values. "Have it *your* way," a fast-food entrepreneur insists on a dozen spot television commercials every evening, trying to sell the country another hamburger. And an advertisement for the insurance companies of America announces:

> You're more than a face in the crowd to us. The impersonal future? That's not our way of doing business. We'll talk to you person to person.

But the promise comes from one of the biggest, most mercilessly profiteering bureaucracies in the economy.

Personal bankers and brokers. Personal travel agents. Personalized checkbooks. Personalized lipstick and perfume and hair styling. Every hustler in the market place seems to be out to give us our very own personal choice of something they have tricked or trapped us into buying. All we have to do is pay the price. In America, every human need, even the needs of the person, becomes somebody's commodity.

Currently, we are at a stage in which our high industrial technocracy is buying time and playing along with the rising spirit of self-discovery, testing out the possibilities of accommodation and co-optation. In later chapters, we will look more closely at some of these experiments in adaptation to see how far they can go in serving the rights of the person. But to anticipate my conclusion: It will be that no concession whose true purpose is to prop up the urban-industrial dominance can be anything but the counterfeit of an honest, personalist reform. Efforts at accommodation like those I mention above may deserve some attention as symptoms of a timely and pressing need; and they may somewhat heighten the appetite of people for personal recognition in ways the manipulators scarcely intend. But where personalist values are authentically at work, their effect upon our institutions must be a disintegrative, never a supportive, one. They must reach out toward smaller, decentralized, participative social forms, and toward an economic style that rests lightly on the planet's resources.

We can be certain that, if a significant movement toward such a personal scale of life should appear in our society, those in charge of the commanding institutions of government and the economy will turn sharply from any further efforts at clever accommodation and will become rigidly intractable. At that point, we can expect to hear a great deal more about "discipline," "duty," "hard work," "competitive achievement"—and not only from voices on the far right, with which we most readily associate this repertory of old-fashioned virtues, but from intellectuals and academics of a liberal or radical stripe who cannot help but see their cultural authority seriously threatened by the anarchic tendencies of the personalist ethos.

Anarchy and Culture

In all these quarters—left, right, and center—the disintegrative pressures of self-discovery, which we inherit as a significant social force from the counter cultural movements of the 1960s, have given rise to the same urgent concern for order, excellence, and social responsibility. Whatever values may otherwise divide liberal, conservative, and radical, all defend a common front against the dangers they see in much that is intimately connected with the manifesto of the person: in the human potential therapies and the inwardness of the new religions, in the various forms of consciousness exploration and the renewed interest in the occult, in the social fragmentation that results from situational groupings, in the taste for unrestrained confessional self-expression, in the spreading fascination with the mystic, the introspective, the openly erotic, the formlessly spontaneous. In all this, they see a challenge to everything that reason and excellence have traditionally meant in Western society. They see a barbarism and vulgarity which seem all too willing to dispense with civilized standards of conduct, a demand for personal autonomy that threatens to reach antinomian extremes. Understandably, they draw back in fear and outrage, for there have surely been excesses that merit rejection: the crass commercialism of some religious leaders and therapy entrepreneurs, the horror of the Manson family murder cult. Out of that principled rejection, one already discerns a formidable cultural backlash forming that may yet ally liberal intellect and radical conscience with the antipersonalist resistance of the state and the corporations. The formula that would hold this alliance together is a simple but persuasive one that represents some of the finest aspects of the tradition of the Enlightenment: without respect for dispassionate rationality, no respect for objective social standards of ethical conduct and intellectual achievement; without objective social standards, no culture and no conscience. On the basis of that argument, we may yet see the rights of the person confronted by an invincible coalition of raw political power and articulate ethical conviction.

The vices upon which this backlash falls are usually called "narcissism," "subjectivism," "hedonism," "privatism," "irrationalism." Anything remotely associated with mystical religion is automatically condemned, for here both agnostic liberals and pious conservatives share a common hostility. The introspection and spontaneity that accompany most forms of self-discovery are dismissed as "anticognitive," "anti-intellectual." The God-word "Reason" is wielded like the sword of the righteous, as if it still possessed the pristine and unequivocal meaning Descartes might have assigned it three centuries ago, before Rousseau and the Romantics, Freud and the psychiatrists dared to question the proper place and power of that most unexamined of faculties in the human personality. The entire antipersonalist critique is grounded in a tragically bifurcated psychology that persists in pitting the rational against the emotional, the intellectual against the instinctive, the analytical against the inspirational—an age-old warfare of the self against the self which remains the prime symptom of Western society's dissociation of the sensibilities. Again and again, these old, familiar psychic polarities are thrust forward as a supposedly viable choice, and we are pressed to take sides, without the least recognition that neither side can stand alone as a guarantee of decency or sanity. For the personality is an organic whole and the mind is a spectrum of possibilities; the problem is the dichotomy which rends the continuum. Each time it is reasserted—and especially when it is presented as a moral imperative—we sink deeper into the spiritual despair that blights the powers of self-discovery.

Yet the intellectual forces that defend that dichotomy are mighty both in numbers and in influence. Just to limit the discussion to recent years, we can begin by mentioning the prescient critique Phillip Rieff developed in his seminal work, *The Triumph of the Therapeutic* (1966). There, Rieff lamented the corrosive effect the post-Freudian psychiatries were apt to have on moral discipline and cultural tone. "Psychological man," Reiff observed, "is born to be pleased." The result, he feared, would be "a permanent dises-

tablishment of deeply internalized moral demands" and a culture
that "demands less, permits more." Echoes of Rieff's concern continue to reverberate through the weightiest journals of opinion—as
do the dour conclusions John Passmore reached in his *Perfectibility of Man* (1970), a historical survey of perfectionist, Romantic, and Utopian images of human nature which finishes with
a stern rebuke to "the new mysticism" for encouraging "Pelagian
pride, pride in one's 'creativity' or originality" and, in general, for
raising unrealistic expectations of joy and innocence.

The same doubts are as alive as ever in Daniel Bell's *Cultural
Contradictions of Capitalism* (1976). In the current "megalomania of self-infinitization" Bell sees a vulgarization of Faustian
élan and Bohemian artistic rebellion. He tells us:

> Modern culture is defined by this extraordinary freedom to ran-
> sack the world storehouse and to engorge any and every style it
> comes upon. Such freedom comes from the fact that the axial
> principle of modern culture is the expression and remaking of
> the "self" in order to achieve self-realization and self-fulfillment.
> And in its search, there is a denial of any limits or boundaries to
> experience. It is a reaching out for all experience; nothing is for-
> bidden, all is to be explored.

But, Bell's critique continues, once this high and heady cultural
ideal has descended into the streets as "the new sensibility of the
sixties," once it has spawned its own "hedonistic" psychotherapies
that seek to " 'free' the person from inhibitions and restraints so
that he or she can more easily express his impulses and feelings,"
the result is "an attack upon reason itself" in favor of "pre-rational
spontaneity" or "shamanic vision." Bell asks,

> Do these exhortations add up to anything more than a longing
> for the lost gratifications of an idealized childhood . . . a denial
> of those necessary distinctions—between sexes and among ideas
> —which are the mark of adulthood?

With good reason, Bell fears that such a sensibility works to undermine "the social structure itself by striking at the motivational
and psychic-reward system which has sustained it." In his view,

this represents a loss of "*civitas,* that spontaneous willingness to obey the law, to respect the rights of others, to forgo the temptations of private enrichment at the expense of the public weal."

An even more aggressive version of the same argument can be found in Russell Jacoby's pungent analysis *Social Amnesia: A Critique of Conformist Psychology from Adler to Laing* (1975). Here, the point of departure is well to the left of Bell or Rieff. Jacoby speaks from the viewpoint of the Neo-Marxist Frankfurt School which has given us Herbert Marcuse's efforts to amalgamate Marx and Freud; but the line of attack is much the same. We are told that the post-Freudian and Humanistic psychologies (from Adler and Fromm down to Laing and Cooper) have yielded to a "rampant narcissism" that devastates "sustained political energy and theory." Under their treacherous influence, "theory seems politically impotent and personally unreal and distant. Only human subjectivity—the personal life—is meaningful and concrete."

The resulting "cult of subjectivity," Jacoby insists, is not "the negation of bourgeois society but its substance."

> The endless talk of human relations and responses is Utopian; it assumes what is obsolete or yet to be realized: *human* relations. Today these relations are inhuman; they partake more of rats than of humans, more of things than of people. And not because of bad will but because of an evil society. To forget this is to indulge in the ideology of sensitivity groups that work to desensitize by cutting off human relations from the social roots that have made them brutal. More sensitivity today means revolution or madness. The rest is chatter.

Exactly so. The deeper an authentic personal sensitivity goes, the more vivid, the more painful the awareness of alienation. But how does Jacoby believe such a subversive sensitivity is to be aroused in large numbers of people in our still inhuman and prehistoric society? How are the trapped rats to become conscious of their condition? Is it to be done by still heavier doses of sociological scholarship in marginal radical journals, by still more ideological pamphleteering, by classroom lectures and street corner harangues? Or does he expect it to be done by the Freudian psychoanalysis he so strongly defends in his study, a form of therapy (and theory) that has never reached more than an elite and affluent handful—and then, often after years of costly analysis, has produced what politically significant change in people's lives? These are questions which the historical record answers unambiguously in the negative. So we have new therapeutic departures that start with the unrealized potentiality of the person, individually or in small groups. And how can Jacoby (or Rieff or Bell) be so certain that all the new consciousness and therapy movements—*all* of them without exception—lack the power and intention to create the right kind of sensitivity?

Significantly, the introduction to Jacoby's book is written by Christopher Lasch, who has taken many of these criticisms into the pages of the highly influential *New York Review of Books* in a major essay which concludes that "narcissism holds the key to the consciousness movement and to the moral climate of contemporary society." But once again, one has no sense that Lasch knows anything more about "the consciousness movement" in all its bewildering variety than he has learned from dismissive books and articles or from hearsay accounts. What goes unrecognized by such critics is the possibility that there may be stages and phases of self-exploration that require extremes of introversion and intervals of unbecoming emotional revelation, even moments of infantile regression in which people tunnel back into the earliest, most blocked and troubled period of life. Where the unconscious and the repressed are meant to be liberated rather than merely analyzed, experienced rather than merely read about and lectured upon, there may have to be risky exercises that bring the psychically bizarre and unsettling, perhaps even the demonic, close to the surface. At least temporarily and within the boundaries of therapeutic discipline, it may be necessary to experiment with what Kierkegaard (in a theological context) called a "teleological suspension of the ethical"—with the result that our social nature, our sense of decorum and rational discrimination are, for a time, subordinated to another, more personal objective. Even Socrates, that most articulate and analytical of Western gurus, fell into periods of trance as part of his philosophical vocation, attending to voices and visions that belonged to a wholly private world. It is only fair to ask: If, in the name of reason, sound politics, and good manners, no one is to be permitted such intervals of inscrutable withdrawal and "irrational" rumination, are we not in fact making self-knowledge an impossibility?

Daniel Bell is candid enough to admit the contradiction involved in such a position. He sees in the counter cultural experiments of the sixties an extension of the long-standing liberal struggle against Puritanical repression. But the preachings of liberalism were now being translated into practice; in the streets or in therapeutic encounters, liberal values were being acted out and acted upon as only a Bohemian few had dared to do in the past. They were taken "to a point in *life-style* that the liberal mentality— which would approve of such ideas in *art and imagination*—is not prepared to go."

Yet liberalism finds itself uneasy in trying to say why. It approves a basic permissiveness, but cannot with any certainty define the bounds. And this is its dilemma. In culture, as well as in politics, liberalism is now up against the wall.

The Antipersonalist Consensus

Both liberal and radical need only glance to the right to discover that they share that wall with some stout conservative defenders— for example, with the political theorist Robert Nisbet, who makes the same slashing attack upon the "environment of subjectivism" that supposedly dominated the decade of the sixties. In his study *The Twilight of Authority,* Nisbet draws as heavily on Edmund Burke as Russell Jacoby draws on Karl Marx; but the target under fire is again the personalist ethos of the time, which Nisbet characterizes as an "individual retreat to innermost areas of consciousness and . . . a kind of consecration to self, self-awareness, and the undilutedly subjective." Once more, the result is seen to be "cultivated infantilism, irrationalism . . . a retreat from mind and its disciplines" at the expense of social duty.

When subjectivity is a pervasive state of mind in arts, letters, and philosophy, in the social sciences, and even in social protest, it is bound to rank high among the forces which have negative impact upon not only culture, reason, and the whole sense of membership in a social order, but the political community itself.

From time to time in the course of the middle and later seventies, these criticisms have been reflected in the mass media—in the newsweeklies and slick magazines, the daily press and television reports. But, by and large, the position of the media has been a mixture of indecision and treacherous ambivalence. Always eager to move with the latest fad, they have been quick to recognize the growing popular appeal of self-discovery and have generally sought ways to exploit its more sensational and frivolous aspects. They have seen the possibility that the new therapies and consciousness movements could become a promising psychic commodity—the latest fashion in self-improvement and middle-class fun and games. Accordingly, most of the commentary and reporting one finds at this level dotes on the worst excesses of silly self-indulgence and commercial opportunism—vices that are always there to be found in anything that attracts a sizable audience in America. Sex, nudity, and the most bizarre forms of uninhibited self-expression are given prominent attention, usually in that tone of calculated disparagement that implies more fascination than disapproval. Where the ethical and social criticism becomes any heavier in the popular media, it presents an intriguing problem in cultural politics.

For example, in a brutally sarcastic (and shamefully misinformed) piece of parajournalism written for *New York* magazine, the satirist Tom Wolfe dismisses the popularity of therapeutic self-examination as a decadent expression of the "Me Decade" and traces the fascination to nothing deeper than clever Madison Avenue huckstering and "groin spasms." Similarly, at the conclusion of a major *Newsweek* feature surveying the new religions and therapies, the editors, affecting a dark Augustinian solemnity, decide that "by ignoring the demonic side of man and smothering tragedy in a cloud of consciousness," they "offer a sentimental journey for those who cannot stand too much reality."

Now, here we have magazine journalism that is wholly supported by high consumption advertising whose only "reality" is financial profit and loss, and which employs every form of unscrupulous deception, erotic delusion, and self-indulgent temptation to sell its wares. Yet the articles purport to write off the growing taste for self-discovery as hedonistic, escapist, and socially irresponsible. Apparently, then (as far as the editorial policy of the publications is concerned), to buy a product—*any* advertised product—is morally acceptable, socially commendable. But to buy something that one believes (rightly or wrongly) to be a means of self-knowledge is not. *Why* not?

The same jarring discrepancy mars a far more compelling critique by Peter Marin published in *Harper's* (October 1975). The article scathingly condemns the new therapies for their "retreat from the worlds of morality and history," for their "refusal to consider moral complexities" and the "neglected others—dying in Asia, hungry in Africa, impoverished in our own country." But Marin's harsh denunciation of "The New Narcissism" appears across the page from a lush advertisement for the new Cadillac Eldorado. Similarly, we have a sweeping condemnation of "popular therapies and consciousness disciplines" in the journalistic survey *Psychobabble* by R. D. Rosen, who again makes much of their "narcissism" and "unabashedly materialistic" vices. But Rosen's career as a writer is that of a restaurant reviewer for *Boston* magazine, which, like Tom Wolfe's *New York,* is another of the new metropolitan slicks whose main source of revenue is advertising none but the swankiest liquor, perfume, and vacation tours. I am not suggesting that such connections invalidate the criticisms that Wolfe or Marin or Rosen raise; some of what they say is appropriate enough, for they have picked obvious targets and score many easy anecdotal points. But are they aware of the uses to which their ethical concern is being put by the very forces that provide a forum for their writing? A question all of us who write, teach, and lecture would do well to ponder.

While most of these critics seem unaware of the fact, all the issues they raise have long since surfaced in the new religions and therapies, and within the general province of the human potential movement, where they have remained a highly charged focus of debate. This has been true at least since Esalen Institute held its 1973 conference in San Francisco on "Spiritual and Therapeutic Tyranny" and other ethical dilemmas associated with consciousness expansion. The breakaway and steady leftward politicization of the Radical Therapists since the early 1970s is an obvious, even earlier sign of that inner ferment. More recently, at the 1977 conference of the Association for Humanistic Psychology, the "self/society" issue emerged as the most constant and heated topic under discussion; it promises to maintain that status for some time to come. In an article in the *AHP Newsletter* published just prior to the conference (July 1977), Rick Gilbert of the Humanistic Psychology Institute put the challenge as sharply as any "outside" critic:

> In contrast to our public self-image as cosmic transformationalists, I see us as a slightly lost group of middle-aged, well-heeled, paunchy seekers after a little fun and relaxation. . . . I believe our concern with individual transformation and the new consciousness causes us to turn away from the rest of the world, as Peter Marin and Tom Wolfe have pointed out. Humanistic psychology has much to offer in helping to solve problems of the real world. If, however, we continue to shift the locus of our models of human experience into the cosmos, or deep into the "inner me," we will truly have failed the human potential.
>
> My concern is that the brutality of the 1960s, Watergate, Viet Nam, etc., has caused many of us to give up on the real world and to turn inward, feeling that we are essentially powerless to change things. The human potential movement is leading the way in that direction.

Gilbert's recommendation for the future of humanistic and other third-force psychologies is that they cut themselves free of the human potential movement in an effort to "strengthen our credibility" and to undertake a solid academic and research effort that would build "a substantial, cognitive (left brain, if you must) tough-minded base upon which to rest humanistic psychology." Once again, then—this time from within the psychotherapeutic community where Gilbert's appeal hardly stands unsupported—we have the call for social relevance and intellectual rigor against what is seen as the spreading anarchy of self-discovery.

There is a weighty and formidable consensus forming in these evaluations, one that could rally some surprisingly diverse intellectual forces, conservative and radical, in a principled rejection of the dangers they see threatening from permissive therapeutics and Eastern mysticism, privatism and unreason. The ranks of this united front might stretch from *Dissent* and *Commentary* to *The Public Interest* and *The National Review,* from the chic satire of *Esquire* to the heavy scholarship of the learned journals, from Herman Kahn's Hudson Institute to the dissenting Institute for Policy Studies, from the Radical Therapists to the strict behavioral psychologists and the orthodox Freudians. Admittedly, a strange alliance. Yet, I can speak as one whose criticism of science, technocratic politics, and the urban-industrial dominance has invited just such a widely eclectic range of critical fire. The "Romanticism," "mysticism," and "a-politicism" with which I have often found myself charged seems finally to be directed at my conviction that there is a self beyond culture, a person above politics whose identity includes a transcendent vocation—hence, my concern in this work to salvage the best values of self-discovery. It is, therefore, no great difficulty for me to imagine these otherwise antagonistic ideological and intellectual camps making common cause in what they would understand to be a heroic defense of reason, intellect, and social responsibility. For those on the political right, social responsibility would doubtlessly mean subservience and conformity to private corporate power and the national defense; for those on the left, it would mean dissent and resistance in behalf of social justice. But it would mean, in all cases, the subordination of the self to social duty, the total politicization of the personality, and, at last, the closure of the inner life, except as it might be experienced vicariously in critically well-received literary works, or possibly in discrete doses at the hands of orthodox, professional psychoanalysts.

In fact, what this would represent is a mighty reassertion of the greater cultural orthodoxy that has always bound left, right, and center together in the common project of advancing the urban-industrial dominance. At the level of a deep psychic compulsion, it would be a summons for our return to all the alienating sublimations and dutiful repressions which are the bedrock of that system. It would indiscriminately condemn as narcissism and the betrayal of reason every resort to contemplative withdrawal and solitude, every discipline of self-examination, whether high or low, shallow or deep. And yet somewhere among these practices are the means which self-discovery must have if it is to free our lives from the impaction of industrial culture and the alienating pressures of the scientific world view.

It is not easy for those who have devoted their lives to an all-consuming political vocation to admit that there is anything more, let alone more sacrosanct, than civic duty to occupy our attention. All of us in the Western world, believers and agnostics alike (and sometimes the agnostics more so than the believers), live beneath the judgment of the prophets of ancient Israel, who commanded that justice be done even if the heavens should fall. Especially those on the political left have, with the highest ethical resolution, bowed to that prophetical calling, often sacrificing their right of self-discovery on the altar of relentless social engagement—an act of self-imposed spiritual alienation in which one can doubtless take a bitter and stubborn pride. It is, therefore, all the more impressive when a good radical like Irving Howe candidly questions what the relationship is between socialist conscience and the "ultimate questions" regarding "man's place in the universe, the meaning of his existence, the nature of his destiny." Supposedly, in classical radical theory, such questions belong to the victorious socialist stage of history. Yet here they are being raised in the new religions and therapies, pressing in upon more and more "ordinary" people while we are still living "within a context of class domination and social snobbism."

We would [Howe warns] be dooming ourselves to a philistine narrowness if we denied that such questions do beset human beings, that they are significant questions, and that in our moment there are peculiarly urgent reasons for coming back to

them. . . . What we must do is to recognize the distance, perhaps the necessary distance, between political strategy and existential response. We are saying that many things requiring rem-
edy are open to social-political solution. . . . We are also
saying that we live at a moment when problems beyond the
reach of politics—problems that *should* be beyond the reach of
politics—have come to seem especially urgent and disturbing.

Howe's effort to find an honest balance between social action
and philosophical solitude is essentially the project the French Personalists set for themselves as a movement during the 1930s and
1940s. We will touch upon that effort in the chapter to follow; but
here I will anticipate their position, quoting the leading Personalist
spokesman Emmanuel Mounier, who insisted that a sane politics
must recognize that

man is only man through engagement. But if man were only his
engagements, he would be a slave, particularly in a world where
the net of collectivity is drawn ever closer and the interplay between individuals and groups always more restricted. The guarantee of our freedom within engagement is the relative nature of
engagement, relative to an absolute which it invokes, sets in action, and at the same time betrays.

The emerging liberal-radical-conservative consensus against self-
discovery, insisting ever more tough-mindedly on firm standards of
objective excellence and citizenly engagement, might well carry
over into questioning any number of ameliorative and progressive
social policies with a momentum that its more liberal and left-
radical members never intended. In a publication like *The Public
Interest,* one detects just such a neoconservative, antipopulist hard-
ening of former liberal intellectuals: a certain somber willingness
to "rethink" the permissiveness and laxity that produced "the sixties" . . . indulgent child rearing, lenient grading in the schools,
"Mickey Mouse" coursework like social-life counseling and ethnic
studies, rehabilitation programs in the prisons, and the sort of
slackness in the welfare system that allows opportunistic dropouts
and chronic nonachievers to get by on food stamps and handouts.

Of course, one need not imagine this neoconservative tide running its course free of resistance. Those to the left of the consensus would surely continue to speak out bravely for society's burdened, disadvantaged, and handicapped members. There could still be that sort of political split between the compassionate, crusading left and the niggardly, mean-tempered right. But "feeling sorry," "being kind," calling for equal justice and fair access are *not* what is centrally at issue when we speak of the rights of the person. These are worthy sympathies and ideals, but they belong to another set of issues on another level of experience. Here, it is not the miseries and injustices of people we must place at the center of our concern, but their *personhood*—the person each of us is within and beyond our afflictions. It is not pity for unfortunate people, but joy in the flowering of their buried personalities we must call for as an integral, immediate, and paramount aspect of their liberation. The goal is not simply to clear away the stones that cover the social ground, but to find and water every human seed that lies beneath, each closed in its own darkness. The question I raise, then, is: What does it require of us to liberate these personalities, to let them grow proudly and discover their unique destiny? And the answer—so I argue—is the repeal of all assigned identities, together with the radical scaling down of urban-industrial institutions that would necessarily follow.

Once again we return to the key point that self-discovery is a *disintegrative* force, one which now rises to importance in response to the ecological emergency. It is an alliance of person and planet born of their common need. Seen in this light, self-discovery brings us up against one of the stubborn facts of political life. There is no way to assert the rights of the person without entering the province of anarchist politics—or at least a certain, special region of that province which we will examine in the chapter to come. Self-discovery is inextricably a value born and harbored within that tradition. And neither liberals nor orthodox socialists are anarchists. At this important crossroads, especially where anarchy appears to threaten cultural orthodoxy as well as political authority, their course leads in another direction—toward, not away from, the urban-industrial dominance.

A Tyranny of Excellence, a Culture of Guilt

With this much said in reply to those who have chosen to reject the adventure of self-discovery, let me add a few of my sympathies to their honest doubts. For I would be the last to deny the amount of sheer nonsense and outright fraud one can find in this bewilderingly mixed bag of therapeutic practices. I fully recognize that the follies and false starts of people striving to create new identities can make easy targets for criticism and satire. That is one reason why I will not take up much space here to repeat the denigration these obvious vices have already abundantly received. One does not have to be clever, only quite cruel, to take advantage of such open vulnerability. For many people, the search for personhood begins with a second infancy; they are struggling through a strange rebirth, often with no more to help them along than desperate need and makeshift means. So they must learn to feel, to relate, to breathe, to move, to dream all over again. They grope, as the newborn must; they yield to histrionic self-indulgence and astonishing gullibility, as children will. Very likely, coming as they do from a society whose psyche is ego-dominated through and through, they do go through phases of narcissism and self-absorption. How does one even begin to practice introspection without at least *looking* self-absorbed from somebody else's viewpoint? And perhaps those who receive poor guidance find no inner dynamic that will carry them beyond that stage. Undeniably, there are opportunists at hand eager to exploit these moments of confusion and uncertainty—dubious gurus, "psychic facilitators" who rush forward with cheap therapeutic gimmicks that leave their clients stranded in an unbecoming or lethal cul-de-sac of the personality.

But what does one do in the face of this problem? To heap wholesale cynicism on the anguished spiritual plight of people is hardly what our cultural condition demands. That is the very poison we are dying of—the cynicism that pervades all the major structures of our society and leads us to see everything about our lives as vile and false. That cynicism comes in many varieties. Those who crassly exploit the personal needs of people for their own profit or power are guilty of one kind of cynicism. But there is another that is even worse. That is to mock the exploited *together* with the exploiters, to revile the need as well as its abuse. That is plain nihilism.

For my own part, I prefer to treat the projects of self-discovery I see about me with all the mercy I can summon (except perhaps where they are contaminated by some clear form of "spiritual fascism"). My conviction is that there is an honest, if confused, struggle for authenticity taking place among the many flaws and blemishes I see as clearly as any critic. I say this even though I have at times found myself put off by the maudlin self-dramatization that accompanies many consciousness-raising exercises. I admit that it has also set my teeth on edge to hear people going on and on about themselves, loitering over every minor nuance of their feelings, their motives, their miseries . . . carrying on, that is, as if *they* mattered in the world. I bridle, as many critics do, at the vogue words one hears too much repeated: "growth," "sensitivity," "awareness," "relationship" . . . though I cannot say what better vocabulary our culture gives us for discussing the inner life. Has the language of Freud (so barbarically scientistic) or of Jung (so metaphysically murky) worn any better? One need only sample the introspective complexities of Indian or Tibetan philosophy to realize that our culture does not give us an exact and eloquent psychological vocabulary; we are forced to make do with rough improvisations.

Unquestionably there is a terrible amateurishness about many of the new therapeutic practices that offends by its lack of intellectual precision, by seeming absence of "seriousness." I have found myself wondering, in the midst of some vapid or cloying sessions: "Have these people never read anything by Dostoevski or Proust or John of the Cross? Where are the torments and searing ambiguities of the matter?"

But then I think again. How fair is it to raise such a crushing standard of comparison? The essence of what is going on here before me is not high cultural excellence, but personal urgency and participation. Am I saying that the only introspective rights in this world belong to tortured saints and eloquent artists? That the rest of us are suited only to the role of admiring spectators before these prodigious heroes of self-examination? Here, after all, are "ordinary" people, as torn and troubled and ungifted as myself. And I think, in moments like this, they are doing their best to search out an honest personhood. They cannot write great novels or paint great canvases; they do not pretend to such talents. Yet, they also live in the shadow of death and have suffered the weight of despairing hours. Are they not making a brave beginning here at the difficult project of self-knowledge—and perhaps with wholly inadequate guidance? Is it the worst I can accuse them of that they are not creating elegant and immortal literature for my enjoyment? In fact, they are not doing anything here for my critical approval; this is not a cultural performance. This is their private adventure in authenticity, and perhaps the best introspective road they have yet found to travel. Have I, for no better reason than disappointed taste, the right to ridicule them back into embarrassed silence? What sort of smug fastidiousness is this I yield to? Am I not allowing "excellence" to become a censoring tyranny that would leave all but the superbly literate few mute?

I know, as I pursue these thoughts, that I am weakening toward a hazardous permissiveness. But, for the moment, I will run that risk for the sake of letting an issue arise that is frequently driven from consideration by too quick and censorious a display of impatience with the intellectual shoddiness of many new therapies. I fully realize that there are therapeutic fashions on the scene—like Transactional Analysis or Transcendental Meditation—which have made their promoters rich overnight by promising easy and rapid enlightenment. I would agree that such facile systems, with their quickly mastered methods, their endless supply of neologisms, their ostentatious analyses of the obvious, may do more to obstruct self-knowledge than to facilitate it. There are therapies that are out to accomplish little more than to massage the psychic surface with catch phrases and platitudes. Nevertheless, I want to trust that there is some valid instinct that draws people in such numbers—even well-read and decently educated people—to these exercises. I want to suggest that, even here, we may discover a cultural symptom that has something to teach us about the need of the times.

So then, I ask myself—and all the more pointedly when I see people gravitating to shallow and faddish therapies—where would I send them to learn a more becoming and accomplished standard of self-discovery? Where, in our culture, are there the traditions and techniques of personal exploration I would have them adopt as models? And pondering this, I think I begin to understand why these efforts are so abrasive. It is not really their sentimentality or banality that makes me uncomfortable; that is very largely my defensive pose in the face of something far more challenging. The true reason is: *There is no sense of sin here.* Neither in the situational groups nor in the new therapies do we find people *apologizing* for what they are. They do not grovel; they make no act of contrition. Or, if they do, they do not stop there. They do not delve within merely to accuse themselves of evil, but finally to claim a significant kind of *innocence.* They presume to put away guilt and stand unashamed in the world. At the extreme, in the Oriental forms of self-examination, the self in search of its personhood even becomes God—so these traditions teach. Through them, supposedly, one sets forth to experience one's essential divinity—a teaching I doubt that many Westerners can claim to understand accurately.

These are purposes that few in our society will approve. On the contrary, we cannot help but to be distressed by their presumptuousness, if not their outright blasphemy. What our culture knows of the art of introspection it inherits from religious traditions that have a heavy investment in fear and trembling. The major forms of deep self-analysis that have been developed in the Western world are all related to the experience of sin and the fear of divine displeasure: the Catholic confession, the Puritan diary, the camp-meeting testimonial. For us, the inner life is what St. Paul, St. Augustine, Luther, Calvin, Jonathan Edwards, Kierkegaard, Karl Barth have taught us it must be: shame and unworthiness. And behind this body of moral theology there hovers the dark biblical teaching of human fallenness, the act of disobedience "that brought death into the world and all our woe." One does not turn inward to claim innocence or to experience the powers of creative growth, let alone the splendors of divinity. Rather, one begs forgiveness beneath the shadow of death and the dread of damnation.

That same harrowing image of the self is still with us today, even in the atheist existentialist artists and philosophers who show us the inner life as a private inferno of failure and "bad faith." Again and again, they confront us with the same annihilating experience: the self as a chamber of horrors and den of iniquity. It is there again waiting for us in all the classic psychological literature of our culture, with the exception of some notably unashamed Romantic spirits who are among the pioneers of our contemporary efforts at self-discovery. What, after all, is Freud's psychoanalysis but, inevitably, an agonizing search for guilty secrets buried in the unconscious mind: incestuous longings, sexual perversions, patricidal fantasies, death wishes, the cowardly flight from mortality? With Freud, we finish with the minimal sanity of catharsis and purgation, hard-won and sobering.

Here, we confront a significant aspect of the antipersonalist resistance under discussion in this chapter. With a remarkable consistency, the critics of the new consciousness disciplines revert to Freudian analysis as the single acceptable technique of self-exploration, as if to say "thus far into the personality, and no further." They do so despite the fact that psychoanalysis remains the most restricted, expensive, and time-consuming form of psychiatry available, the one school that could most accurately be charged with being an elitist, high bourgeois, even "narcissistic" prerogative. In comparison, most of the new therapies (even those that may run to a few hundred dollars for fifty or sixty hours of intensive workshop sessions) are dirt-cheap, vastly democratic, and produce far fewer well-heeled practitioners than we find among the orthodox psychiatrists, most of whom, it would be a safe wager, are as politically conservative or apolitical as the great majority of physicians. Why, then, does psychoanalysis pass muster with these critics as an acceptable form of introspection and self-revelation? Lionel Trilling offers the answer:

> The nature of guilt as Freud conceives it is precisely that it does not originate in actual wrong-doing. . . . It takes its rise from

an unfulfilled and repressed wish to do wrong . . . and it is experienced . . . as the denial of the possibility of gratification and delight, even desire.

This morbid vision of ineradicable guilt, of a guilt that arises not from action but from the very nature of our being,

> preserves something—much—of the stratum of hardness that runs through the Jewish and Christian traditions as they respond to the hardness of human destiny. . . . it has at its heart an explanation of suffering through a doctrine of something like original sin: not for nothing had Freud in his youth chosen John Milton as a favorite poet, and if he gives no credence to the idea of redemption, he yet acquiesces, and with something of Milton's appalled elation, in the ordeal of man's life in history.

So, too, Daniel Bell insists that all therapy which deviates from Freudianism is "hedonistic," with no more than an "instrumental and psychologistic" intention. "Fun morality, in consequence, displaces 'goodness morality,' which stressed interference with impulses." Russell Jacoby goes even further. For him, the whole value of Freud lies in the fact that his psychiatry works to *lower* expectations and inculcate resignation. As Freud himself explained to one of his patients, psychoanalysis is content to leave people in a condition of "everyday unhappiness." Yet, as Jacoby sees it, such ingrained joylessness turns out to be the prerequisite for revolutionary change by proving how intractably inhuman the existing social order is. This would seem to be a psychological extension of Marx's embarrassingly simple-minded assumption that social upheaval can only arise from the unrelenting "immiserization" of the masses. Hence, one proves how wicked capitalist society is by refusing any amelioration and working to defeat reform. Of course, the argument is muddled. A psychiatry that works to inure people to the insistent punishment of the superego and which limits their hopes to "everyday unhappiness" can only play into the hands of those social forces that impose an unhappy reality. People who have tasted little of their thwarted potentialities are not apt to ask for more than they are allotted by the powers that be. Indeed, the social authoritarianism to which Freud's psychiatry leads shows up in his own writings again and again—as when he tells us that the pleasure-seeking unconscious may "be compared with a modern state in which a mob, eager for enjoyment and destruction, has to be held down forcibly by a prudent superior class."

I am not suggesting that it is the inherent authoritarianism of Freudian psychiatry (both in theory and in practice) which appeals to its supporters. Rather, it is the punishing severity and fatalistically tragic flavor of psychoanalysis that give it its air of authenticity and seriousness. These are qualities that echo our deep conviction of fallenness. And this, in turn, answers to the secret grief we experience in the presence of our wounded personhood. The guilt is surely there within us; but it is guilt born of our unfulfilled destiny, our failure to become what we are. In that experience—once it has been clarified and its cultural context illuminated—there is, I suspect, a powerful force of political discontent.

Traditionally, this sense of fallenness was meant to drive the hounded and humiliated soul toward God begging for grace. First, unbearable guilt; then, the blood of the lamb. In our day, the religious context of this tormenting scrupulosity has fallen away for most moderns, but the search for hidden terrors still denotes *serious* introspection, *real* psychiatry to many intellectuals. Self-knowledge must never be ennobling. It is supposed to be a hard road to guilty resignation. That, at least, has been our cultural orthodoxy. And for many of the critics of self-discovery I have cited here, it remains the foundation of the personality and the bedrock of all moral resolution. So, like all the moral authorities of the past, they continue to preach morality: to scold, to command, to intimidate with moral rhetoric. And wherever they do not see much ethical language in evidence, they cannot believe there is an ethical intention, a moral possibility. From this traditional, Western point of view, the only way one makes people moral is to keep *telling* them they aren't and that they must be, until, at last, they are shamed into good conduct. Or perhaps there is one other way—something that has only lately appeared in the work of our behavioral psychologists. One cleverly *conditions* people into being "good" by the strategic use of bribes and punishments. But then this may only be a secular variation of the old appeal to the "loss of heaven and the pains of hell."

A Liberation of Innocence

But now, around the edges of our culture, a very different sensibility comes into play—one that I admit I do not find it easy to endorse, though I will not lightly spurn it. I have, for example, found myself among the Swami Muktananda's disciples, surrounded in the ashram by scores of people of all ages and backgrounds for whom introspection no longer means meditating on one's sins. For them (so they claim) it means ecstatic oneness with Shiva, the god of the divine self. "Become your own beloved," the swami teaches them. "Meditate on your Self. Worship your inner Being. God lives within you as you." I cannot say how authentic the Shivaite Hinduism of these people is; perhaps it has not been deeply studied at all. But that does not seem to me the important question. In fact, it is a pedantic issue to raise. It is not even important to me to know whether they find the ecstasy they seek. What is more to the point is the unaccountable spontaneity with which these people rush toward religions and therapies of guiltlessness. *They dare to be innocent.* Like Whitman in his great Song, they dare to celebrate themselves. So there is no torture or humility to their quest, but a mood of exaltation and joy.

Joy and innocence. *That* is the offense that many critical minds find in the "triumph of the therapeutic." They correctly see our entire cultural tradition being shaken to its ethical and psychological foundations by these pretensions of sinlessness. "Human nature," Abraham Maslow, one of the founding fathers of Humanistic Psychology, suggests, "is not nearly so bad as it has been thought to be. In fact, it can be said that the possibilities of human nature have customarily been sold short." The language of the statement, like that of Carl Rogers, Rollo May, and so many of the major spokesmen for the new therapies, is aggravatingly bland; it will hardly match the somber, misanthropic brooding of an Augustine or a Calvin. Nor is there the struggle and fury of a Nietzsche asserting human nobility against a still formidable religious opposition. Nevertheless, some two thousand years of Christian moral theology is being called into question by such voices, and by all those to whom personhood means having nothing to be ashamed of, nothing that makes one afraid to stand up in the world and display one's uniqueness.

Speaking from the conservative psychological viewpoint, Alan Mintz has every reason to be concerned for the radical departure the growth therapies represent.

> In terms of a social and historical vision of man, we have here the Enlightenment's doctrine of perfectibility without its commitment to rationality, Romanticism's exaltation of subjectivity without its acceptance of agony and suffering, the nineteenth century's scientism without its insistence on the primacy of society. For anyone alive to the contradictions of history, the persistence of so self-assured a vision of man in the second half of the twentieth century, with all the willful denials of human reality that vision entails, must be a curious and troubling phenomenon.

> In such fears, we can sense the perverse, consoling pride all of us have come to take in an unflinchingly cynical view of human nature—even when one makes oneself its principal victim. We can come to have a desperately vested interest in our own psychic wounds and ugliness. We can learn to savor the scars of our remorse, until we finally take our whole identity from them. As if we were reduced to saying, "At least I face up to the shame and waste of my life and make no excuses for the sorry mess I have made of myself." *That* is what seems rock-solid and ultimately "serious" to many of us—that harshly jaundiced candor and grim resignation. It is this sense of tarnished creatureliness, now unrelieved by even the whisper of grace, that we retain from an obliterated religious heritage. We finish by believing that sin is the reality of the self; we may even pin our hope of moral action to the shame that comes of that belief.

But the matter goes deeper still; it takes on a sociological dimension. For do we not sense, with a fearful intuitive certainty, that the discipline and productivity of our industrial order—all the mighty compulsions we know as the work ethic, capitalist acquisitiveness, deferred gratification—are tied to our inherited culture of guilt? It is out of this restless sense of guilty fear that the entrepreneurial energies are born, together with the inner urge to obey and serve which that energy must find in its work force. These are the displacements of a tormenting self-discontent into the surrounding world. We turn out and away from ourselves because inside is terror and the abyss. Our escape is into history; our penance is "progress." We have every reason to wonder, then, what price in economic security and social discipline we will have to pay if these reservoirs of self-loathing are now to be dried up. Where will we find the bottled-up aggression and alienated energy that now support the affluence of the industrial system?

I confess that I too, as one born into the culture of guilt, remain more than a little uneasy with a psychology that does not give supremacy to these darker dimensions of the personality. I was also raised to believe that severely critical introspection is the prime sign of "seriousness" in life, and that honest introspection must be an unsparing act of self-crucifixion. My first deliberate effort at self-examination took place as a child of nine in the Catholic confessional. And what had I been trained to do in that interval of solitude? To think on my sins, to weigh and ponder each one, to grieve for the offense I had caused God, and to tremble at the prospect of eternal damnation. There was nothing more I had been instructed to do, nothing more I had been prepared to search for in myself—only these experiences of shame and dread. And if I found no sins to confess, then I was to call up my "evil thoughts": sexual fantasies, secret pleasures taken in disobedience or willfulness, unspoken words of rebellion and anger. Here I was, practicing the oldest introspective discipline in Christian history, and this was its entire content—a humiliating and wholly trivial exercise in self-condemnation intended to shape me to the expectations of social authorities . . . to make me a "good boy." This was the single form of inner exploration I was now to repeat through the rest of my years—this ugly and anxious appeal for forgiveness.

Only lately have I come to see, perhaps from my experience with the new therapies and mystical disciplines, how truly petty such moral anxiety finally is—and how unnecessary. So little of it derives from anything I would now respect as real wickedness: from treason against one's fellows, from indifference to the suffering of others, from the doing of violence and injustice. It is my conviction that, buried away in the core of the Western conscience, there is a festering accumulation of "sin" that is simply unworthy of serious adult concern, and should never have been dunned into our children. Rather, it is compounded of our pathetic childish shame about the body, sexual insecurities, thwarted aggressions that could not be displayed in the home, and a vast backlog of role-playing anxieties. Yet this is the shallow ballast of our moral nature, and we let it hound us through a lifetime of "good behavior," "high achievement," and "responsibility," as we try to prove again and again that we are pure, nice, and lovable. I often wonder how much of the moral scruple of ourselves and our ancestors has been grounded—sullenly, resentfully—in the guilt of old masturbation fantasies.

But do we not now begin to sense within us the possibility of a finer, more positive and mature ethical sensibility—an authentic conscience that responds naturally to the good and needs no shame to make its influence felt? Can we not begin to feel that conviction stirring inside us, beneath the inhibited anger, the silly little sexual hang-ups that people now, quite remarkably, find it so easy to declare to the world without shame? Wherever that experience does enter our lives, I think we are in touch with the brightest promise of self-discovery: a morality born of innocence, a decency that springs from delight. One by one, the layers of worthless and unworthy guilt are stripped away. The body, the sexual needs, the aggressive, animal energies within us are openly acknowledged and given their chance for humane expression. Until, at last, beneath all these, we come to the guilt that underlies the rest—the nagging culpability we feel for failing to live up to what *They* (our parents, teachers, social authorities) expect of us. We discover that we have been haunted by the shame we feel for never fully answering to the role *They* have designed for us in life, never entirely acquiescing to the ready-made identity the world has imposed upon us. Here is the force that has oppressed our erotic drives, our passionate need to grow; and, resenting the imposition, we rebel against it overtly or secretly—and then berate ourselves for the transgression.

The experience we call "conscience" is a mixed and many-faceted thing. I fear that very little of it relates to matters of justice, compassion, good fellowship. For the most part, it is nothing more than the whip society uses to drive down our instinctive impulse toward personhood. It is a punishing demon shaped from our thwarted growth.

The struggle for self-discovery is indeed a claim upon innocence —a presumptuous claim by all the moral and psychological standards of our world. But that is exactly what I have come to see as its redeeming moral quality. In that presumption lies the possibility of our liberation from a vast array of alienated and trivial ethical demands—demands whose whole purpose is to force a false social identity upon us, and so to maintain a civilization that has become toxic to the entire planet. If we are ever to become moral beings in any higher, more life-giving way, it will be by freeing ourselves of the guilt we now carry about for not living up to our assigned roles. I do not doubt there is a morality of the person, but we will only know what it is after we have experienced the innocence that comes of free self-discovery.

There are bound to be stern, censorious authorities in our midst who will rail against the social and economic disintegration such a liberation of innocence must bring—and their fears are well founded. Even more efficiently than police force, it is distrust of self that makes people vulnerable and obedient; it is self-loathing that opens them to emotional intimidation. These are the "mind-forg'd manacles" of social domination. Beyond the use of naked physical power, society has very little leverage with innocent people. It cannot manipulate or mystify them into endorsing their subjugation. It cannot make them despise themselves and so bow down to their prescribed duty.

We have already seen what happens when blacks, Latinos, Native Americans, homosexuals, women, the handicapped throw off their subservient and guilt-ridden mentality and assert their natural identity in the full pride of innocence. Is it not obvious that the ethos of self-discovery is simply that same liberation pressed forward toward a universal assertion of unashamed personhood? Those who have already achieved something of that freedom are teaching us that, when we look within, we do not find only guilty terrors, but—at the core of our personality—autonomous powers of growth, creativity, and renewal. Here, for example, are the words of the feminist theologian Mary Daly, describing her struggle to create a personal identity beyond the religion of God the Father with all its intimidating assumptions of masculine superiority. In her voice we hear the tribulation and the insurgent pride that attend the adventure of free self-discovery.

The beginning of a breakthrough means a realization that there is an existential conflict between the self and the structures that have given such crippling security: being possessed by husband and his "estate" of children, house, job, etc. This requires confronting the shock of nonbeing, of not being one's self, with the courage to be. It means facing the nameless anxieties of fate, which become concretized in loss of jobs, friends, social approval, health, and even life itself. Also involved is anxiety of guilt over refusing to do what society demands, a guilt which can hold one in its grip long after it has been recognized as false. Finally, there is the anxiety of meaninglessness which can be overwhelming at times when the old simple meanings, role definitions, and life expectations have been rooted out and rejected openly and one emerges into a world without models. This confrontation with the anxiety of nonbeing is revelatory.

A society based on such experiences of self-affirmation would very likely lack all the psychic compulsions on which industrial discipline is based. For innocent people will not submit to the punishment of an alienated life; they will demand too many rights in the world—not least of all the right to relax and enjoy.

Conscience and consciousness. How instructive the overlapping similarity of those two words is. From the new consciousness we are gaining of ourselves as persons perhaps we will yet create a new conscience, one whose ethical sensitivity is at last tuned to a significant good, a significant evil.

Chapter 4

The Third Tradition:
The Individual, the Collective,
the Personal

The Movie Star and the Commissar

I am watching an interview filmed for television in the early seventies. The scene is a Chinese agricultural commune. On one side of the exchange is an American motion-picture star visiting China as part of a women's delegation; on the other side is a young Chinese teacher, a Communist party member who is serving as their guide. The subject under discussion is the education of children. The young ideologue is expounding the Maoist ideal of "service to the people," explaining how children are educated in the New China to subordinate themselves to the needs of their comrades: never to compete, never to browbeat, never to take advantage, but to lay all their talents at the disposal of others. I am reminded, as I hear him speak, of Joseph Needham's contention that China has become the only true Christian society on Earth, for this is indeed an impassioned appeal for secular saintliness—though it sounds too much like catechism learned by rote.

When the teacher finishes, the film star raises a question. She asks, What if one of the children should turn out to be a Michelangelo.

The teacher is stymied. He does not understand the question. The actress elaborates. What would the commune do with a pupil of extraordinary talent who wished to go his own way, pursue his own private fascination . . . a genius who desired to excel at his art and had no interest in public service?

The teacher does not hesitate for a moment. Such a student

would have to be taken aside and "rehabilitated." He would not be forced to conform, but he would be subjected to collective criticism until he acknowledged that he must devote his talent to the class struggle.

It is a revealing exchange of misconceptions. What is the movie star talking about when she mentions Michelangelo? I think she is talking about "art" as a film celebrity would understand it: fame, fortune, independence, the chance to make a glorious great name for oneself. Otherwise why does she choose a glowing historical superstar like Michelangelo—hardly an example of the avant-garde artist and rejected pioneer?

And what, on the other hand, does the zealous Maoist educator see in that example? Egotism, selfishness, greed . . . an antisocial square peg in one of the commune's round holes. Not that there isn't a place for art in the People's Republic. But it is the place of popular entertainment, official propaganda. What is it, after all, that the communist societies excel in producing? Virtuoso musicians, athletes, acrobats, gymnasts . . . superbly trained performers, specialists in impersonal technique, who reflect glory on the state, but do not question a single social orthodoxy. The ideal is art that never goes beyond what the millions can immediately understand, never requires them to reach out—to surpass familiar standards. In the words of a collectively composed Chinese student song:

> There never could be any poetry
> In individualistic ideals.
> The ideals of revolutionary youth
> Must be fashioned by the whole proletariat
> Calling on millions upon millions
>   to participate!
> Our beautiful reality
> And glorious ideals
> Are tightly linked
> By the red line of revolutionary struggle!

The movie star and the commissar. How neatly they epitomize the ideological conflict that tears our world. The individual against the collective. The individual as champion of self-interest and competitive achievement. The collective as defender of social duty and egalitarian conformity.

Horatio Alger versus Chairman Mao. The Robber Barons versus Big Brother.

We need a third choice.

Michelangelo, in fact, is a close approximation of that choice— though I do not think in any sense either movie star or commissar would understand. I do not mean the Michelangelo who became a leading light of the Renaissance, a celebrated and well-kept favorite of the Medici court and the Vatican, but the Michelangelo who painted himself among the damned of the "Last Judgment," a twisted face on a flayed human hide in the unpitying grip of St. Peter: the artist who had learned how contemptibly worthless the world's celebrity finally is beneath the judgment of God. There is a towering victory of the spirit in such gestures of self-annihilation, perhaps even a holy and prophetical pride. To strip away one's public face like the mask it is . . . to become the common sinner neither pope nor prince ever grows wise enough to acknowledge in himself. In such images of the wrath and majesty of God, we take an exacting measure of ourselves, of our failed possibilities and incompleteness. There is a humility only great souls can know and bear.

Understand—I am not recommending the way of art or sainthood as our third choice. What could that be but a counsel of perfection? Visionary power, high aesthetic talent may always be the gifts of a few. But the inwardness, the introspective candor on which these gifts draw—this is within the reach of all. In that experience of self-discovery, we find an identity that transcends the murderous clash of individual and collective. It is our identity as persons.

Individual and Person

There have never been many persons in the world. There have never been many people who even knew they had the option of becoming persons. Instead our world has always been invidiously divided between leaders and followers, idolized elites and anonymous masses. But whether we rise to the one status or fall to the other, in neither role do we assert the ideal of personhood; we only assume prefabricated identities bound by custom and function. Society—this collective fiction we make of ourselves—allows (or rather requires) that there should be leaders, heroes, celebrities. But these privileged few, for all the rewards they enjoy, are still only people playing assigned roles. Taskmasters, exemplars of the official virtues, objects of veneration or awe . . . their job is their life. They exist to muster allegiance, ensure unity, enforce conformity. To perform these functions they must flatten themselves into the printed pictures and electronic images that clutter the world's newspapers, magazines, wall posters, television screens— until, at last, they become that utterly depersonalized social force which seems always to be mysteriously, invisibly *there,* upholding the official culture, the rights of property, the sanctity of the state. They merge into the all-seeing, ever-present *"They"* we speak of when we tell one another (and ourselves) that *They* will not let us . . . *They* will not like it . . . *They* will disapprove. Those who perform that oppressive service may be given the chance to fatten their egos along with their purses; but whatever their rewards, they do not gain the freedom of authentic personality. They do not enjoy the right to discover and become themselves. As much as the masses they lord it over, the elites of the Earth belong (in Marx's phrase) to the "prehistory" of our species, the long, dreary chronicle of human underdevelopment.

I want to be careful to stress this distinction between *individual* and *person,* because any hasty confusion of the two is bound to distort all I have to say from this point forward. I write in the full and troubled awareness that it is the individual who has, for centuries if not for millenniums, dominated the meaning of personality. It is the excesses of the individual which have at last generated the vindictive excesses of the collectivist ideologies. The bourgeois tradition of individualism has taught us to regard all concern for the self as . . . "selfish." Whether we regard selfishness as a vice or a precious right, it has for generations been the whole moral content of self-awareness. There has seemed no way to be interested in the

self that is not an expression of "self-interest" in the crudest, Social Darwinian sense. Individualism has laid a dark and stubborn
curse upon all forms of self-discovery, making them seem feeble
apologies for social injustice, political elitism.

Yet, in reality, this aggressive bourgeois ideal of life has nothing
to do with personality. Or rather, it is personality warped beyond
recognition by fear and defensiveness, harnessed to the demands
of industrial progress. Individualism drives the person into the narrow fortress of the ego and locks it up there, an isolated, opportunistic, ever-watchful presence. In the individual, no depth or
mystery is permitted, no inwardness beyond secret and ulterior
motives. There is only the hard, public surface of self-interest
thrusting itself forward (at times even courageously) against all
restriction—against the tyrannical restrictions of public authority,
but also against the legitimate moral opposition of the common-
weal.

The individual may be filled with lavish self-importance, but
never with a sense of inherent personal worth, because as individuals we are measured—and we measure ourselves—only by exter-
nals: by acquisition and conquest, by *having,* never by *being.* And
this is the very opposite of self-discovery; it entails subordination
to an exterior, competitive standard. That is the heart of the matter. Self-discovery makes the person, but competition makes the
individual. That is why individualism is as antipersonal as it is antisocial, as much an alienation from our own subjectivity as from
our fellows.

Think, for a moment, what it means to run a race—any race, a
foot race, a race for public office, a race for cash and status. We
begin by accepting a goal, a goal that is "out there" like the finish
line on a track. It is not *my* goal or *your* goal. It is *the* goal. It
does not emerge as a free and original invention of my feelings,
tastes, interests. Its purpose as *the* goal is only to be objectively,
externally *there.* And it must have one other feature. It must be
scarce, so scarce that very few can possess it. Ideally, it should be
absolutely unique—not in the sense that only I may want it (that
would amount to personal choice), but in the sense that only one
of us *can* have it. That is why "being first" is the ideal competitive

goal: Only one contestant can be first, and then all the others in the race can be precisely located in reference to first and treated accordingly—a strong second . . . a poor third . . . a negligible field of "also-rans." Competition is the perfect expression of an economy of scarcity; it gives an immediate and unambiguous calculus for distributing rewards. Especially where finishing "out of the money" may result in intolerable penury, it serves as an excellent device for forcing people to give up being their own persons and to become whatever the game requires them to be. That is the basic competitive assumption: that all contestants can be measured by a single, external standard. They must acquiesce in being homogenized, and not only by their fixation upon a uniform goal but by their acceptance of the rules, the qualities of character, the preparations that go into qualifying as a contestant. Thus, the conventional wisdom regarding social competition has it that "nice guys finish last" . . . so let all comers be warned. The contest makes the contestant.

To compete means that, for the duration of the competition, I cease to be my own master, cease to live my own life. I enter a contest others have designed. I may, then, as a competitor, be "selfish" in the sense of being greedy to win; but this is not an assertion of my self-as-a-unique-identity. How can it be? Uniqueness provides no ground for contest or comparison—only for self-evaluation. This is why competition makes sense only where, as in games and athletics, there is a criterion as objective as a simple measurement of speed, distance, amount, technical precision.

But I no sooner say this than I realize that there are qualifications that must now be added to the discussion of games and athletics. Even here, where we deal with the perfect model of competitive individualism, the personalist sensibility of the day has begun to make imaginative inroads. For example, if we shift our angle of vision just a little, we can see any competitive game as a *collaboration* between players who are, consciously or not, co-operating to produce an exciting and mutually rewarding event. Nobody loses a game played in this spirit, any more than either of the actors playing hero and villain in a drama can be said to "win" or "lose." Similarly, any game that is pursued as an exercise yoga ("tennis flow," "Zen golf," "the inner game of running," aikido, and other Oriental martial arts) loses its competitive, public quality and becomes an inward exploration. Such games do not even have to be played "well" in any conventional sense—though they may actually take on a new and easy grace.

In recent years, this approach to athletics has been pioneered at the Esalen Sports Center in California by Michael Murphy and George Leonard as part of a comprehensive jocks' liberation effort. It is also a sign of the times that we have in our midst an increasingly popular social invention called "New Games." In these big, festive events, created by Stewart Brand and Pat Farrington, the object is style, spontaneous innovation, communal enjoyment for all concerned. They are "games without losers and without spectators," slightly zany but cleverly designed to require maximum improvisation and universal participation. This is the ethos of self-discovery invading one of the citadels of competition to show us a better way.

But let us grant that conventional games and athletics have their place as episodic activities undertaken for the exhilaration of the contest: islands of diversion amid the greater, more imponderable pursuits of life. What happens, however, when life as a whole comes to be seen as one endless, competitive game? Then we do not make a provisional and temporary adaptation to the contest; the adaptation becomes lifelong. Perhaps the contest is not even something we enter into voluntarily. We can be born into the competition, or it can be imposed upon us by parents, teachers, employers. We may be given no choice but to run the race, because we are made to believe that life *is* this race, and to lose is to fall off the edge of the world. So the game becomes the whole meaning of "responsibility," "discipline," "excellence." That is what bourgeois individualism poses as its ideal: life as an all-consuming race for money, status, acclaim, perhaps for bare survival. It creates a society that never stops judging everything we are and all we do by crude, quantitative measures: sales appeal, voter appeal, income, audience, grades, rank, power. And it allows no "time out" until we flatten every rival in the field or collapse with exhaustion . . . unless, of course, we resign the contest and "drop out."

In contrast, the search for the person is a quiet and solitary exploration undertaken in candor and curiosity. Its aim is neither success nor celebrity, but self-knowledge—a knowledge of the self for whatever the self happens to be, as much to confront its weakness and shame as to discover its hidden powers. The joy of the quest does not lie in working up the competitive energies that allow us to outdo others. Rather, the search is for those unique qualities to which no competitive standard applies. On this private ground, there are no measurements of "better than," "farther than," "richer than." There is nothing of the game or race. There is a road wide enough for only one traveler. Perhaps I can be helped along the way by a trusted guide, but no one can follow the road except me. Because the road is myself—my experience of a lifetime waiting to be searched for its shape and meaning. For the progress I make along the way, there is no reward beyond a deepening wisdom whose gratifications are wholly private. Nothing to boast of or display. Nothing to feed the ego.

We become persons in the degree to which we understand the subtle but profound difference between isolation and solitude—a distinction that has been all but wholly lost in our culture. For the person, solitude is an indispensable resource. It is that moment of stillness in which we strip away our received identities and seek to become as naked and nameless as the day we were born. It offers us the opportunity to salvage our original nature—the self we were before the world laid claim to us and began to make us over. Yet, though we may experience solitude as some measure of rebirth, what we discover at the core of that effort, if we delve far enough within, is the fact of our death, waiting inside us, a dark, masked, and unspeaking presence. In solitude, we learn how to be alone with our death; we learn how to use that unfathomable prospect as a means of telling the urgent from the trivial, the noble from the base. We learn how death may be used to cleanse us of distraction, waste, and unworthy ambition.

But for the individual, solitude is nothingness and annihilating despair—and all the more so as the awareness of death presses itself forward for recognition, because death turns everything the individual values into total absurdity. So the individual experiences solitude as a crazy and nauseating zero in the center of life's bustling business: a bottomless chasm in which there are no familiar landmarks, no sure directions. The individual, after all, exists only by competitive reference and external status. Therefore, as individuals, we crave the company of others, not out of love or true sociability, but because others provide our diet of invidious comparison. We take direction and identity from them. What individuality wants of life is never solitude—which it finds wholly meaningless, wholly terrifying—but only *isolation:* a secure ground in the midst of combat. The ego in us is a creature of isolation, standing off from the rivals it needs to lend it a sense of reality, laying plans against them, devising strategies, calculating advantages. Isolation is always isolation *from.* That is what the ego seeks: a way to be safely apart *from,* while still among the hostile others, like a well-defended tower in a battlefield. All the emotional connections of the ego—jealousy, fear, resentment, dominance, self-pity, vindictiveness, arrogance—are relations of antagonism; they presuppose the arena, hence, the inability to be alone. Yet that is just what the solitude of the person is: a private space filled with oneself—and perhaps with God, who is beyond all comparisons. It is a directionless abyss; but the person knows how to enter it without terror. And once within that space, the person learns a radically new relationship with others, one that is purged of envy and fear. Paradoxically, authentic solitude, solitude well used, may be the basis of the healthiest conviviality—because only whole and autonomous persons make clean friendships.

Undeniably, from an outer and conventional viewpoint, the project of self-discovery, especially in its recurrent use of solitude and introspection, is bound to be seen by many as passive, irresponsible, narcissistic . . . a retreat from the "real" world. I confess I am not entirely certain how terms like "narcissism" are used in such criticism. In many cases, it seems only to mean that there is no obvious pursuit of achievement, nothing that gains us a pay raise or public reputation, nothing that attracts the awe or gratitude of others or brings a glowing tribute in *Time* magazine. To see the matter in this way is really only to confess how chained we still are to measurements of performance and productivity. Is it remarkable, then, that, during the hazardous transition we are in from a culture of individuality to a culture of personality, there should be meditation-and-therapy-mongers on hand who seek to make self-discovery "pay off"? Health, wealth, popularity, success . . . they promise the world. On campuses where I have taught, eager promoters from Transcendental Meditation periodically visit, assuring students that TM will raise their grade-point average by two letters, while leading them along the road to beatitude. Perhaps the promise is only bait; but it surely appeals to exactly the wrong appetite. It speaks to the need of the ego, not the person.

Robert Heilbroner has raised the question whether the values of human uniqueness and creative self-consciousness will be able to outlive the demise he foresees of bourgeois culture and its business civilization.

> There are assuredly glories to the civilization of capitalism as there were glories to slave Greece or feudal Europe or ancient China. . . . Of all these attainments, that which is most difficult to appraise in terms of the future is the cultivation of the individualism that is so much a part of bourgeois economics, politics, thought, and art. . . . the great question to which an enlightened and humane "socialism" will have to address itself is the degree to which the individual will be encouraged to develop his or her unique attributes, differences, eccentricities. . . .
>
> No doubt the answers will depend to a large degree on the stringency of the constraints with which "socialism" will have to contend. But this is not the only problem. Much will also hinge on the conception of the nature of man himself—on his depiction as an infinitely malleable and plastic social creature, or as a being whose individualism ultimately reflects the uniqueness or the final autonomy of each person. The philosophy of individualism, which the capitalist epoch has nurtured and expressed, albeit in the grossest form, takes its strength from the assertion that there exists such a uniqueness, a final autonomy, within each individual.

Here we have exactly the confusion of individuality and personality which has so severely thwarted the pursuit of self-discovery. As the outgrowth of competition in the market place, capitalist individualism has nothing whatever to do with "uniqueness" and "autonomy"—unless we are to interpret "autonomy" in the lowest possible terms as isolated self-interest. That is why capitalism devolves so effortlessly into the era of corporate regimentation and the organization man. That is why it so easily adopts the strategies of mass media advertising, a shameful assault upon "uniqueness" and "autonomy." Having no familiarity with the virtues, it does not hesitate to violate them utterly. Indeed, it is precisely the yearning we now see among us for a unique and autonomous experience of personhood that calls into question every standard by which bourgeois society has guided itself for the last three centuries. If the right of self-discovery survives at all in our culture, it is thanks to a marginal minority of artists, visionaries, mavericks who have managed to win their way through to a sense of personhood against the grain of "business civilization." Marshall Berman, tracing the "politics of authenticity" from Rousseau down to the radicalism of the turbulent 1960s, gives the issue a sharp historical definition:

> The New Left's complaint against democratic capitalism was not that it was too individualistic, but rather that it wasn't individualistic enough: It forced every individual into competitive and aggressive impasses . . . which prevented any individual feelings, needs, ideas, energies from being expressed. The moral basis of this political critique was an ideal of authenticity. This outlook was new and yet old, radical and yet traditional. Thus, the New Left's lasting cultural achievement—one that may outlive the New Left itself—has been to bring about a return of the repressed, to bring radicalism back to its Romantic roots.

What Berman refers to as radical and Romantic individualism is the personalist sense of identity, the raw, autonomous self whose rights, Rousseau felt, predate culture and transcend politics.

At most, the capitalist societies of the world have spared the personality a few sheltering inches along their fringes. At times, they have done this by lavishing upon certain great talents who never sought it a belated—and commercially profitable—celebrity. One generation of merchant princes turns Rembrandt into an outcast and a beggar; the next reaps a handsome profit from his once-despised work. It says something of importance about capitalist society that the sense of authentic personhood has managed to survive within it one way or another. But that is not the same as saying that personhood is a creation of the capitalist market place and now faces extinction with it. On the contrary, it is a matter of recognizing that, in harboring the person within its interstices, capitalism, like all social forms, has nurtured one of its own internal contradictions.

Sad enough to see misunderstandings of this kind abroad in our society. What is far more disheartening is the failure of the collectivist societies to redeem this tragic confusion of the individualistic and the personal as part of their revolutionary mission. Instead, they have also confounded the two—and then, in the name of equality and fraternity, have condemned *both* as expressions of antisocial egotism. So the two ideological camps of the world go at one another; but, like antagonists in a nightmare, their embattled forms fuse into one monstrous shape, a single force of destruction threatening every assertion of personal rights that falls across the path of their struggle.

We need a third choice.

Eclipse of the Sacramental

Clearly, there have been terrible contradictions at work in the history of the individualist and collectivist traditions, ironies that defeat their highest intentions. The heart of the dilemma is their common blindness to the demands of the person, a failing that is only explained when we search the deep psychology of revolutionary politics in our culture. A great and troubling truth waits there to be learned, one that many radicals understandably resent and reject: the realization that the pursuit of social justice has not been a sovereign force in our history, even in the lives of its greatest champions. Rather, it has been the adjunct of a larger cultural movement, a transformation of the sensibilities which has severely impaired the quality of our experience. If we have not, in the modern world, made place for the personality in our politics, it is because we have not experienced personality in ourselves—or rather have not allowed ourselves to admit the experience. At some point in our history, we learned to be ashamed of that experience, and so to hide it away like a guilty secret.

How did this extraordinary act of self-censorship come about?

Start with the classic target of modern revolutionary dissent: the *ancien régime,* with its institutions built upon assumptions of blood superiority and dynastic privilege. In the modern world, we would regard the surviving examples of aristocratic elitism as discredited and degenerate remnants—or possibly, as quaintly charming where they are harmless. Yet, there is one trait of the aristocratic tradition which deserves far more careful appreciation than it has received from its democratic opposition. I mean the intimate relationship of aristocracy with the charismatic.

Aristocracy assumes that there is a point in our political life where the sacred and profane resides—by birthright—in people. Not in *all* people, of course, but only in a class apart: a born-special and privileged few whom the many must approach in deference and awe. To these few the aristocratic principle grants a certain boundary—a sovereign and personal boundary, much like the boundaries we know today only as the frontiers of nations.

Over the generations, though revolutionary movements have struggled fiercely to displace the feudal past, they have retained one precious souvenir from their fallen aristocratic enemy: the doctrine of inherent sanctity. This they keep, not as the invidious social privilege it once was, but as a democratic claim to personal inviolability—as "natural rights," "human rights." How better to characterize the highest humanitarian purpose of democratic revolution: to universalize nobility, across all lines of race, class, sex until it becomes an inseparable part of our human condition? Indeed, the project of a *personalist* democracy (my main interest in these pages) is to ennoble all people as no aristocrat ever was— by liberating us one and all from the class roles and assigned social functions which have imprisoned even aristocrats, making them perhaps the most artificial of people. The personalist ideal is to appropriate the aura of inviolability with which aristocracy once enveloped itself, to make that sanctity our common human quality, and then, within this charmed circle, to allow the person to work out its unique vocation. After all, what was the divinity that once hedged the kings of the Earth but a projection of our personal grandeur, waiting to be recognized once again as our own and reclaimed?

And yet . . . and yet . . . something has vitiated the experience that underlies this great democratic project. We may speak, with Shelley, of the revolution making "man King over himself"; or declare, with Saint-Martin, that "All men are kings." But we do not *feel* this universalized royalty as the living presence of royalty must once have been felt in king, pharaoh, emperor. The concept has grown prosaic; it has been planed down into a political theory, a mere constitutional principle. There is no pageantry to it, no lore, no ritual; there is no *magic*. This is a critical and revealing loss, one that explains how it can be that the sanctity of kings should, for millenniums, have survived as an experienced mystery of state, while the rights of man have, in less than two centuries, devolved from an impassioned rhetorical sentiment to a contemporary legal fiction. This is not to be set down to the automatic effects of age; it has come about for a very definite reason. It has happened because the forces of the democratic revolution have, from the very beginning, been allied to the strict logicality and ruthless skepticism of science. The two have marched together under the banner of "Enlightenment." Science and liberty. Skepticism and equality. Indeed, the principle of political equality was itself born as part of the general scientific leveling down of all natural hierarchies in the cosmos.

From Galileo to Rousseau, from Saint-Just to Mao Tse-tung. The same revolutionary movement that made the universe safe for democracy made it no fit home for such archaic superstitions as "sanctity" of any kind, because sanctity is no empirical finding, no verifiable hypothesis. Rather, it is an intuition of the sacramental. We are dealing here in political mysteries that trace back to the charisma of kings, the taboo of tribal priests. This is the sacred ground which, once upon a time, could only be entered by one who was armed with the Golden Bough. Whenever humanistic spirits rush forward to defend our personal dignity from invasion or insult, though they may not know it, they invoke an authority which we inherit from priest and prophet. They are asserting the personality as a locus of magical powers. *But* the idea has been cut off at its historical and psychological roots, because the severely logical eye, obedient to the best scientific standards, finds no place for magic in the universe; it simply cannot admit the legitimacy of sacramental experience. So, when a tough-minded empiricist like B. F. Skinner turns his attention to political discourse, he has no qualms whatever about mashing our most cherished values—our so-called freedom and our so-called dignity—into so much sentimental sludge. For where, he asks, are the observable data for these attributes? What are their criteria of verification and falsification? Of course, the questions are barbarous. But is there not a certain intimidating intellectual simplicity and logical consistency to the man's argument?

Here we begin to see why the revolutionary movements of modern times have dealt so outrageously with the mystique of aristocracy. If the democratic cause has borrowed and expanded the idea of inalienable right, it has, along other lines, cruelly debunked that mystique, discarding it as so much pious obfuscation. "Religion," as De Tocqueville observed, "has been for a long time entangled with those institutions which democracy destroys." In this, then, we find the darkest irony of the revolutionary tradition. The justified anticlericalism of the Age of Reason has become a sweeping rejection of all sacramental experience. Revolution has become, along the leading front of its attack, a war not only upon all forms of elitism but upon all forms of mystery as well, including the mystery of the person.

Science and Secular Humanism

Consider the two major revolutionary traditions of the modern world: bourgeois liberalism and social democracy, the primary carriers of individualist and collectivist politics. Our debt to both is great for the liberating forces they have released into the world. But, in their impassioned dissent from the culture of the *ancien régime,* both have ridden the great running tide of scientific skepticism that appears in our history as an integral part of the revolutionary appeal to reason. Science (too often in its most rigid form) has provided both with their intellectual style and world view; it has been their talisman and their weapon. And science, whatever its virtues, is at best a language of objects, not subjects. It belongs to the world of empirical fact and practical manipulation, not to the life of the spirit. At most, the liberal revolutionaries of Jefferson's day were willing to retain a tame and minimal piety. "Natural religion," as they called it: the religion of common sense. The Ten Commandments, the Sermon on the Mount, and a polite respect for Jesus as the best and wisest man who ever lived. A religion one need not blush to bring up in gentlemanly conversation.

But where religion became a vexation to sound logic and good intellectual etiquette, a thing of mystery and paradox, the man of reason would have none of it. *On principle,* he closed himself to such capacities for experience. They were driven into the dark "irrational" quarters of the mind. It is by way of such squeamish, if highly motivated, self-censorship that the greathearted humanitarianism of Voltaire, Jefferson, Mill has cooled into the frigid positivism of Comte, the deep-frozen behaviorism of B. F. Skinner, the icy Objectivism of Ayn Rand. In pursuit of reason, we finish in the spiritual Antarctica of the Brave New World.

Meanwhile, where has social democracy, the other great tributary of revolution, carried us? In the major socialist nations of the modern world, it takes us along another route to much the same destination. Social democracy, for all its ethical heroism, has made the identical mistake of adopting scientific skepticism as its beacon. "Socialism," August Bebel insisted, "is science applied to all domains of human activity." Not that it had to be so. But if we dissent, we have the heavy authority of Marx against us—Marx, who fancied himself the Darwin of political economy, the creator of a "scientific" socialism. Again, the intention is high, the promise bright. Yet there is no sensitivity for the person—only for "the people." Instead of the sacramental experience which the person requires, we have sociological abstraction, a feeble guarantor of personal inviolability. Once more, with a terrible inevitability, the hard skeptical edge of the revolution, ignorantly at war with all forms of religious tradition, transforms "the people" into a mere behavioristic herd to be conditioned and indoctrinated into virtuous conduct. We finish with socialist societies whose image of human nature is bounded by Pavlov's reflex arc.

Admittedly, there have been more humane versions of both traditions. Again and again, there have been commendable efforts to moderate their dismal reductionism, especially of the left-wing ideologies. A Liberal Socialism. A Socialism with a Human Face. A Marxist Humanism. But none of these breaks with the cultural dominance of science or with the imperatives of high industrial integration, and so none can defend our personhood as it needs to be defended. Even in China, despite Mao's fervent commitment to a barefoot populism, the technocratic forces represented by Teng Hsiao-p'ing now show every sign of being powerfully placed. Indeed, Mao's paternalistic centralization of state and party, his heavy use of indoctrination by "consciousness-raising" cadres during the Cultural Revolution, and his own massive personality cult may, in the years to come, contribute to making China the world's closest approximation to Orwell's 1984.

The drift of the modern cultural mainstream is obvious enough. It runs toward an ironic convergence of bourgeois individualism and socialist collectivism. To the one side, Pavlov's dogs; to the other, Skinner's pigeons—and between them, a world where the human mystery has been abolished forever and people become mere personnel, manipulated, for their own good of course, by a "technology of behavior." And what comfort is it to observe (as I would agree) that the full horror of 1984 is never likely to be consummated, that we are far more apt to finish in a broken-backed technocracy of chronic emergency and wild improvisation? It is enough that we must live under the relentless pressure of these dehumanizing intentions, forever beating back new assaults upon our dignity.

The Modern Idolatries

But now double the irony twice over. Here we have the twin revolutionary currents of the modern world whose common objective it has been to bring Enlightenment to mankind. Two great skeptical streams of carbolic acid striving to wash the world clean of mystagoguery and superstition. But, as Alfred Whitehead once remarked, "man cannot live by carbolic acid alone." So, by way of perverse compensation, the old superstitions have re-emerged in our time as vicious mythologies of race and nation, finally culminating in the revolt of modern fascism against civilization itself. Where have these murderous idolatries of blood and soil sprung from? They are born of a thwarted longing for the vanishing enchantments of religion and aristocracy. That is what we see in movements like Social Darwinism, imperialism, Prussian Junker militarism: a sort of lumpen-elitism, well laced with demonic fury. It is as if the old aristocratic mystique would not lie down and die without exacting a last, terrible revenge: It infects the masses with its arrogant delusions of grandeur, transforms the mob into a collectivized caricature of itself. At last, "we" the millions—the faceless party, the race, the nation enslaved to the *Führer-Prinzip*— are master and messianic elite, privileged to exploit, bully, and kill.

We have not expunged the mystical from our politics. We have only made it, more than ever, the devil's unreason. We have seen that ancient evil come alive in the mass movements of our time, asking the blood sacrifice of millions: the beast we thought we had buried forever under a mountain of skeptical self-assurance. Of course, people do not find what they want in this secularized Satanism. They do not find their way to sacred ground, because the sacred can only become real within the person. And in these idolatries of race and nation, there is no more tolerance for the person than in the individualist and collectivist traditions. There are only the same mass and class identities, now even more viciously enforced upon the persecuting mob and its scapegoat enemies. We finish again at the same destination: the war machine and the technocratic powerhouse.

The Oldest Politics

We need a third choice. By which I do not mean the choice supposedly presented by third world socialism. The societies of the third world are still in an early stage of nation-building and economic development that makes them, at best, younger, smaller, and therefore somewhat less rigidified versions of what the major powers have become. But they have yet to find their way through the mass and class identities which seem (alas!) to be an inevitable phase of national liberation and modernization.

The third choice I speak of is a new human identity, neither individualistic nor collectivistic. And for this, we need a politics that has outgrown the modern infatuation with science and industrial necessity, a radicalism that opens itself to the spiritual dimension of life.

For some time now in my writing, I have been carving out that choice for myself—a third tradition that makes me part of an odd and exotic political ancestry. Most directly, it links me to that rich vein of mystical anarchism—Tolstoi and Buber, Whitman and Thoreau, Peter Maurin and Dorothy Day, Gustav Landauer and Paul Goodman—in which there is always an abiding concern for the sacred center of life, for the drama of salvation that can only be enacted in solitude or in the intimacy of authentic dialogue. Buber spoke of that concern as "a custody of the true boundaries" —a politics that knows the limits of the political. I suppose Gandhi, who learned his politics from Tolstoi and Thoreau, is the major representative of this brand of anarchism in our century— though I doubt he ever described himself as an anarchist. (Most of the best anarchists never bother to call themselves anarchists.) Nevertheless, as large and as militant as Gandhi's movement for Indian independence became, he insisted (if not always successfully) that the roots of the Congress party be kept in the ashram and in an economy of autonomous villages. I am reminded how similar has been the style of leaders like Martin Luther King and César Chávez: the same commitment to personal scale, the same respect for folk tradition and spiritual fellowship.

Anarchists of this stripe manage to ally themselves with any number of religious traditions—though, invariably, within any tradition they profess, they find their way to a characteristic kind of mysticism, to a warm, intuitive trust in the essential goodness of God, nature, and human community. They have known the darkness, but never despair. Tolstoi's Russian Orthodoxy, Buber's Hassidism, Maurin's proletarian Catholicism, Gandhi's caste-destroying Hinduism, Gary Snyder's Buddhism—all of these share the same transcendent delight in the creative possibilities of human fellowship. Certainly, the Quakers and the Bruderhof communities are variations on the same theme. As are, I think, the works of many of the supposedly non-religious members of the anarchist family—figures like Gustav Landauer, Herbert Read, Murray Bookchin. Not far below the surface, these too turn out to be essentially mystic sensibilities, trusting with unswerving faith in the organic harmonies of the world. Kropotkin is typical of these more secular anarchists. Though he fancied himself a rigorously scientific anthropologist, Kropotkin always let himself be swayed by his reverence for folk wisdom and the subtle reciprocities of nature. I am almost tempted to say that it is impossible for anarchists not to be mystics, unless they try very hard.

When Paul Goodman looked about to find an appropriate philosophical context for his decentralist politics, he decided that Taoism was most suitable. It is an evocative choice. It reminds us that this blend of the mystic and the anarchic grows out of that ageless tradition of tribal and village communitarianism which Lao-tzu commemorated in his elusive meditations. For all but a bare fraction of human history, this spontaneous folk anarchism was the only politics people knew. It is in truth a paleolithic politics, and it comes down to us still filled with a certain "primitive" vigilance for the signs and sacraments that nature offers us for our instruction. It is, all together, a politics that keeps close to the soil, even when it becomes the pure theory of very citified intellectuals (which Lao-tzu himself was) and that never lightly discards what the peasant, the nomad, the hunting folk have to teach us about the ways and rhythms of untamed nature. It is no coincidence that a political style which cultivates so strong an appreciation for the spiritual autonomy of people should also possess a precocious ecological intelligence. What is this but another example of how the planet calls out to the person, how the person opens out to the planet—both in defense of their endangered rights?

Anarchist philosophers, pietist Christians, Taoist sages, somewhere mixed up in the lot, a number of Romantic poets and nature mystics . . . I grant this makes up an ungainly family tree. How many of these often cantankerous artists and thinkers could so much as have shared a conversation with one another? Yet, I am sure they belong together. Not as an ideology, but as a sensibility— for the sacred, the organic, the personal. How to sum it up? At the center of nature, the human personality in its unique project of self-transcendence; at the center of the personality, "that of God" within us all.

"That all the Lord's people might be prophets"

For what we want to know about ourselves as masses and classes, we need look no further than to the last two centuries of industrial culture. Elite and rabble, victims and oppressors—the industrial system grinds out these alienated identities in grim obedience to its needs. It carves and slices us to fit its iron necessities. We are its work force, its taskmasters, its mass market.

But personhood belongs to a very different history—a planetary history, and yet a history of the margins and shadows. The person has always been an endangered species, cleaving to the fringes of society, searching out the untrodden paths, keeping the sacred flame alive in secret places. Sometimes, astonishingly and delightfully, one or another of these reclusive few attains the glory of saint or sage. Or perhaps we should say, an occasional prophet troubles us into bestowing that lofty status upon him or her. In that way, by the very act of granting them such devotion, we strategically shield ourselves from the claim they make upon us. We make them gods in order to guard our comfortable mediocrity.

St. Anthony among his visions in the desert solitude, Blake writing a poetry that brought him the reputation of madness, the Tibetan sage Milarepa abandoning the world for the mountain wilderness, Gauguin fleeing to the most isolated islands to become his own man . . . these are the champions of personhood, these and untold others who have left behind no name, no work. Nevertheless, if there is any portion of our still "prehistoric" species which contributes to an authentically human history—to a history of growth, truth, and spiritual adventure—it is this creative minority. We deal here with those towering spirits whom Nietzsche taught us to think of as supermen. In his rage and vengeful anguish, Nietzsche portrayed them always as men of rugged and world-beating grandeur: tyrant artists, stormy prophets. But Tolstoi (whose piety and populist compassion Nietzsche deplored) was obviously among the supermen of our time; and Tolstoi was convinced that true greatness of soul dwells unobtrusively among the wretched of the Earth—among the peasants, the convicts, the humble folk. He believed the world teemed with obscure saints whose hidden magnificence revealed itself only in acts of Christlike humility. Again and again he fills his pages with this heroism of the shadows: secret crucifixions of the ego, simple goodness that puts to shame the pretensions of the learned and mighty. Tolstoi is among the supreme artists of the enlightening instant—the moment in which ultimate truth tears away our veil of lies and touches the most ordinary lives with a resplendent capacity for self-transcendence.

Nietzsche and Tolstoi. The herald of the superman and the prophet of the peasant millions. Can one tradition hold them both? It can—and must, if it is to be a tradition of the person. Because to speak of personality as we do here is to speak of the natural aristocracy that is the unrealized promise of every human being. This is what Tolstoi discerned beneath the wretched surface of the masses. Not simply the claim to justice Marx saw there; not simply the collective heroism Mao has brought forth; but something finer still. The yearning for self-discovery which gives to each soul its unique vocation. For Tolstoi, the peasant masses were not a faceless wave of humanity—a force and weapon of the revolution. They were so many lives in pursuit of truth. And to each one he granted privacy, inwardness, adventure. It takes an artist's knowledge of mortality to fathom such depths of the person, to know that, however much of us our mass and class conformities use up, we die one by one. And nothing, in the moment of our death, makes us more than a soul alone with its fate.

But this is the concern of Nietzsche as well—and of the other great philosophical elitists of our time: Kierkegaard, René Guénon, Ortega y Gasset. If their harsh, critical edge draws blood from the democratic ideal, it is in behalf of our endangered potentialities. What they disdained in democracy was what De Tocqueville had so shrewdly discerned: its underlying psychology of resentment—for the daring, the different, the unique. The elitism they represent is that of self-transcendence: the willingness to make hard demands of *oneself,* the willingness to risk growth, above all the willingness to renounce power. Even Nietzsche, in rare moments of compassion, could recognize this as, just possibly, a universal potentiality.

> The men we live among [he once observed] are like a field of magnificent sculpture lying in ruins, crying out to us, "come, help us, make us perfect . . . we yearn to become whole."

There is a point where Nietzsche's aristocratic disdain and Tolstoi's tenderhearted populism intersect. Their common ground is the unexplored frontier of the third tradition.

A remarkable passage in Scripture comes to mind, one of the most striking I know. I quote it here because I believe it captures the whole meaning of a politics grounded in self-discovery (Numbers 11:26–29).

> But there remained two men in the camp, and the name of one was Eldad, and the name of the other Medad. And the Spirit rested upon them and they prophesied. And there ran a young man and told Moses and said, "Eldad and Medad do prophesy in the camp." And Joshua the son of Nun answered and said, "My lord Moses, forbid them." And Moses said unto him, "Art thou jealous for my sake? Would to God that all the Lord's people were prophets."

In Defense of the Person

There is one group of thinkers that holds a special place in the genealogy of my third tradition: the European Personalists.* No movement of our times has articulated the manifesto of the person with more precision or against heavier odds. Certainly there is little I say in these pages about the right of self-discovery that is not indebted to their instruction. I have in mind the work of Nicolas Berdyaev, Gabriel Marcel, and especially Emmanuel Mounier and those who gathered around Mounier's celebrated journal *Esprit*. Why have these remarkable minds not enjoyed the visibility they deserve in America? Possibly because the Communist party never wielded the influence among American intellectuals that it has in France. Personalism speaks to a crisis of conscience that arises from the moral default of organized Marxism—the ruthless partisanship, the dirty intrigues, the shabby surrender to totalitarian leadership. It is a banner where those rally who have been too many times bruised by the corrupted idealism of their comrades. Still, the elements of the Personalist sensibility have filtered into American social thought here and there—in the works of Lewis Mumford, Thomas Merton, and Paul Goodman, in the poetry of Kenneth Rexroth and Denise Levertov. Dwight MacDonald's little postwar journal *Politics* was an outstanding expression of Personalist values; his essay "The Root Is Man" is perhaps the classic American Personalist pamphlet.

Personalism is a movement of the left that began by bravely rejecting the foremost revolutionary leadership of its day—that of the Soviet Union and the Communist party. Why? Most obviously, because, like all democratic socialists, the Personalists saw in the bureaucratic collectivism of the Stalin regime, and especially in the nightmare of the Moscow trials, as terrifying a violation of human dignity as any capitalist injustice. But the dissent of the Personalists went further. It possessed a metaphysical dimension which took issue with Marx's materialistic dialectics. This is the

---

* In reference to the political movement, which dates from the early 1930s, I will capitalize the word.

very feature that supposedly makes Marxism uniquely "scientific." But not so, the Personalists argued. It is not scientific validity we gain from an exclusively materialistic interpretation of history and society, but a terrible caricature of science—a harsh and inflexible skepticism that refuses, as a matter of principle, to recognize the freedom, creativity, and transcendent aspiration of the person. And how does this finally differ from the deadly cynicism of capitalist culture, which also refuses to value anything in life but getting and spending, money and power? Regardless of the cause that espouses it, in such a degraded image of human nature there is no subtlety, plasticity, or tenderness. There are no delightful surprises waiting in the human heart to befuddle the economic calculus. Instead, we have only a fanatical obsession with physical need and physical power that wholly swamps the personality in what Mounier called "the spiritual imperialism of the collective man."

The Personalists (except perhaps for Berdyaev) never tried to elaborate their position into a system, let alone an ideology. Rather, they set themselves the task of being the Socratic conscience of revolutionary politics, a stubborn ethical sensibility that applied itself to all systems, all ideologies. The core of their political insight was this: that moral sensitivity will always be obliterated by a moral indignation that loses itself among mass and class identities, abstract historical movements, issues, causes, party lines. These are the verbal phantoms of politics, and they do not become the least bit more "real" because we cover them with blood or embittered rhetoric. So the Personalists put their challenge: Here is the whole human being, *this* man, *this* woman before us, a fragile union of time and eternity, public and private, social duty and personal vocation. Does what you propose do justice to this being in its fullness? Does it enhance our awareness of ourselves as moral and creative agents struggling to understand a strange destiny? Does it recognize that there is a certain genius within us that makes us more than the mere ciphers of historical necessity?

The demand was for an answer unclouded by propagandistic alibis or illusions of "realism," by collective measures of success or distant historical vindications. In a phrase Dwight MacDonald liked to quote from Whitehead, what was demanded was "the concrete contemplation of the complete facts." Personalism was a pertinent inquiry in search of the flesh and blood, the here and now behind all ideological apologies. But it was always an inquiry predicated upon action; it went forward into the world as a *working* philosophy prepared to ally itself with many camps—on more than a few occasions, at least in France, even with the Communists. These could be delicate, sometimes hazardous collaborations; but Mounier was insistent that Personalism must never let itself be tempted into the moral luxury of isolated purity. Though the movement reserved a place for solitude and for contemplative calm, it never turned its face from the streets, the factories, the battlefields of the world. Mounier could be astonishingly optimistic in his conviction that industrialism, the nation-state, the entire institutional apparatus of modern life—including its mass political structures, the trade unions, the party system—might yet be made to serve the person. It was a task he understood to require organized effort, the courage to attack self-interest and misguided power, a willingness to struggle in league with others who were at least provisionally accessible to the Personalist inquiry. Under Mounier's leadership, the *Esprit* groups were prominent in many united front efforts and served honorably in the wartime Resistance. For all his spirited eloquence, I am not at all certain that I can endorse Mounier's optimism regarding the humanistic possibilities of urban-industrialism or the promise of conventional politics; but I can only admire his *élan* for action and engagement.

Similarly, there is too little ecological sensitivity in Mounier's politics for my tastes, too little respect for nature as "the uncarved block," there to act as a limit and instruction to human conduct. Too often he slips into the habit of equating progress with a domineering "mastery" over nature. As a group, the Personalists are very metropolitan French, oversophisticated and too strenuously citified; they are unmistakably the children of the *philosophes*. Not much of the raw, organic Tao shows through their urbane intensity. Yet, for all that, theirs is an authentic strain of ethical mysticism, a quality of experience we should hardly expect to find surviving in our desolate cities, applying itself with such courageous persistence to the emergencies of the day. The last thing Mounier wished to have his spirituality become was "a holy eloquence that floats between heaven and Earth and betrays both equally." He would never content himself with being a "Stakhanovite of anathema" pouring out a "lofty and solitary disdain for the abandoned world." "Be Not Afraid" is the translated title of one of Mounier's last essays—and it is an appropriate motto for his courage and energy.

Despite their stout resistance to its oppressive materialism, the Personalists were willing to make use of the Marxist critique as a severe self-discipline for their thought. They acknowledged the vices Marx saw in conventional religion—its moral delinquency, its "idealistic anemia." Berdyaev never hesitated to observe that the human weakness for self-enslavement attaches itself to nothing more tenaciously than religious dogma and ecclesiastical mystification—a human failing that may, paradoxically, make the principled rejection of religion in our time part of a profoundly religious project. There is a toughness to the Personalist religious sensibility, a severe impatience with all forms of spirituality that evaporate into mere psychic self-indulgence. The new religions and human potential therapies of our day would greatly profit from a strong and steady exposure to Personalist conscience. For here is a moral passion that speaks their language; the dialogue would surely lend ethical solidity to many of their ecstatic flocculations. Too often we find in these movements exactly the sort of "devitalized spirituality" Mounier consistently repudiated as "decadent self-complacency, the fruit of luxury and idleness."

Mounier was adamant on the point: "no spiritual revolution without a material revolution." He saw the personality always as an *embodied* spirit whose physical and economic needs require urgent attention. Indeed, he interpreted this as the distinctive, if much-neglected, teaching of Christianity. For Mounier, the incarnation of the savior was a divine finger pointing steadily at the reality of matter and history—and therefore at the prophetical mission of doing justice. "Essential Christianity," he argued, "offers a more open dialogue to contemporary materialism than it does to idealistic subtleties and evasions."

Mounier's Personalism has been described as a *sociologie des profondeurs*—an effort to connect solitude with society, transcendence with engagement. And what is this, after all, but the politics of sanity—of the higher sanity that lies beyond both one-dimensional religion and one-dimensional revolution?

There is [as he wrote in "Be Not Afraid"] a madness of those who treat the world as a dream, and there is a madness of those who treat the inner life as a phantom. The second lunatic is scarcely less frightening than the former. But whereas the former gets locked up in an asylum, the other slowly acquires an ascendancy amongst men who forget what it is to be man. Personalism may hesitate as to which road to follow, but it knows that if there is one single justification for its existence, in spite of all possible errors, it lies in barring the way to this madman.

II

THE PERSONAL SCALE
OF LIFE:
HOME
SCHOOL
WORK AND
THE CITY

Chapter 5

Too Big . . .

Too big . . . and yet not big enough. The lethal paradox of modern life.

On the one hand, we live in an age of gargantuan institutions whose vastness makes pygmies of us all. On every side, we find ourselves penned in by political and economic systems whose lust for limitless expansion makes it impossible for them to minister gracefully to our personal need. Even where we deal with public institutions whose intentions are benign and which make no effort to exploit us for private advantage, we are nevertheless weighed down by the facelessness and rigidity which are the inescapable results of mass processing. At work, at school, in the streets, in the market place, we are ciphers and masses; and so we come to know ourselves and one another—as manpower units, welfare loads, unemployment statistics, public opinion polls, media ratings, body counts, computer printouts . . . rarely as you and me in our ornery and incommensurate uniqueness.

On the other hand, these same world-girdling systems which burden our personal destiny prove again and again to be so parochial in allegiance, so limited in ethical perspective that they betray our duty as planetary citizens. The leaders who aspire to global influence through these massive institutions do not act with any steady and reliable sense of responsibility to the well-being of the planet, but only for petty national advantage or corporate profit. What are the two aspects of modern life that have most perfectly achieved the planetary dimension? War and industrial technology. Both effectively straddle the globe in their actual physical presence; they fill the seas with weapons and sludge; they fill the air with terror and noxious exhaust. The one threatens the planet with slow, environmental death, the other with instant ecological calamity. But there is nowhere in sight among those who govern these awesome forces more than the most cautious display of a planetary ethic.

I cannot think of a more succinct way to summarize the crisis of urban-industrial civilization. All our troubles hinge on the same fact. The great forces of political and economic life which crush us as persons by driving us into people-eating collectivities cannot rise to a planetary level of responsibility. When our ruling elites think big, it is only to think power and profit. Their Promethean dynamism is not matched by Promethean vision.

I have always found it odd to hear practical-minded people criticize Utopian communities and social experiments on the grounds that they often fail and so quickly vanish. I am not at all sure it is the worst thing that can be said of a human institution that it possesses the organic pliancy that will allow it to decompose after it has failed and so leave the ground clear for new growth. There is a more ominous possibility: It can refuse to die when it has outlived its usefulness. It can continue functioning at its obsolete task, forcing itself upon people to whom it is no longer of value, draining away their allegiance and energy. That, I think, is the situation we are in with the overdeveloped institutions of industrial society. They endanger the person and the planet, and yet they will not die and give way. They are not biodegradable. They are our creation, conceived in many cases with high ideals in view, but built on so enormous a scale that they have taken on a brutal and impersonal automaticity. They are a legion of zombies meant to serve us, but lacking the organic sensitivity. Perhaps, in some of the smaller nations of the world, life is somewhat sheltered from their influence. But even the little nations are often little only in size, not in spirit or aspiration. By choice or by force of circumstances, they too often imitate the style of the superpowers. They, too, urbanize, mechanize, systematize, and eventually are tied into larger alliances and markets. The Swedes and Israelis must have military establishments of the highest push-button efficiency, plus nuclear firepower; the Swiss profit proudly off the intricacy of the international money market. The first thing almost every wretchedly poor third world nation wants to do is to build a metropolis filled with luxury hotels and high-rise bureaucracy.

My argument here is that the personalist sensibility, with its passionate regard for the right of self-discovery, has come into prominence precisely in order to moderate the threatening colossalism of urban-industrial life. It is a spiritual force generated by the planet itself as a defensive response to the bigness of things. The aspiration for personal identity on which that response fastens is not, of course, a novel feature in human history. Societies of the past have always had their mavericks and deviants, a surrounding fringe of unaccountable originals who either sought or were driven to go their own strange way—and who might, in consequence, be regarded as saints, prophets, or village idiots. But such types were always understood to be a strict and segregated minority. There were no patterns or institutions for these types; they were looked upon as unpredictable oddities and left to rattle around loosely in some free space of their own making. The sages and hermits took off for the woods; the artists and outlaws gathered in tiny Bohemian neighborhoods beyond the city wall; the lunatics might be treated as town jesters or scapegoats . . . or locked away in the madhouse. Political theory, sociology, cultural anthropology still rarely set foot in such precincts of the world; they are natural anarchies that defy social analysis.

Now, quite suddenly, we find growing numbers of "ordinary" people searching in all the ways we have mentioned in the first section of this book to find just such unstructured spaces where each may go his or her own way. Just as urban culture threatens to monopolize the globe, there is a longing abroad to live beyond the prescribed identities. No society has ever attempted to accommodate that demand with more than benign neglect; no society has ever tolerated it as a legitimate need. The first objective of all societies, even those that pride themselves on their freedom and openness, has been to tell people who they are; all of us arrive in life assigned a name, a sex, a social class, a cultural style. How, then, are we to invent political and social structures that expand personality instead of boxing it in?

In the nature of the case, nobody can blueprint a society that has no precedent. Therefore, in the section that follows, I limit myself to the discussion of a few of those basic and intimate needs that must be looked after in any society. Whatever else we may wish to strip away and do without in a personalist social order, there must be a home where the family meets to exercise its responsibilities, there must be provision for teaching the young, there must be work to make one's livelihood by. Family, education, work—they make up the sustaining web of daily life. And precisely because they touch our lives so closely and constantly, they are the social material we can most readily take hold of and experimentally transform. If I keep the following discussion close to home, I would hope it thereby gains a kind of homely practicality.

So I ask: What is a personalist family, a personalist education, a personalist livelihood? I ask, recognizing that no one knows, that there is no corpus of authoritative research we can turn to, no guides who can provide more than some sparks of inspiration. We must each set about inventing the answers we need out of our own experience, perhaps most of all out of our unhappy knowledge of what has *not* worked. We must let our wounds make us wise. In all the history of the world, the function of family and school has been to shape the newborn to society's pre-existing standards; the task of boss, lord, and master has been to enforce the interests of economic elites upon the laboring many. Always, there have been all-knowing social authorities and inherited paradigms wise with the tradition of the culture, armed with the power of legitimate coercion—there to assign identities.

Here, however, in obedience to the rights of the person, I propose that we reverse the course of the cultural river, so that it flows out from the inherent needs of the person into the structures of society—on the assumption that the human personality is the most precious resource of all, one which enriches the entire species and ennobles the planet. I ask, what manner of home life, education, work will support the adventure of self-discovery? I raise the questions as separate discussions, but they are, in my thinking, a single social constellation—and essentially one continuous educational project. It is, indeed, one of the worst corruptions of modern life that this single process of cultivating the personality should be segregated into separate compartments, the home in one place hopelessly dependent on resources, services, and income from remote sources; the job elsewhere connected to the home only by a pay check; schooling in still another place entrusted to specialized professionals who will only teach at a special time, in special facilities, and whose primary obligation is to prepare children for the demands of the economy.

My intention here is that these three should come to be seen as a continuum whose main goal is not to *make* something happen, but to *let* something happen. For personhood cannot be imposed; it can only emerge in its own good time. How easy that is to say, but what a blessing of conviction it takes to believe—that people are indeed persons, that their growth can be trusted. The ideal we must honor is that of an open childhood—from prenatal days into adolescence. Home and school blend together inseparably in the responsibility of maintaining that openness; perhaps they even become one and the same institution, parents and teachers sharing episodically in this or that aspect of the child's growth. The challenge throughout is to provide a security that does not stifle, a guidance that does not dominate. It is a difficult art for all concerned: to stand as a model of mature adulthood before the young, and yet not to overshadow the originality of vision and talent that is born into every child. The culmination of childhood is the discovery of one's vocation in the world, the calling which it is one's peculiar destiny to answer. Unless this vocation is then translated into a viable livelihood, our education has been a fraud and a frustration. Work is but the adult phase of education, self-discovery carried forward into each day's labor.

Finally, in this section, we will turn to a discussion of the city. Not because the city is a basic social structure; human beings have, after all, lived out most of their history in a world without cities. But the city is a basic structure of contemporary life. It is the context for all we discuss here; it contains our homes, our schools, our work. Cities govern the nations and service the industrial apparatus. Above all, cities monopolize our culture. They own the brains, the expertise, the literate knowledge of the world. Even what we may want to say of rural life and the land must begin with talking about the city, because the land is owned and ruled by the city, together with the resources of the wilderness. At some point, we must ask what the place of the city is in the personal scale of life. Can cities—*our* cities, these sprawling, all-consuming leviathans—contribute to the right of self-discovery? Or are they the trap in which our personhood must surely perish?

The chapters that follow offer few social prescriptions. They confess to a deal of the doubt and failure I have experienced in seeking to find my own way home through the urban-industrial wasteland of modern life. My family life, my education, my work have been as badly damaged by the person-crushing pressures of our time as those of anybody I know. And I have wasted much time looking to this reform or that movement to provide them shelter. Yet, I become less and less certain as the years go by that any mass action or official policy can do more than ameliorate those pressures—very likely by displacing them toward other victims, other areas of life. If there is to be a revolution of the person, it will have to be an intimate revolution, one that pledges itself first of all to rebuilding the basic structures of life I turn to here. It will have to put down roots in the home, in the neighborhood, in the school, on the job; it will have to discover the villages that have been buried by our cities; perhaps literally, it will have to reclaim the fertile soils beneath the smothering pavements.

Everything I speak of here begins with the person; but in every case, I see those needs building community. Companionship is of their essence. The home requires a supportive context: an extended family, a neighborhood, a commune, a village. Work that expresses vocation reaches out toward companionable forms of self-management. Education needs a pedagogical environment defended by its community from the economic forces that would exploit our children's energies and appetites. The city must be won back from its collective anonymity by becoming a commonwealth of urban villages. On all sides, to use Mounier's words, "the *thou*, which implies the *we*, is prior to the I—or at least accompanies it." One slogan hovers over these pages: *Personhood is a convivial fact.*

I know that such an approach—homely, immediate, piecemeal—amounts to moving by inches. But it is movement by way of real projects, here and now, and at least each inch we gain is real ground won for the rights of the person and the health of the planet.

Chapter 6

Home: In Search of a Practical Sacrament

We are of flesh born of flesh into a long babyhood. However oddly a people may draw their bloodlines and divide the duties of the home, their newborn enter the world needing kinfolk and mothering kindness. Our lives as political animals begin in the politics of the family.

Yet, for as long as we have been sociable animals, the burden of the family has been to stamp the young with an ancestral image and bind them to their social fate. The violation of personhood begins in the cradle, if not in the womb.

So we have the dilemma: biology at war with personality, the right of self-discovery ransomed away for our mother's milk. In childhood each of us is an angel looking homeward, toward the one destination we would call our own, the one life that can be nobody else's life but ours. But first we must make ourselves welcome in another home—our parents' home. And it is filled with jealous authorities: the ghosts of the ancestral past, the pretensions of social power. We are born into other people's intentions. We learn our names and our natures at their hands, and they cannot teach us more truth than they know or will freely tell.

Can there be families whose love is not treason against our natural vocation?

Demystifying the Family

I have lived in only two families in my lifetime—the family of my birth and the family of my marriage. Two very legal, very unbroken homes. I say *"only"* two because I suspect this makes me part of an obsolescent cultural pattern. There are any number of statistics on the breakdown of domestic life in the Western world that could tell me as much, but none of them more vividly than my daily experience. Each year, I count fewer friends and neighbors who have not been through one or more divorces. Others—especially younger friends and students—avoid divorce by avoiding marriage. They form "relationships," an option that keeps things legally casual and limits the expense of splitting up to the cost of renting a truck to move somebody's belongings to another apartment. Although somewhere between a third and a half of American marriages end in divorce (and in some parts of the country, like California, divorces outnumber marriages), the official census figures say that 99 per cent of all cohabiting couples are still married. But experimental relationships ("free love," as it used to be called) are a sharply growing trend (they have increased fivefold in the past decade) and—even more importantly—nobody bothers to be reticent about them any longer. I can recall when the most popular movie star in Hollywood could have her career ruined by one unlawful pregnancy. Now it seems almost mandatory for celebrities to advertise an unwedded love life.

It was only a few years ago that my daughter came home from school complaining that she was the only kid she knew who didn't have an extra mother or father, or some half-brothers and stepsisters scattered around the country in homes here and there where she might spend weekends or vacations. She had discovered the extended family, American style; and, being no part of it, she felt odd and left out. All the reports I come upon tell me that she would find herself surrounded by as many broken homes if her family belonged to any other race or class. Wherever the law allows, wherever there is money enough to make a down payment on an attorney's fee, marriages break up in increasing numbers—in the ghetto and in the suburbs, among the junior executives and among the unemployed. Even the attorney's fee may no longer be that much of a barrier. For a few dollars, one can buy a Do-It-Yourself Divorce Kit in most bookshops, complete with the necessary legal forms. And very likely "no-fault" divorce laws will soon be the rule throughout America.

"No Fault." The concept reveals so much about the plight of

modern marriage and the family. No fault . . . nobody to blame. A marriage comes apart, a home breaks up—often amid outrage and anguish. But we decide not to contest the liability. We say the complexity of sorting out the rights and wrongs is too great, the expense prohibitive. Let us simplify the matter. Let us eliminate the ethical issue, do without blame, without punishment . . . as if a natural disaster had befallen us. A clean, sharp break and no re-criminations.

Perhaps there is a certain moral maturity in admitting that the guilt of a failed marriage is too diffuse to be assigned punitively. Or it may be that, like the automobiles that hurtle along our free-ways at murderous high speed and whose collisions we have also elected to regard as "no-fault" accidents, we too, in our homes and marriages, feel ourselves careering through a mad traffic of human relations, traveling too fast, changing direction too sud-denly. We impinge upon one another, flying fragments of a disinte-grating social order, surrounded by too many pressures and temp-tations. Inevitably, there are marital accidents, bruises, and heartbreaks along the way. But who can hold us responsible if we lose control of our runaway lives now and then?

I feel uncommonly fortunate to have come this far in life un-scathed by the emotional carnage of a broken home. These days there are any number of books and workshops that teach how di-vorce can be approached as a liberating, even a "creative," oppor-tunity for beginning life all over again—almost like a rite of pas-sage. But I know that in my case, the waste and punishment of the experience would be immense; I would be losing more than I could recover. In the homes I have been part of, I have found all the love I will have to go on in this life, and more than I have earned. I have known a loyalty that may be as close as I will ever come to the sacramental meaning that once underlay the pledging of troth between people. There have been wrenching strains in the homes I have belonged to; but I have come to see that there is more desperation than malice behind the wounds we inflict on each other in a family. Our worst anger is often a way of calling out for help, laying claim to a tenderness and acceptance that cannot be reliably found anyplace else in the world.

I say all this to make it clear at the outset that my own family life has been warm and rewarding. In thinking back over it, I easily weaken toward an almost embarrassing sentimentality. But even so, I have again and again experienced the frightening vulnerability of this overburdened institution. It is there at the core of the family, an instability that is not primarily due to the merciless pressures of urban-industrial life. Those pressures are real enough, and they play their part in grinding the family down. But the vulnerability I speak of goes deeper than that. It reaches down to the family's fundamental responsibility as guardian of the sexual identities and moral orthodoxies on which societies are built. The weakness is *inside* the family itself, because it is inside every member of the family. I feel it within myself—a restless, hair-trigger intolerance for the censorship I experience at the hands of loved ones, for the manipulation I have suffered in the name of love and for the sake of love. My sensitivity in this respect is hardly unique; I share it with a generation that has become peculiarly alert to the treacherous mystifications on which the family has always been based. That perception may be the stock in trade of our greatest novelists and dramatists over the past century or more; but when have these subtle insights entered more poignantly into the common experience of people to work such damage upon family life?

In our bones, we know something about the family that no earlier generation knew as vividly or could bring itself to acknowledge. We know that every ideal that supports the family has been used to tell a lie. Its love has been used as a lever of power; its trust and allegiance have been the masks of social domination. People find that bitter truth plainly before them, gashed across the grain of their lives—women in search of their liberation, children in search of an autonomous adulthood, men who have suffered domestic rebellion against their masculine authority—and they are not afraid to declare it, even though, at the word, the bonds of the family strain and break.

It is good that this should happen, good that all forms of mystification should be undone, even if we must—as we do here—call into question an institution that is rooted a million years deep in our history, in the very foundations of human biology. Yet, there must now be a family *beyond* the family so many are struggling to escape. Because if there is not, then we will not achieve any sort of liberation by destroying the family; we will only finish unattached and drifting.

A Crippled Tradition

Whenever I hear people—usually politicians, clergymen, or journalists—bemoan the breakdown of the contemporary family, I wonder what they have in mind as the better state of affairs we have supposedly left behind. Do they know where the modern family comes from? Do they know what function it was created to serve?

The family as we know it is one of the most damaged and pathetic by-products of industrial upheaval. Its heritage is a drab tale of victimization. If we reach back less than two centuries into the social history of the modern world, what do we find? Factory towns and mining camps sweeping dislocated rural masses and immigrant multitudes into their burgeoning job markets like a vast global debris. By all their tradition and experience, these laboring folk were tied to a domestic economy of household and locality. Then, suddenly, within a few generations in every Western industrial society, they were rudely dumped into a very different economic order—a world economy whose engines were savage cities that systematically pulverized their human material into the footloose fragments economists euphemistically called a "free and mobile labor force" capable of instantaneous response to the market. Such "free" labor came to the cities as uprooted, propertyless, mainly youthful men and women whose sex lives and love lives now became unprecedentedly promiscuous and unstable, on such a scale and with such suddenness that Edward Shorter identifies their condition as the first "sexual revolution" of the modern era. The only family these new economic "individuals" could be expected to create was the tiny human cluster we now call "the nuclear family." But that was all the new economy wanted of them in their domestic life: their status as minimal units of labor power.

There should be a man to be drained of his full-time energy in the mill or the pit; a wife to keep his home, bear his children, and assume primary responsibility for their nurture (even when she might herself become a mill hand); children to be raised as the next generation of cheap labor. As an organizational base for the industrial system, the nuclear family was irreducible and utterly efficient, the smallest conceivable social entity that could man the factories and replenish the work force.

Moreover, the industrial household was, by virtue of its isolation and insecurity, a savagely competitive bundle of self-interest that neatly reinforced the fierce aggressiveness of the capitalist market place. It was forced to fight incessantly for employment and upward mobility. All sense of community was quickly wrung from its consciousness. The very architecture of industrial towns expressed the family's isolation and selfish defensiveness: row upon row of beehive tenements crowded with distressed and anonymous masses, held together as powerless household units at most by desperation and basic erotic need. In time, the competitively successful might move out into the more affluent isolation of a private home in a residential neighborhood or even in a suburban garden spot, and there, illusions of romantic love, family sentiment, devoted motherhood might be cultivated as more refined, middle-class bulwarks of family life. For such families, the insidious mystification of romance and erotic fulfillment, presenting itself as a free expression of autonomous choice between man and woman, rapidly became the staple of popular culture: novel, drama, magazine, eventually the film. And in all these forms, it also became the acid that ate away at the bond between the generations as the children born of supposedly romantically fulfilling marriages quickly took off in search of the same gratification in their own nuclear families.

In the industrial cities, even when there were efforts to support and fortify the precarious life of the toiling masses—friendly societies, trade unions, co-operatives—all were built atop the nuclear family. The only appeal for allegiance they made beyond the home was to ethnicity or "class consciousness," abstract collective identities that might become a basis for embattled social solidarity at the proletarian level, but which have never held those who manage to drift upward into the middle class. In bourgeois society, only single-minded devotion to the building of a successful family business and the greedy defense of property among the well-to-do have provided any sure ground for a robust extended family life. But for every prospering clan of Forsytes and Buddenbrooks, there were millions of fragile working-class households that had to look to makeshift expedients like trade unions, socialist parties, immigrant associations, church social groups to find some part of the stability their preindustrial ancestors had once found in the family.

This is the crippled tradition from which the modern family takes its course: a century and a half of institutional shipwreck, a long, bone-wearying struggle by millions of deracinated men and women to improvise love, loyalty, and the responsibilities of parenthood out of the social ruins left in the wake of industrial disruption. Still today, the troubled families that come to pieces all about us are reeling in those great winds of change. They are pitted against the brutal historical fact that wherever the industrial city takes over, it comes, not to preserve families and strengthen community, but to erect cities, assemble a work force, build an economy. And for that, it needs power at the top and helpless human fragments at the bottom.

In the United States, where the pressures of urbanism only began to make themselves felt after the 1840s, the most marked social response among the middle classes was a wishful cult of idyllic domesticity that was meant to defend the family from the crime and grime of the encroaching city. It was also a sad, faltering effort to save the natural innocence of the New World from the mounting threat of mammon and machinery which the city represented. The American state of nature was to be turned into a well-kept front yard and private garden. Every humble cottage would become a domestic paradise presided over by an angelic wife whose mission in life was to scrub the house clean and keep her family pure. Kirk Jeffrey calls the episode a "utopian retreat from the city" and believes it achieved little more than an oppressive exaggeration of sexual stereotypes and paternal authoritarianism.

Later, when transportation allowed, the retreat became a flight to the suburbs. But it was still the city that called the tune—as much for the affluent commuters at the end of the train tracks as for the wretched immigrant families they fled from in the inner city. Financially, culturally, sociologically, all were tied to the industrial economy. And so we remain. Nothing that has come along in the past century—no major social movement or significant reform—has diminished the dependency and isolation of home life in industrial society. The fragmentation of all natural community continues—in the high-rise ziggurats that fill the central city and in the housing tracts of suburbia where each home withdraws from streets and neighbors to become a bastion of selfish consumption. All we have done is to resign ourselves to our domestic isolation and call it "privacy." To every home its own power mower, burden of debt, and nervous breakdown. Just as I set to work on this chapter, I received a letter from a woman in the Midwest, someone who had read my book *Where the Wasteland Ends*—a cry for help which I could answer with little more than sympathy:

I don't know where the wasteland ends (annihilation or insanity?) but I know that it goes right through my house here in suburbia: the wasteland is my life. I am a housewife (or as we say, *"just* a housewife"). My children live in the wasteland of department store toys, the TV set, and books which tell them what it's like to watch a sunset or walk in the woods or live on a farm. I have no co-workers, and my children have no playmates other than one another. Here our yards are fenced in, and we have no sidewalks. Neighbors keep to themselves. Each private home on the street has its own snowblower, lawnmower, and a car for every person over sixteen years of age. In the evening, a different supper is served in each house on the street, and at the end of the day a lonely housewife puts the dirty dishes into the dishwasher. Here in suburbia there is no sharing and no caring.

Mounier once observed, "The charms of private life are the opium of the bourgeoisie or its hiding place from the misery of the world; the values of privacy need rescuing from that profanation." But clearly the opium is no longer taking effect on everyone.

The Torments of Respectability

How often do we hear the families of primitive societies spoken of as "extended families"? The adjective suggests that what we find among these people is an outmoded modification of some basic institution called, simply, "the family." *We* have "families"; *they* have *"extended* families." But no. The truth is, they have families; we have *diminished,* if not absolutely minimal, families. One step further along, and we arrive at the single-parent household which must scramble frantically for public assistance or state-supported day-care to survive at all.

Yet, consider how much we continue to demand of this diminished institution. Ideally, it is where children are to be born, reared in the care of inspiring adult models, and successfully prepared to take their productive place in the world. It is where men and women are to find unfailing companionship and lifelong sexual gratification. It is the commissariat and dormitory to which the work force of the economy returns each evening to be rested, fed, and to have its morale boosted for the next day's tribulations. It is the haven to which all of us are expected to take our failures and heartaches for solace. It is the asylum where our psychic kinks and tangles are to be made straight or to be contained with tender, loving care. It is where we are to look for support whenever we prove incapable of earning our own way. It is where our laws place the final responsibility for most consumer debt, taxation, citizenly duty, and the disposition of noncorporate private property, income, and savings. It is where we are expected to grow up healthy, seek the greater part of our love and fulfillment, find personal acceptance, grow old gracefully, and die in peace.

Only think how many social services and specialized "helping" professions have had to be awkwardly grafted upon the nuclear family over the years to help it carry this impossible load. And even then, do the professionals and the agencies support, or do they undermine the family? Do they not, in their totality, almost make the amateurish family seem superfluous?

We expect absurdly more of the family than so tiny and embattled an institution can ever give. And yet there have been families that tried to do it all: fanatically respectable, high-achieving, house-proud families that have insisted on doing their duty to society. But how could they even begin to manage the task and still hold together in their irreducible smallness, except by resorting to rigid internal discipline? And that is exactly the style of family life we look back upon and call "stable" and "responsible." In Victorian England (to cite only one example I am especially familiar with) the middle- and upper-middle-class family achieved an almost proverbial solidarity—or rather, those families that survived the competition did so. But who were the people who inhabited these respectable homes? Compulsively authoritarian fathers, frigid and hysteria-prone wives, obsequiously timid and frustrated daughters, sons who were afflicted with a collection of pathological symptoms that ranged from stuttering and bed-wetting to sexual impotence. This was the social system on which modern psychiatry, in its early days, patterned all its standard neuroses.

In most cases, these disorders of the Victorian mind and spirit achieved some generally acceptable kind of sublimation—like competitive games, economic acquisitiveness, empire-building, social snobbery; either that, or they flowed off into subterranean channels of sexual kinkiness and puerile pornography—aspects of Victorian middle-class life that have only lately attracted scholarly attention. But the inner anguish was always there, not far below the stilted good manners and social rigidities that characterize the period and give it the charm we may now find so quaintly depicted in television serials like "Upstairs, Downstairs" or "The Forsyte Saga." I will accept any number of exceptions to the generalizations I make; there is no need to exaggerate the point to defend its overwhelming validity. The truth reveals itself to anyone who examines the tortured lives which we now know so many eminent Victorians lived in their gingerbread prisons—Ruskin, Mill, Swinburne, Elizabeth Barrett, Cecil Rhodes, Lewis Carroll. It is there to be seen in the lives of the women who became the first generation of feminists. It is there, too, in Samuel Butler's *The Way of All Flesh,* which offers a ghastly anatomy of the family which all Butler's contemporaries could recognize.

There he writes of his hero, Ernest Pontifex, bent beneath his father's domestic terrorism:

He believed in his own depravity; never was there a little mortal more ready to accept without cavil whatever he was told by those who were in authority over him: he thought, at least, that he believed it, for as yet he knew nothing of that other Ernest that dwelt within him, and was so much stronger and more real than the Ernest of which he was conscious.

The words are a shrewd personalist insight into the mystifications of domestic authority. They tell what a terrifying human price the middle-class home, in its classic historical form, paid for stability. It became a machine for grinding down all personal vitality—but at the same time, the perfect social foundation for the necessities of industry and empire.

When families like this break down, it is because their members want to break out. They know they are in a jailhouse that will suffocate all that is most original and authentic in them if they do not escape. Yes, the oppressiveness of the family has been softened since Butler's day. Many forces have played their part in the amelioration: the dislocations of war, the comforts of affluence, the rising pace of social transiency, the automobile, the mass media. Humane reform has also contributed to making family life more permissive, even to the point of making it shapeless and untenable: the liberation of women, increased legal protection for children, the greater sexual candor we have learned from modern psychiatry, the cushions and buffers of the welfare state. All this helps make Ernest Pontifex's ogre of a father look like a prehistoric beast.

Yet, in our own day, we find R. D. Laing insisting that the politics of the family is still rooted in "unknowing violence and terror." Every baby, he contends, is subjected to "forces of violence called love, as its mother and father have been, and their parents before them. . . . The family's function is . . . to create, in short, one-dimensional man: to promote respect, conformity, obedience . . . to promote a respect for 'respectability.' . . . We have all been processed on Procrustean beds." Laing's work and that of his followers mounts to an apocalyptic vision of family life as mass-produced madness. But it has become best-selling psychiatric literature if not social prophecy, because it tells a truth people are ready to hear, a truth they discover in their own experience. "We are destroying ourselves," Laing argues, "by violence masquerading as love."

The old domestic despotism mellows; but as it does so, a heightened awareness of subtle restriction and violation comes to the fore. People—to begin with, mainly the wives and adolescent young—demand more latitude, more space to range and grow in. Where they are denied so much as an inch, they hurt, they fight back, and with each blow they begin to feel out the dimensions of an invisible cage: unspoken cues, subliminal expectations, hidden scripts. With remarkable rapidity, our generation has developed a historically unique sensitivity for the emotional manipulation that has always underlain the family's role as the primary socializing agency. It is as if the inner mechanism of a sacred idol had suddenly been revealed for all to see, and we realize that we have been hoodwinked by those who purport to love and serve us—though, of course, they too were taken in by the same deception. Where does the discovery leave us? Perhaps in a limbo of social dislocation. But at least we have named the wrong and given it the visibility of a "problem." Even if we do not yet know what our personal destiny is in the world, we recognize that it is not to be any of the roles the family has predesigned for us: man/woman, husband/wife, boy/girl, obedient citizen, grade-grubbing student, loyal employee. Before we find out who we are (if we ever do) we must find out who we are *not*. Self-discovery begins with suffering the loss of false identity.

Maybe this, paradoxically, is the great virtue of the modern family. In the course of the urban-industrial process, it has at last been so enfeebled that all its deceptions become transparent. The intimidation that hides in its intimacy shows through. So the family becomes the first target of personal rebellion in our time: the easiest to strike at, the most vulnerable in our immediate field. And it falls apart. There is that much to be said for it: It is fragile enough to break when it can no longer bottle up the discontent of its members. We may not have families that know how to nurture the personality; but at least the families we have no longer find it easy to beat us into submission.

Open Marriages and Plastic Wombs

Marriages come apart, homes break up . . . but the statistics show that most people who divorce remarry. Of the women who divorce, 75 per cent remarry, and of the men, over 80 per cent within three years. As weak a reed as the family may be, it is all most of us have to hold against the engulfing loneliness. It is also the one little corner of the world where we find the chance to experience responsibility—not much perhaps, minor decisions about household budgeting, where the kids should go to school, what color to paint the kitchen . . . but as much of a chance as the big, busy world gives us to feel grown-up and in charge of something more than our private lives.

There are many frothy ideas around these days about "open marriage," "being close but free," "Harrad experiments," proposals that would "save" marriage by detaching it from the continuity of the family and diluting its loyalties still further. What do these liberated life styles promise? Unfettered transiency, promiscuous sex, a dead minimum of responsibility and commitment. They turn a once-sacramental relationship into a frivolous liaison between swinging singles. Such an ephemeral encounter of surfaces may serve as an interim arrangement for "young marrieds" with easy money on hand and a heavy backlog of adolescent eroticism to burn off. But they will never offer the sustaining loyalty or personal recognition people continue to look for in marriage and family. After a point, there is a pathos in casual relationships that tears the heart more than disappointed love.

Proposals of this kind are too lacking in moral weight to merit serious attention. In the name of freedom, they do little more than flow with the tide of our hedonistic, high-living economy. A disposable love life is ideally suited to the competitive ambitions and rootless mobility of advanced industrial culture. It keeps us footloose and lets us travel light. These are values that belong to the world of the careerist individual, not to that of the person.

This study is predicated on the assumption that our society has overwhelmed the human scale of things. I began this section with the lament that our world has become "too big." But there is one institution that has become too small, and that is the family. It has wasted away to the bare minimum and is desperately in need of expansion. In fact, this is not an exception to our thesis: it is a corollary. Things have gotten too big at the expense of basic structure. Some of these structures—the neighborhood, the village, the community of work—have simply been driven into the ground as obstacles to big system efficiency. The most basic structure of all, the family, lingers on. It remains a biological necessity—until perhaps it is someday replaced (as in *Brave New World* and many another futuristic fantasy) by a public hatchery of sperm banks and plastic wombs, a possibility already before us as a serious political proposition by one feminist militant (Shulamith Firestone) who believes artificial gestation would be a means of "freeing women from their biology." Meanwhile, the family is tolerated— but only in its most denatured, nuclear form.

It might be an axiom of our thesis: The bigger the industrial apparatus, the weaker the family. The one subtracts its human resources from the other. Any reform we propose for the diminished family that disintegrates it still further will only expand the public welfare bureaucracies and make official expertise that much more indispensable to millions of isolated and floundering human fragments. If our solution to the problem of the family is simply to dissolve it out of existence by way of divorce and "open marriage," then we can only expect to see the role of the state increase in our lives. No libertarian politics should have any interest in providing still more excuses for such incursions.

The First Law of Voluntary Association

Scaling down the industrial leviathan means building bigger families—or rather bigger households. It is not more children we need in families, but more family we need in the life of every child: more adults to share the home and participate in parenting the young. And such families are being built, as experimental models with many shapes and under many names. We hear them spoken of these days as communes, collectives, rural homesteads, ashrams. The forms are many, but they point in a common direction—toward homes that can hold their own against the crushing pressures of the urban-industrial dominance.

On the shelves across from me as I write, there are scores of recent books, monographs, articles on these new extended families. I have visited some, collected files of letters and reports on others . . . and I have gone looking for a few which, like mirages in the desert, were no more than a failed dream when I got there—an experience which many students of communal life report all too often.

I have wrestled with this sprawling body of contemporary experience, trying to evaluate its occasional triumphs and frequent disappointments. By its sheer bulk, the reportorial material available announces that we are living through a period of exuberant communitarian experimentation, one of the great episodes of the Utopian tradition. Here is where much of the best counter cultural energy of our day has gone—if only to be dissipated again and again along the route to an elusive goal. But how much of this thought and work can I do justice to here? I have not seen a report on the subject that does not become dated within a few years of its appearance. The fluidity and variety of experimentation is immense, and it moves on many fronts at once, challenging our concepts of child rearing and sex relations, work and property, authority and freedom, privacy and participation, consumption and distribution. Even the best students of the scene settle for tentative conclusions.

One *has* to be tentative, not simply because the communes are new and untested (not all of them are) but because our society at large, and many communitarians themselves, no longer possess a fixed standard of success and failure to work by. That indeed is the weight of my thesis in these pages. We are at a cultural juncture where the meaning of success, progress, achievement changes shape and eludes our grasp. Almost automatically, people ask of a communal effort: Will it last? Will it grow? Will it prosper? But are those the relevant questions? True, they reflect the values we still look for in the social mainstream . . . bigness, power, affluence. But the "success" of Chase Manhattan Bank and the Pentagon is the very blight of our lives, a force that flattens both personality and conviviality.

If, then, the communitarians devote themselves to the search for intimacy and simplicity, if they pursue personal fulfillment, camaraderie, democratic sharing, environmental harmony, spiritual growth, how is the world outside their boundary to judge their achievements? How much does any of us know about these virtues and their hidden intricacies? If people take the risk of social invention, if their work and their lives come apart with the strain, can we tell what insights they may have salvaged for all of us from a noble failure?

Or again, even in many sympathetic studies, one comes upon the Israeli kibbutzim or the Chinese agrarian communes presented as experiments that took root and worked; so they become the criteria of success held up as the measure of all communitarian efforts. But the comparison is neither valid nor helpful because it does not fathom the depth of the problem. Both the kibbutzim and the Chinese communes have been nation-building endeavors, and both have enjoyed the binding heritage of a culture they could affirm and follow. Their identities were given, their nationalist commitments move with one of the modern world's strongest currents. These are great advantages to have in the wilderness of social innovation. In the case of the Maoist communes, the advantage was even greater, if more compromising to its libertarian significance. The entire effort was initiated by an idolized national leader, guided by official policy, and now continues under strict state supervision as a prime factor in China's industrial development. Even in a people's republic, power at the top does not tolerate autonomous structure below.

In sharp contrast, communitarianism in our society is born of dissent and appears at the precarious margins. Its purpose is to *disintegrate* the national identity and, in most cases, to throw off much of the dominant culture. It is the work of some of the most damaged human material in our society—the estranged and oppressed, the emotionally crippled and disaffiliated, drawn together in anger and discontent by the bonds of shared sufferings. A young friend I know in the Hare Krishna movement tells me he can name few members of the order who did not arrive by way of hellish drug trips and acute psychic alienation. So, too, communities like Synanon and Delancey Street (both in California) are social experiments being created from the misery and emotional terror of addiction: John Maher, founder of Delancey Street, speaks of his people as "society's garbage." Other agonies bring people to these surrogate families: the experience of prison, of persecution, of moral bankruptcy in the most lucrative professions and careers. Not least of all, there is the punishment of a hard divorce, a jolt that can teach the most complacent among us how false and fragile our institutions are.

We deal here with people who are the victims and casualties of our troubled system; they have exhausted their assigned social and sexual identities. It is not so much that they have elected to drop out; they have fallen through the bottom of their society. There are not many people who come through traumas like this prepared to affirm all the old roles and rules. With the exception of a few evangelical Christian movements (like the Reverend Moon's Unification Church, which seems to be working from a hidden political agenda that calls for old-fashioned anticommunist patriotism) all the new intentional communities sound a clear note of dissent. Even those that prefer to remain politically unobtrusive are permeated with cultural disaffiliation. They eat differently, dress differently, live to a different schedule, work to the rhythm of a different incentive. They rear and educate their children by different standards. They avoid the rat race in favor of modest earnings; perhaps they even become mendicants in the streets. If they take to the land, it is under the sway of a strong ecological ethic: thrift, conservation, and simple living.

Not all of this is done competently; not all of it works. (One of the best authorities on the subject, Rosabeth Kantor, estimates that communal experiments have about the same tenuous survival rate as small business in America.) But every serious and humane communitarian effort, no matter how small or short-lived, does something to keep alive the hope of scaling down and loosening up our impacted industrial order. It is, at least, a gesture that works to increase the living variety around us.

But with that much said in sympathetic support, there remains a serious problem about the new families—one that poses a fierce dilemma for the personalist ethic. With only a few significant exceptions (I will mention them further along) the new communities are repeating a classic pattern; it might be called the First Law of Voluntary Association. Where there is authority and prescribed orthodoxy, the community holds together; where there is anarchist permissiveness and free growth, it comes apart. In the one case, we have permanence, but with less and less self-discovery as time goes on. In the other, we have self-discovery (maybe), but quick disintegration.

I would agree that permanence, in and of itself, should not be made a social fetish; failed experiments and antiquated institutions should be allowed to die and make way for new growth. But that is not the same as saying that impermanence and chronic transiency are positive virtues. There are far too many communes I know of that have been a sheer human chaos of cross-purposes and pathological incompetence. Their "freedom" was little more than ramshackling disorganization, as if perhaps the entire enterprise was never really meant to do more than provide casual sex and a cheap crash pad. The dishes collected in the sink, the house filled up with unpaid bills and mangey pets, everybody kept their backpacks ready to go under the hall stairs. My wife and I once inherited a house from such a commune. They were gentle and soulful people who had held out against the landlord and irate neighbors for nearly a year before the membership drifted off to new "relationships" all over the globe. It took us the better part of another year to clean up the mess and repair the damage they left behind. Misadventures like this are no solution to any of our problems; they are merely more symptoms of spiritual malaise.

But on the other hand, we have the solid sectarian communities that are built to last. They are orderly, disciplined, reliably financed . . . and a perennial vexation to libertarian social philosophy. What to do with those who use their freedom to create unfree communities? One rough compromise some anarchists settle for is to locate freedom *between* voluntary associations, rather than necessarily within them. Let a thousand flowers blossom, and let the measure of our liberty be our unrestricted right to come and go among them. I think this is an adequate solution where we are dealing with adult or celibate communities—like monasteries or convents. These are also families for their members, and among the most durable that history has ever seen. They belong to a wise and well-tested tradition that requires no comment here.

But what happens when we are dealing with closed or sectarian communities that intend to include children? The first generation on the ground may have every right to choose for itself; many may find, even in the severest discipline, the style of life that suits their personal need. That choice is their exercise in self-discovery. But what are the rights of the next generation? It will be born to the faith—to the dress, the diet, the ritual, the beliefs, the authorities. The children will not choose, they will inherit.

And of course, what they inherit derives from their parents' best and most loving intentions. That is the pathos of the doubts I raise; they are a criticism of people who believe profoundly in the sanctity of the family. The Nation of Islam, the Hare Krishna movement, the Healthy-Happy-Holy Organization, many of the Jesus People communes—all of these recognize the horror of what has happened to the family in the modern world; they all know, more urgently than I could ever state the need, that something must be done to repair the damage. A high and solemn sense of parental responsibility stands at the core of their spiritual life, and that is nothing to be lightly dismissed.

In an earlier book, I sharply questioned the decision of the Hare Krishna order to raise its next generation in strict parochial segregation from the surrounding society. A young man in the movement has since written to me in protest, asking,

> What is wrong with raising children in a largely Vedic milieu? Is Donald Duck, Mickey Mouse, and McDonald's better than the great saints, sages, and kings of Bharata? . . . Vedic culture, paintings, music, stories can all be shown to be healthier for the

human and child psyche than their Western counterparts. . . .
I shall send my four year old boy to the Krishna conscious school
system as the only sane alternative to having his senses, mind,
and intelligence rotted away by the decadent lifestyle that mas-
querades for human life by members of the right, left, and center (and which rotted me for so many years).

In reading his impassioned letter, I felt humbled and troubled
by his remarks. He cannot know how deeply I feel his concern,
nor how strongly I can sympathize with his decision made in the
midst of a dilemma to which I have found no solution. Our children's natural dignity *is* violated by the corrupted culture around
them; they have a right to a sane and supportive upbringing.

But how do the sectarian communes go about fulfilling their responsibility to the young? They reach back into tradition and received doctrine to retrieve a legendary image of happy and stable
family life grounded in fatherly supremacy, wifely submission,
puritanical sexuality, and heavy parental dominance. They resur-
rect the old, assigned identities; they salvage all the ancient
mystifications; they rebuild the authoritarian home. And of course
it "works" . . . for their purposes . . . for the time being . . . because they come to the community starving for structure and spiritual sustenance. These they find in the tradition and in the identities they freely elect to adopt as their own. No doubt, with enough
isolation, they can defend their special ethos indefinitely against
the outside world, as the Hutterites and the Amish and the Men-
nonites have. A libertarian politics will always defend the right of
people to establish close, confessional communities; perhaps, if
their number is great enough, they will help to scale down and
ventilate our impacted industrial order. But the right of self-discovery will never take root in these homes. They stand as instructive reminders that "small" may not always be "personal."

Parochial censorship is one kind of restrictiveness from which
experimental communities may suffer. There is another that can
develop where no sectarianism is on the scene at all. This is the
psychological uniformity that occurs where situational groups
transform themselves into families. Here, the force that brings

people together is shared suffering or common grievance; so the members of the household are apt to be like-minded, from similar backgrounds, bearing identical scars. Everybody turns out to be young, old, male, female, divorced, gay, handicapped, an ex-convict, or an ex-addict.

Situational households can become very narrowly based indeed. Here in the San Francisco Bay Area, young women who have turned militantly feminist after too many treacherous relations with men have assembled in extended families restricted to divorced and unmarried mothers. I have met some women who regard this as an ideal arrangement and talk of planning a wholly impersonal pregnancy with a father they never intend to marry or live with; he will simply be the sperm in their lives. I have even come across a few households of lesbian mothers—a rather specialized population. And things can become more bizarre still. One woman I know has been entertaining the notion of bearing a child by one man and then giving it to another man to raise. The prospective foster father is a friend of hers who happens to be gay and lives in a homosexual male commune . . . but he would dearly like to experience the responsibilities of fatherhood.

In the opening chapter of this book, I touched upon the personalist contribution of situational groupings. They are a necessary defensive gesture and a significant stage of contemporary social development. But what happens when we begin thinking of situational networks as families? Do we not lose something of great value to our personhood and to that of the young who may be related in these households? One of the major roles of the family is to be somewhat of a microcosmic human society. This means it should contain, as all traditionally extended families do, a sampling of life's variety. At the very least, the two sexes should be there, along with the major phases of the life cycle: children, young adults, the middle-aged, the old. No doubt a complete household should also make a place within itself for birth and death—experiences now usually screened from us by hospital care. It is one of the worst vices of our times that we now see many people segregating themselves by age—on top of all the other social segregation we live amid. We have the old in "retirement communities" and the young hiving off into "singles-only" apartment complexes. Where situational networks become families, the households may take on size, but they reduce diversity by refining the criteria of segregation still further.

Exceptions to the Rule

I mentioned earlier that there are notable exceptions to our First Law of Voluntary Association: groups which have refused to throw up parochial barricades, and yet have found a way to endure and grow, in some cases over a period that dates back to the 1940s. Let me name a few of these experiments here—mainly to suggest one significant truth they seem to teach.

The groups I have in mind include Boimondau, the French watchcase-making commune; Lanza del Vasto's Community of the Ark, also in France; Charles Dederich's Synanon and John Maher's Delancey Street, both in California; Steven Gaskin's Farm in Tennessee; Sri Aurobindo's city of Auroville near Pondicherry, India. I am inclined to include also two well-seasoned and prospering Christian communities: the Bruderhofs in New York, Pennsylvania, and Connecticut; and Koinonia in Georgia. Both of these have strong religious commitments that somewhat modify their openness; but each has managed to avoid a tight sectarian closure. The Bruderhofs, for example, have made it a policy to require their teen-aged children to experience the outside world through several years of school and work; then they must apply for membership of their own volition if they wish to return. (Most do.) Koinonia, which began as a pecan farm dedicated to a Christian witness on behalf of racial brotherhood, has developed so many alliances and local programs (farming, housing, education, handicraft industries) that it is open on all sides to the surrounding community.

Now, there is one striking fact that all these communities have in common: Each stems from a charismatic founder. (The Bruderhof was begun by Eberhard Arnold in Germany in 1920, Koinonia by Clarence Jordan in the early forties—both inspired prophetical figures.) We might do well to ponder the importance of this factor. It suggests there is a certain radiance of the enlightened soul that can unite people in comradeship as powerfully as any religious doctrine or sectarian discipline: a bond of personal trust within the group that does not need to build a wall around the community's children or to raise barriers against the world outside. We have no political category for this magical quality of leadership. We may speak of it as "charisma," but naming it does not explain its power. To call it "benevolent dictatorship" hardly does justice to the impassioned democracy of its faith and intentions. We are up against the mystery of Plato's philosopher-king— the leader whose genius it was to embody the noblest consensus of the polity and to govern by the power of truth.

We are wise to resist that power where it aspires to govern nations or marshal armies to battle. In doing that, it contradicts its own subtle humanity; it becomes a giant's face on a colossal placard—the overblown great leader, dwarfing each of us and massifying the millions. But in the small community, in the tribe and family, there is a place for philosopher-kings after all, an intimate arena where they may look us in the eye and summon up the best that is in us. They become teachers to whose judgment people will tend to defer. They are trusted, and they do not betray the trust.

Perhaps this sounds as if nonsectarian communities must wait until some rare charismatic lightning strikes. But there is another way to see the matter. We might ponder how many there are who carry that lightning in them. Perhaps it lies quiescent in the hearts of millions, an untapped resource that we have not given much chance to show itself. After all, among the communitarian geniuses I mention here, it is not only philosophers and gurus like Aurobindo that have inspired durable experiments; that is also the achievement of an ex-alcoholic like Charles Dederich, a former jailbird like John Maher, a hippie dropout like Steven Gaskin. And certainly during my visits to Synanon, I have met some mighty convivial talents that had been salvaged from the social dregs and looked ready to make their community last forever. My hope would be that, as the right of self-discovery comes to be more widely exercised, many of us will find more communitarian creativity in us than the world has ever let us know was there.

The Birthright of Loyalty

To a significant degree, the successful communities I have mentioned answer the question that was raised by our First Law of Voluntary Association. Yes, there are alternatives to sectarian exclusiveness and centrifugal permissiveness. There *can* be a personalist communitarianism, open, strong, and free. We need these experiments, and many more like them, because they represent some of the deepest thought and experience available to us about the place of the family in the life of the person.

But theirs is not the course I want to follow here. I do not wish to go where the attractive alternatives lead, but to bring our discussion back to the scene of the crisis—to the homes we are born into, and marry into, and are still tied to, even if the bond is strained and frayed. For the remainder of what I say here, when I speak of "family," I am not referring to alternatives that need to be invented or experiments that have to be tested, but to the blood family which begins no further away than the parents and children, the brothers, sisters, and assorted kin that come to us by way of birth and marriage. For I think we are inclined, in our desperation, to give up too quickly on this battered and much-abused institution, even before we have looked to see what contribution it might make to the needs of the personality.

There is now available to us a vast body of research and reportage dealing with intentional communities, collectives, situational groups, communal households; but there is very little literature that addresses itself to saving the family that amounts to more than conventional marriage counseling or pious platitudes. Rescuing the family is not a project that seems to attract the energies of renewal in our day. Why not? Perhaps because those who have set their minds to inventing substitutes for the family have been driven to their task by bitter disappointment in their own homes. Their efforts, born of rebellion against parental oppression or the despair of bad marriages, take no interest in reclaiming the family, only in replacing it.

Very likely this is a phase of storm and stress we will have to pass through as the rights of the person work their way through urban-industrial society, shaking all our institutions to their foundations. Yet, I cannot let go of the fact that the family is a community in its own right; it is our basic, biologically given community. In its better, more extended days, it has always included a variety of life—the two sexes, the major stages of youth and age, the facts of birth and death, even a range of eccentricities—that few communitarian experiments manage to embrace. There is that breadth and substance to it. And as it is with our natural resources, so too with our social resources: It is intolerably wasteful to throw away and build from scratch, when the old and worn-out might yet be recycled.

At this point, I want to pursue a difficult argument. I want to speak in behalf of salvaging the blood family, of building it bigger and stronger, and of reviving its domestic economy. But it is obviously not the traditional authoritarian family I have in mind, for that would make no contribution to the rights of the person. Rather, my interest is in the *new* family that might arise by metamorphosis out of the old, born from the desiccating husk of the family we inherit. New wine in an old bottle.

Why the old bottle? Because I cannot think of any more practical place to begin the discussion of basic structure than where most of us are now. For all its insecurities, the family is still where most people live out their lives, trying—with varying degrees of success—to hold the pieces together. It is not likely that many people will ever convert to the exotic faiths or unusual life styles on which intentional communities are based. Conversion like that is a leap into the unknown: Few will take the risk until family life becomes totally impossible and has taken a heavy toll. Even then, the conversion may not go deep enough to last—and they may simply drift into the gray legions of the detached and lonely who are the background population of every modern metropolis. For most of us who take up the challenge of social renewal, the family is the raw material closest at hand and most available for reshaping.

But more than this: Somewhere in every family, buried beneath all its assigned identities and traditional authoritarianism, there is one precious need of the person which no Utopian substitute can provide, because it is welded into the biological continuity of human life. *Spontaneous and unconditional loyalty.* No matter how odd or elaborate a society's conception of the family may become, the absolute bond of blood is at the core of its kinship system. At the very least, it is there as the birthright of every child in its mother's care; but it usually diffuses much further into the surrounding world of relatives. None of us could have survived our infancy if that loyalty were not there; but, of course, we take it for granted. Some of us may never have occasion to reflect upon its presence once in the course of a lifetime . . . until we search elsewhere in the world for the same quality of trust and concern, and discover that it cannot be found or easily improvised. It is a loyalty that does not come to us as a reward or as the benefit of a contractual formality, nor because we have proved ourselves worthy by some rigorous initiation or sworn to a common belief. It is not even there because we are liked, or approved of, or agreed with. It is a commitment that undercuts all this; it attaches to our being. It is ours simply because we are blood relatives of those who have it to give.

We enter their circle of kinship, and the pledge of concern is made. We hunger, and we are fed. We cry, and we are comforted. We are in danger, and we are defended. We suffer abuse, and we are revenged. Nobody inside that circle asks, Why do I owe you this favor? What have you done to earn it? It is enough to say that we are "family." That may indeed be *all* we can sometimes say for ourselves. To begin with in life, we cannot even say that much; we are mute and helpless—utterly vulnerable and of no use to anyone. Yet the kindness we cry out for is given. If it is not, then the failed obligation makes itself known in the heart and the conscience of the entire family—a wound that may never heal or be forgiven. Each of us is born into a family that is spontaneously beholden to us for no better reason than that we are its young.

How deep into our consciousness can we trace this strange moral force of nature? There are anthropologists who believe we can find the rudiments of blood loyalty in animals—especially among the birds and mammals, where maternal concern for the newborn looks very like the powers of conscience at work. They do not eat their young; they do not abandon them to predators. Perhaps there is something to this speculation. But if so, what begins so humbly among simpler creatures as an act of instinctive nurture blossoms forth at the human level to become educative companionship—the gift of thought and aspiration passed on from generation to generation. With us, there is far more involved in parental loyalty than protection and nourishment; there is a positive cultivation of faculties—the long process of sharing experience between the generations. If we assume a healthy culture, then, when the child asks, it is answered; when it reaches out to learn, the lesson is given for the immediate joy of giving it. There is a reciprocity here that is so biologically primitive that it can do without a sworn word or legal formality; yet it holds within it the seed of our highest spiritual growth.

When, at last, people do give the form of words and ritual expression to this special loyalty—as they do in ceremonies of marriage—the best they can do is to model their rites upon a primordial relationship of trust and concern. The rites do not create the relationship; they simply declare that two people have now sworn that there should stand between them the bond that has always held between kinfolk: an unconditional loyalty . . . for richer, for poorer, in sickness and in health, for better or for worse. And from that promise there springs the home that will teach the habit of unconditioned loyalty to another generation.

I make no attempt here to sentimentalize family life. We all know how often the loyalties of marriage and kinship are abused, and how bitter relations within the family circle can become. The oldest tragedies in our literature are family tragedies—great stormy dramas of hatred and betrayal that come to a murderous finish. No doubt betrayal is as old an experience within the family as trust. But that is exactly why family strife can become so fierce—because the trust that is violated within the home is so deeply rooted in our biological and spiritual needs that we cannot help but to regard it as sacred.

And this is the heart of the matter; this is where the metamorphosis of family life must center. It is the universal teaching of human society that the bonds of the family are *sacramental;* and all the love and need and trust that tie us to the family tell us that in some deep sense this is true. But *what* is sacred? To *what* do we pledge the troth of kinship?

Every society in human history has taught its members that the sacramental loyalty of the family belongs to the assigned identities people assume through childbirth and marriage: to this woman as wife and mother, to this man as husband and father, to this infant as their child and heir, and beyond them perhaps to innumerable kinfolk, each defined by a customary station. Is this not still how we come to know our families—as if all these awesome grownups were actors in a ritual drama, bearing titles and performing archetypal roles, looking larger than life, seeming to know so much, telling us things that must certainly be so, deciding what to do, showing us how, giving orders? We arrive in the theater of the family to be their understudies; we stand in the wings, watching how they play their parts, trying to pick up the cues, learning How to Be Like Them.

That is how it has always been—until now. I cannot think of another society or another period of history that has realized so vividly that the grownups of the world are only tall children after all. Think of the laughing stock we have become at the hands of humorists like Lenny Bruce, Woody Allen, Jules Feiffer—all of us in our well-fortified roles and stations. They see us for the bewildered incompetents we are, stuffed to bursting with subversive little anxieties, mixed-up sex, and feeble alibis. We strain to keep up a good front, but jesters like these catch us out. *They* know that *we* know what *poseurs* we are. Our television comedies are filled with those bathetic images, and we are expected to recognize the humor. It is not the old satire of manners and morals whose purpose was to reveal the corruption behind every noble social façade. Here, the psychology is far more involuted, and the cynicism reaches deep into the politics of the family. It shows us what victims of crazy mystifications we all are, struggling to keep our "act" together . . . and never succeeding; a population of worried clowns plagued by unreliable repressions, giving way to all-too-human hang-ups and infantile impulses. It is the comedy of radical self-doubt—a very Socratic comedy that hinges on the great truth that we do not know who we really are.

For increasing numbers of people, there is no credibility or charm left in the old family drama. Neither the rules nor the roles are sacred any more. Too many of us have learned how this traditional make-believe has been used to denigrate and oppress. We do not wish to be *dramatis personae* any longer, but real persons in a script of our own making.

Yet, somewhere behind each mask of the old drama, there has always been a real person, struggling dutifully to fit his or her uniqueness to the demands of the assigned family role. The parents we may never have known, and who may never have let themselves be known as anyone but "Mother" and "Father," are persons. The lovers and lifelong companions we may only have known as "Husband" and "Wife" are persons. And these personalities *are* sacred; they crave and deserve our unconditional loyalty as much as any newborn child, because without it, they will keep themselves hidden away and safely guarded, until they wither for never having seen the light of day.

There is within each of us a capacity for loyalty to those we grow up among and make our homes with. That nourishing human power grows uniquely out of the biology of the family. Thus far in our history, it has always attached itself to prescribed social roles and has served to reinforce those roles. *Can that same loyalty now be given to the person rather than the role?* Can we bring ourselves to say to our children, our parents, our lovers, as we would have them say to us:

We meet as strangers, each carrying a mystery within us. I cannot say who you are; I may never know you completely. But I trust that you are a person in your own right, possessed of a beauty and value that are the world's richest resources. So I make this promise to you: I will impose no identities upon you, but will invite you to become yourself, without shame or fear. I will defend your right to find an authentic vocation. For as long as your search takes, you have my loyalty.

Where do people look today to find such an invitation to guiltless self-discovery? Psychotherapy, situational groups, intentional communities . . . contrived expedients, though, for the time being the best many of us can hope for. Still, when we join such improvisations, we are bound to be haunted by the fact that we are together in this group only because another group—the family—has fallen away from us. There will always be a failed loyalty behind us that we know can never be duplicated. The provisional and contractual arrangements we invent to take its place will rarely achieve the continuing intimacy of a good marriage; they can never supply the biographical continuity that the family alone keeps in trust for its members: the lost memory of our earliest years, the recollection of ancestors whose influence lingers in the depths of our experience. All this that has passed before our conscious years began is also part of our self-knowledge; in some respects, it is the most vital part.

Psychiatrists may dig for some of this material in our unconscious; the new Primal Therapy even seeks to burrow back into the prenatal period. But all these formative elements of our life are in the family, remembered by the parents and relatives whose experience braids inextricably into ours. R. D. Laing has come up with the idea that families are so many "knots" of recycled biography—a macrame of borrowed hopes and hatreds, cheated dreams and thwarted ambitions, visited upon later generations to be lived out vicariously. He is right in warning us that ancestry can be a subtle tyranny, but too bleak in overlooking the fact that it is also the substance of our personal destiny. The odd and unpredictable interplay of ancestral influences is the promise of each child's uniqueness. There is the same artful blending of continuity and novelty here that we see in the continual scrambling of the genetic material. In both cases, both the inherited old and the emergent new are *us*.

What we need in order to become what we are is not liberation from the family, but a family that lets its young weave their knots into an original fabric. The proper place to work out our genealogical karma is not in a psychiatrist's office, but in an open childhood, among those whose lives must always be the prime facts of our identity.

Can we build that kind of family? Can we give the unconditional loyalty that has always held the family together a new sacramental object—the free personality? Since time out of mind, the job of the family has been to socialize persons. Now let us use it to personalize society.

An Open Childhood

Does the ideal of open childhood mean permissiveness? Yes and no.

No, if we intend the word as many have been loosely employing it over the past generation or so. That shapeless and overindulgent fashion in child rearing may represent a groping, early concession to the personal rights of the young, but it has more often been a sort of forced parental retreat before the turmoil of the times: the war (and then the other war . . . and the *other* war) . . . the bomb . . . the pace of technological innovation . . . the insane gyrations of the economy. Philip Slater believes that the American family has always been peculiarly democratic because the dynamism of the society has repeatedly opened "experiential chasms" between the generations. Perhaps so. But this is not the permissiveness that belongs to an open childhood; it is simply the floundering bewilderment of parents who cannot get a grip on the runaway world around them. Parents obviously cannot be authoritarian if, in the chronic flux of the time, they cannot speak with authority about anything.

The psychiatrists have also made their influence felt in the years since Freud, especially with respect to sanctioning open sexual curiosity and outspokenness in middle-class homes. That, in itself, has rapidly liberated a good deal of young innocence from what Herbert Marcuse has called "surplus repression"—again, at the cost of creating another generational disjuncture. But all this has given our children the freedom of a free fall through empty space. It does not speak to the simple truth that the principal project of childhood and adolescence is to grow up gracefully. And for that, children must obviously have stable families that present competent models of adulthood. If they are left to make do with rock stars or television teen-agers for that purpose, they will be stalled indefinitely in a narcissistic adolescence—and they too will finally grow up to be tall children.

A permissiveness that is no better than parental default betrays the young. Yet, if the rights of the person are to become our prime cultural value, we *have* to be permissive with our children; there has to be an honest and central element of self-discovery in their growing up, and so a willingness on our part to let them become their own person. In our parenting, we need an ideal which allows us to be exemplary without being prescriptive. Each of us must know how to be a free personality, without insisting that we are *the* personality our children are expected to become. And there must be an accessible range of adult possibilities near at hand for our children to learn from—meaning families of some size and variety.

The ideal of open childhood is an old one, though one that has never been honored by any social system. It is the ideal of Socratic pedagogy—the same star (so I will argue in the chapter to come) that must guide the education of the person throughout life.

Socrates, we recall, described himself as a midwife of self-knowledge. The image presents the paradox of a constructive permissiveness. The midwife is one who comes to make a "delivery," yet she comes empty-handed because what she has to deliver is already there, somebody else's creation and possession. Thus, Socrates does not come to tell the young what to think or how to live. If they ask for such direction, he stymies them; he purports to know nothing. He will only say, "Let us talk it over." And he adds, *"You* begin." As it turns out, his "ignorance" is a fertile vacuum; it draws out the student's inner resources—tentative ideas, unformed tastes, embryonic aspirations. What the student offers in the dialogue does not always meet with benign indulgence (that would be the course of a treacherous permissiveness). More often it is astutely, but lovingly, criticized. But these *are* authentically the student's own convictions that are being used as experimental raw material. The student opens the dialogue and is encouraged to try out this position and that. Each argument, even if it is angry and abusive, is taken up seriously and examined, until the student sees its limitation or folly. In the course of things, Socrates even criticizes his own convictions and invites the students to join in. He mocks himself a bit, perhaps to make sure he does not over-shadow the new growth he is cultivating. Nothing is sacred in this dialogue, except the human personality as the potential locus of enlightenment.

So the dialectic is paced along by the young. And yet, all the while, there is Socrates at the center of the adventure, embodying in his very presence all the values of mature personhood, making them felt throughout the dialogue. That is the art of the method. By the tone and quality of the exploration, Socrates teaches what he uniquely is; and the young all about him, if they absorb the les-son, comprehend his model. They may finish sharing no single idea or doctrine with their teacher; in that sense, no *thing* has been taught. But they have learned what dignity, generosity, and free-dom are; they have tasted the joy of open inquiry. They become themselves, yet they are forever Socrates' children.

The ideal of open childhood is just such a dialogue between adult and child in the home, spread out across the early years. It is the beginning of what will become a lifelong project—the unfolding of personality. Join the unconditional loyalty of the family to the Socratic commitment to free dialogue, and we have a home that champions self-discovery and defends it against all comers.

Re-creating Domestic Economy

What interesting centers of subversive free growth such families might be—homes prepared to tell the domineering forces of society and economy that they may not have our children (or any of us) for their raw material. But, of course, there is no way to make that defense unless the home that champions the ideal is rooted in an effective independence. All the most durable experimental com-munities—even those that enjoy the benefit of strong sectarian bonds—aspire to some significant degree of economic autonomy. They are not merely ways of living together; they are ways of working together. They realize that self-sustaining, shared labor is necessary to the integrity of their ideal. If families are to become free communities, they too must have an economic ground of their own making to stand on.

We are not used to thinking of families this way in America—not since the family farm disappeared as the basic unit of agriculture. For most of us in the great industrial cities, "independence" means bringing home a regular pay check and having a passable credit rating. On the one side, we take in money as somebody's employee; on the other, we pay it all out as everybody's customer. If we manage to keep functioning as a smooth conduit for the cash flow, we are holding our own and getting by. And certainly nobody who qualifies as an economic expert will show any displeasure with our performance. We will be just what their economic indicators asked for: a unit of manpower in the employment statistics, and many units of effective demand in the market place.

Yet, before the advent of industrialism, every society that was not a slave society included a robust domestic economy. The very word "economics" means a household account: keeping the home in good order. The normal, preindustrial pattern of life was for families to work together—either on the land or in some "putting out" system of manufacturing. This might not make the family any less vulnerable to exploitation, but at least it made the home a practical center of work and of mutual aid. There is a remarkable masculine bias in the usual historical formulation which tells us that the Industrial Revolution deprived only the proletarian worker of *his* independence. The truth is, the entire proletarian family lost whatever economic autonomy the laboring classes still possessed; and it did not exchange what little it had for something better.

From being a place of production, the home became a place of more and more dependent consumption. Especially in its urban setting, it was reduced to the condition of total economic contingency that we now take for granted, and which stands as the ideal of advanced economic planning in the major nations—with the possible exception of a still very rural China. Where the process of uprooting domestic economy is not yet complete—as in some European Common Market countries—official policy is still to move families from the land to the city and to drive the father into more productive (and usually more ecologically wasteful) factory labor. From the viewpoint of such planning, the family should have to look beyond itself for everything—for employment, food, clothing, shelter, utilities, services, consumer credit, amusements, welfare. The result is a society of oversized cities in which millions of households lean ever more precariously on economic powers and sources of supply beyond their control. They must buy everything they need; they are encouraged to spend all they earn; and at last, they live in danger of drowning in their own consumer wastes if the garbage collection ever stops or runs out of dumping space.

Notice how our conventional economics works from the casual assumption that a society's "development" can be measured by per capita cash income. For the most part it is true that where cash income is low, there are many who will be pitifully poor; but the poverty is not there *because* the cash flow is modest. These are two separate economic factors. Where people are able to look after their own needs by primary production and neighborly barter—as might be the case in an economy of productive family farms—they have little need for cash. Poverty really means: no cash *plus* no subsistence. Even more deceptive is the corollary that a people's well-being will increase as cash income rises. Usually, that assumption nicely masks ruinous social processes that drive families from farms and villages into cities where they must, of course, find cash to keep alive. Then, even if they are penurious factory workers or starving beggars in the streets of Calcutta, Caracas, or Hong Kong, they will have more "income" than they had as subsistence farmers or village artisans.

An economics that thinks this way would also assume that we could measure how healthy a society is by the amount of pills and medicines it consumes. It is an economist's sleight-of-hand trick to distract our attention with the coin of the realm, while domestic economy is bundled off the stage and out of sight. Domestic economy, the world's oldest economic form, has little use for cash or the abstractions of the market place. It deals simply and directly in the processes of work and the needs of subsistence. And its intuitive measure of "the standard of living" is apt to have much to do with the happiness and integrity of family life.

Now, it may well be that over the next few generations, as urban-industrialism grows more unstable, the pressure of necessity will force people everywhere toward the revival of domestic economy—with much panic and hardship along the way. We may have no choice in the matter. But I surely cannot unfold a social program here that anticipates such a transition. If I so much as tried, most people, trapped in our high consumption industrial apparatus, would see the proposal as "turning back the clock." Nevertheless, for those who have ears to hear, I submit that any family-saving strategy which deserves to be taken seriously must include some provision for bringing work back into the home and for increasing, at least in some small measure, the economic autonomy of the family. Even our marriage counseling would do well to consider the importance of practical shared labor (by which I do not mean hobbies, games, or camping out) as an integrating force in the life of the family.

This is not a project that need be limited in scope to the family, even though it should focus upon the family. In the city, it may entail the creation of productive and self-governing neighborhoods; on the land, it surely means aggressive reform that will replace agrindustry by family farming and rural villages. At the very least, it means weaning the general public from the big-spending, big-wasting habits that high industrialism encourages, and which only make us progressively more dependent on big systems and high production. Economic autonomy does not simply mean increasing production. It has even more to do with the intelligent moderation of needs and consumption.

In the early 1930s, in the midst of the Great Depression, Ralph Borsodi and his gallant family abandoned their life in the city to undertake one of the great contemporary experiments in the revival of domestic economy. Their effort in rehabilitating a small farm went further than many of us might find the courage or opportunity to go. Borsodi also assumes too readily that domestic economy requires a return to the land, though it does not mean that exclusively. But it is the spirit and the direction of Borsodi's adventure that matters—that, and the major economic theorem that it proved.

I discovered [Borsodi recounts, writing in 1933] that more than two-thirds of the things which the average family now buys could be produced more economically at home than they could be bought factory-made; that the average man and woman could earn more by producing at home than by working for money in an office or factory and that, therefore, the less time they spent working away from home and the more time they spent working at home, the better off they would be; finally, that the home itself was still capable of being made into a productive and creative institution. . . . We began to experiment with the problem of bringing back into the home, and thus under our own direct control, the various machines which the textile mill, the cannery and packing house, the flour mill, the clothing and garment factory had taken over from the home during the past two hundred years.

No, that is not an eccentric old idea. It is an idea whose time may only be arriving now that we begin to feel the full weight of the environmental emergency and as we experience the terrible fragility of city living. For consider a moment: every resource-saving and environment-defending idea that has been hatched in recent years (waste and water recycling, organic husbandry, solar and wind energy, solid waste composting, container gardening, hydroponics, intermediate technology) finds its natural place in domestic economy, as do all the handicrafts that we now see being revived in America as alternate careers. These are not proposals that hold any practical attraction for big industrial systems or the official planning, which views our problems from the economic stratosphere. Their proper place is in another order of things, one that is scaled to the village, the neighborhood, the homestead, the family. Only at that level do they begin to make sense as ways of giving people an ecologically responsible grasp of their economic needs.

These are not the only ways that families can become communities of work. The family farm and the family business are other more obvious possibilities. Nor is urban ecology likely to yield a significant self-sufficiency for more than a few ingeniously resourceful neighborhoods. But that is hardly the goal of the project; for that matter, it isn't even ideal, if one values regional sharing and exchange. Primarily, the revival of domestic economy—even if it must be done by inches—is an immediate commitment that can give the urban family a taste of the independence it needs to defend the personal rights of its members. It is the one force that can make the family bond a practical sacrament. And it is also a way of making peace with the planet.

Chapter 7

School: Letting Go, Letting Grow

"But My Daughter Is a Dancer"

My daughter saw her first ballet when she was three years old: a Christmas production of *The Nutcracker*. For two hours that afternoon, Kathryn sat spellbound by these astonishing people who, as she put it, "dance in their socks." And when the show was over, she announced that she was going to become a ballerina. How long would her childish fascination last, my wife and I wondered. A week . . . a month . . . a year?

Kathryn has now graduated from high school, and the ambition is still there, stronger than ever. All the awkward charm of her first tentative dance movements has long since flowered into high professional promise. She has the gift, she is a dancer, the ballet is her calling. I have no idea (for who can be sure of anything in so mad and fickle a world as that of the ballet) if it will also become her career. Even if it does not, it will still have been the true school of her early life, the tough and lovely discipline from which she learned the music of her body, the meaning of art, the wealth of the imagination.

From the day I first realized the seriousness of Kathryn's ambition to dance, everything I ever believed about education has been transformed, root and branch. I have seen my daughter make an authentic personal choice of work and study. She has given herself to a fine and noble art with the intensity of inspiration; she has grown in that commitment and has found her best and worst qualities in its trials. There, she has discovered with painful vividness the meaning of excellence. The dance has brought her all the lively knowledge of high culture I have labored (largely in vain) to bring to hundreds of students over the years. I have seen the dance blossom for her into all that an authentic education should be: a commanding ideal, an illuminating vocation.

And I have seen something else. I have seen my daughter's exquisite choice of the creative life treated with indifference in every school she has attended in three countries. She has taken a rich and delicate talent into her school life—a talent which has carried her mind to the study of music, poetry, drama, history, literature—only to have that talent treated as a nonnegotiable currency by her teachers. Until, at last, school became a bore and a burden for her, an agonizing irrelevancy from which she begged to be liberated at the earliest practical and legal moment.

What sort of schools has Kathryn been to? Public schools always—in America, in Britain, and in Canada. In every case, schools regarded as among the "best" in their system. My wife and I—both products of the public schools—are more than a little fanatical in our antagonism to private schools. The ingrained working-class background we both share has always made us reluctant to consider giving Kathryn that special advantage. But it would have done no good if we had been willing—so I am convinced. There would have been no shelter or nourishment for her vocation there. Once—in Berkeley, California—we weakened to her insistent demands for succor and went to interview (and be interviewed by) the "headmaster" of the so-called best (and most expensive) private academy in town. Neither Betty nor I liked the feel of what we were doing: giving our child the privilege we had learned to regard as snobbish and unjust. But we went, and had all the elements of educational "excellence" displayed proudly before us: the "academic" subjects, the promise of strict order and discipline well laid on, the assurance of high standards guaranteed by much homework, hard marking, and precisely calibrated college preparation keyed to the entrance requirements of the ten top universities. It was all there, everything I have heard held up as the hallmarks of a *good* school in every discussion of education I have ever participated in. "We work them hard," the proud headmaster clucked, his voice crackling with no-nonsense self-assurance. And he invited us to examine the placement records and careers of his alumni . . . Harvard, Princeton, Yale, MIT . . . doctors, lawyers, research chemists, university professors . . . a roster of "top people." Yes, the tuition was high; but what better "investment" could we make in our child's future?

"But our daughter is a dancer," I observed. "Will she be able to work her dance classes into your curriculum? Perhaps leave early in the afternoons . . . ?"

Ah, *that* would be a problem. It was the sort of thing that tended to distract a pupil from her studies and to unsettle the discipline of others. There *were* requirements to be cleared, after all . . . *lots* of requirements. And Kathryn *did* want to have every chance to compile a superior record for college admission.

But we weren't certain she would want to go to college. "She wants to be a dancer," I explained again. But I realized it wasn't an explanation. It was simply a bald statement of an aspiration for which there could be no explanation, only recognition and acceptance.

Not certain she would go to college . . . ? A mildly disapproving expression came over the headmaster's face. Then why were we bringing Kathryn to him?

Because the public schools were such a time-wasting bore. Kathryn did have a lively interest in academic things. She was a keen student . . . excellent grades, strong intellectual motivations, and all that.

So then we *did* want a college prep school, the headmaster insisted. Someplace that worked them hard.

No . . . Kathryn didn't have to be "worked," we corrected. She worked very well under her own steam; at subjects she liked— mainly things in the arts and humanities, things she could relate to the dance—she would gladly work like a demon. We were looking for a school where she could shape her education to her dancing.

"Ah, well," the headmaster went on, more dubious than ever. "This is an *academic* school . . . for *serious* students." And he began to assure Kathryn—who looked like a *serious* girl to him— that she would certainly regret her lack of college entrance requirements in the years to come. After all, there were so many opportunities opening up for young women in the professions these days; might it not be wise to let her dancing wait until she had finished her education? There was always room in life for hobbies like that . . . later on.

Gradually, as he talked, Kathryn must have realized that a "good" school might be worse for her than the school she was now in. At least where she was now, she could skip classes with impunity, cut out to ballet school early, and never miss an hour's classroom work she couldn't make up later in a few minutes. It might be slack and tedious and often demoralizing, but it offered a kind of vacuous openness. There was space for her to go her own way, mainly created by a few sympathetic teachers who would agree to look aside if she cut class or was late with an assignment. Maybe that was the best she could hope for—though it was a poor enough compromise.

So Kathryn returned to Berkeley High School to serve out her time. And somewhere in the dense thicket of the administration, she finally found a vice-principal who could recognize a serious vocation when she saw one. With a bit of parental prompting, she agreed to steer Kathryn around enough requirements to let her graduate early. It was an artful piece of administrative legerdemain, and the single best contribution any school ever made to her dance life.

Of course, there exist in odd corners of the world special schools for gifted children, artistic pupils, students of the performing arts. But what I have learned from Kathryn's experience is that these are no real solution to the root problem of education in our society. Such schools presuppose a recognized talent already there for development. They exist to cultivate flowers that have already blossomed. And they are, for the most part, as obedient to the goad of "success" as the most competitive of our "good" schools. That is the other, grimmer side of my daughter's vocation—that she must now take her gift into a world, that of the performing arts, whose competitive pressures are possibly the most savage of all, and as great a threat to her creative powers as any she has faced. Already I see her fellow dancers and her teachers (especially those from the big, prestigious schools she has attended) teaching her that promotion means more than joy, that success counts for more than beauty, and that the art of the dance is something one pieces together from textbook exercises developed to machine-tool young talents to the needs of the corps de ballet. Ironically for someone with her independence of spirit, Kathryn has followed her love of music and movement into what may be the greatest educational anachronism of all: the world of classical ballet, where, even more so than in the schools she has left behind, an inordinate emphasis on impersonal precision and assembly-line uniformity prevails, traits which the ballet peculiarly inherits from a history that traces back to the Russia of the czars.

This too has been instructive to me as an educator. As I have sat in ballet schools watching uniformed regiments of children being paced through hours, days, years of relentless technical drill, watching the natural flow of their movement being microscopically dissected and analyzed, I have realized that the ballet classroom is one of the few places left where, as if in a museum, the traditional pedagogy of Western society can be observed in its purest, most authoritarian state, all but wholly untouched by the reforms that have had at least a minimal liberalizing influence on public education since the days of John Dewey. Of course, there are exceptions, but it is remarkable how the ghosts of the old Maryinsky theater linger on in ballet, preserving a psychology of education that still proudly subscribes to rigid discipline, severe put-downs, ridicule, slashing criticism . . . to all that negative reinforcement can do to break the will of the young and squash their originality. Just as classical literature was for so long used throughout the Western world to flatten the mind with the endless parsing of sentences and recitation of declensions, so one can still find classical dance being taught just as cheerlessly and mechanically to achieve the same alienating effect, and with the same misconceived justification: that resignation to tedium and obedient self-effacement are good for the soul, that personal interpretation and free self-expression are the enemies of excellence. In ballet, as Kathryn has had to learn, creativity is the prerogative of choreographers; dancers are performing mechanisms.

So the dance—or at least the classical dance—also threatens to become a competitive rat race and an academic bore for her. And I find myself wondering, where in all the world, if not among the artists, can we expect to find shelter for the idealistic, the original, the personal?

Born Mavericks

It is not my daughter's experience as a dancer that poses the educational dilemma I want to raise, but her experience as a maverick—as a child in pursuit of a vocation that the established curriculum does not recognize. That is our dilemma because we are all born as mavericks gifted with strange vocations. What I want to assert here is the responsibility of those who educate—parents and teachers alike—to make that fact the first and constant theme of education. This is what all of us bring into life and to school: a wholly unexplored, radically unpredictable identity. To educate is to unfold that identity—to unfold it with the utmost delicacy, recognizing that it is the most precious resource of our species, the true wealth of the human nation.

This is why it would be no solution to my daughter's problem even if the schools, as they exist today everywhere in the world, were to "enrich" their curricula with programs in classical dance or in the arts generally. Inevitably, those programs would from the outset become another matter of competition and certification. There would be requirements, lesson plans, tests, graded classes— as there are in most ballet academies.

Moreover, to say that we can improve the schools by simply expanding the curriculum only presupposes all over again that those who teach can adequately prescribe all there is for children to study and become. And they cannot. They cannot, because the human variety is indeed infinite. As Kathryn has discovered in her own adventure as a young dancer, there are unique attributes of style, interpretation, expressiveness which no fixed curriculum in ballet can comprehend. There are special qualities in every dancer which the standard technique can serve, but never create or wholly anticipate. So she discovers, at last, that she does not wish simply to dance, but to be her own kind of dancer—indeed, a creator of dances, a choreographer. But she finds little tolerance for these special qualities in the academies, because her dance teachers are, after all, *teachers*—authorities and disciplinarians who cannot believe there is anything new under the sun, least of all anything new their *students* could ever teach them. The standard curriculum in ballet makes no provision whatever for improvisation, free expression, choreographic invention, let alone for open aesthetic discussion.

Yet, that is exactly the direction in which the education of the person must initially flow: from the pupil to the teacher. In every educational exchange, it is first of all the teacher who has something to learn. The teacher must approach asking, "Who is this child? What does he or she bring into the world? What have I to discover here that no one has ever known before?"

First of all, we must want children to teach us *who they are*. We should think of our meeting with them as a glad encounter with the unexpected, believing that somewhere in these young humans there is a calling which wants to be found and named. That is what I suggest education in a personalist world must be about: the discovery of the child's destiny. It is the task of the educator to champion that right of self-discovery against all the forces of the world that see in our children only so much raw material for more of the same, the established, the "successful."

Again and again, when I find myself in the midst of educational controversy, I come back to one fixed point of reference. "But my daughter is a dancer . . ." And because she is a dancer, there has been no place for her in the supposed best of schools. Further, I ask what if she had chosen to be a rhapsodic poet . . . a visionary physicist . . . an unconventional healer . . . a circus clown . . . a yogi . . . a wood carver . . . a prophet . . . a magician . . . a clairvoyant . . . a social crusader . . . an eccentric inventor . . . a fool of God? What place would there have been for her then? Even less than nothing. An outer darkness of contempt and prejudice.

Yet, what would our human culture be but for such strange, creative spirits? It is a problem I have often put to teachers—and to myself. Let us say we are in a "good" school, laying on the lash of high standards and tough competition, pacing the kids toward college and career at a brisk clip. Heavy assignments, stiff grades, firm discipline. And so the students learn to read by six, to write good expository prose for the college entrance examiners, to cipher accurately, to play their electronic pocket calculators like true mathematical virtuosi . . . all on schedule . . . *our* schedule. And we see the bright academics clamber on up the social ladder to become doctors, lawyers, junior executives; we see the nonacademics take jobs as plumbers, mechanics, typists. There we have all the hallmarks of "excellence," do we not? A good, practical, high-achieving education that assigns everyone to an existing social niche.

But now go back, all the way to the beginning. Suppose back there in kindergarten, in the first years of school, we could have known, before we turned them into what they became, that it was in these unexplored and unformed young to become very different human beings. This one an Emily Dickinson, this one a Nijinsky, this one a St. Francis . . .

What would our "excellence" have gained us that was worth such a loss? What great favor would we say we had done these children to have snuffed out that high, fine promise? What would it mean, then, to boast that at *our* school we had the third-graders reading at the fifth-grade level . . . and the ninth-graders at college level?

College level . . . *my* level of teaching. I have now had more than twenty years' experience dealing with the freshmen students who finally rise to the top of the heap. At Stanford University, I taught the children of some of America's wealthiest families, ambitious high-achievers confidently on their way toward fat professional careers. Now, at one of the California state universities, I teach students who are mainly lower middle class and working poor, including many blacks and Chicanos, all scrambling to piece together a college degree that will keep their heads above blue-collar drudgery or unemployment . . . and not always making it. All the students I have taught would have to be ranked as successful products of our schools, part of the 5 per cent who qualify for college with a B average or better. The system can be proud of them. Their parents can be proud of them. They are the fortunate few who survived the competition. And among them somewhere are the fewer still who will go on to become leaders, celebrities, decision makers.

But when I look at them, I can only see what I myself had become by the time I graduated *magna cum laude* from the Princeton graduate school—and what I largely remain: a casualty of persistent miseducation. I see profoundly bewildered and anxious people who believe education is a matter of doing requirements, totaling up grades, pleasing teachers. I see trained specialists in scripted performances, chasing to win approval at tasks that hold no personal meaning for them.

Some of them do it superbly; many of the Stanford kids had learned all the straight-A tricks back in the first grade. Some of those I teach now are miserably incompetent even at spelling and basic punctuation and will probably wash out quickly unless they are nonwhite and the color of their skin gains them a special indulgence by way of remedial classes and affirmative action. But *both* the winners and the losers are victims of the same pedagogical mutilation. *Both* have been pared down to that minimal identity we call "student." As they assemble in my classes, how much of themselves have they learned to bring to school? A forebrain connected to a voice box wired to two eyes and two ears that have been reduced to word-and-number processors. Only that, nothing more. They sit there before me, bored but compulsively attentive, so many pieces of intellectual apparatus, ticking away, waiting for me to push all the familiar buttons: Important Fact . . . Big Idea . . . Assignment Due . . . Test Question . . . Right Answer . . . Required Reading . . . click-click-click. Watch the teacher—find out what he wants—do it—get the grade—pass the course—take your degree—get the job—watch the boss—find out what he wants —do it—get the raise . . .

Sometimes I try to discuss the meaning of education with my students, wondering if any of them can still remember who they were, what they wanted to learn before schools and teachers made them the trained performers they are today. I have no illusions about how much can be done (or undone) for them now from within the official system, least of all by someone as hopelessly bookish and academic as myself. Still, I ask them if there is not something *more* education might be—something that engages their personal style and taste, something that might give our work together some small touch of reality. But digressions like this only seem to confuse and embarrass most of them. Only some of the older students will take up the discussion—the men and (mainly) women in their forties and fifties who have come back to school after raising families. They are, for the most part, the serious and questing minds I come upon; I would gladly teach classes full of them—as in the Danish folk schools. But as for the others, the job-worried younger students, it is too late for them to reconsider what school means, and too early for them to consider what life means. Their expectations and responses are fixed. They are impatient to get on with what they came to class to do—which is to complete assignments, take tests, get grades . . . all off the surface of the cerebrum. It only distresses them if I suggest they work up some personally engaging line of study, because they have no idea who they are as persons . . . or they do not trust me when I ask them to let me know who they are. Perhaps they think it is a "trick question," as, no doubt, I would also have suspected at their age.

The world owes us all another lifetime of remedial education that has nothing to do with assignments, grades, tests.

The Children's Interest

I can make no claims for myself as a teacher or father. But I have come to take a deep parental pride in seeing my daughter become something I could never have predicted or advised, something wholly without precedent in our family. Until she became seriously immersed in the dance, I suppose I expected Kathryn to go the way both her mother and I had gone—a straight academic path into college and the professions. Not that either Betty or I took that course of life for granted or regarded it without uncertainty. As first-generation college graduates in our families, we were still close enough to immigrant and working-class parents to know that there are other, and honorable, possibilities. Still, that was the general momentum behind the home we gave our child—toward the world of books and mandarin learning.

That is not the way Kathryn has chosen to follow. Perhaps she will yet come back to it. But first she has something of her own to try. And because I have been lucky enough to see that vocation grow and mature in her life, I have learned a great truth about parenthood. I have come to understand that it is not my proper role to shape my child's life for her. If I had done that, if I had worried myself and her about "practical" choices and promising futures, nothing of the vocation that was innately hers would have emerged. With all the best intentions, I would have deprived her (and the world) of whatever beauty she has to offer through her art.

Anyone who has seen the blossoming of a child's personality must know with an instinctive delight that *this* is the heart and soul of education. There, before us, something of our essential nature declares itself: the originality and variety that make us the unique animal we are. In that "great leap forward" by which one generation transcends the expectations of the last, we glimpse the awesome powers of innovation that reside within us—and perhaps a glimmer of our destiny as a species.

I return to the ideal I raised when we discussed the possibility of an open childhood. A single word, an entire philosophy of education: Socrates speaking of himself as "midwife" to his students. *Midwife*—one who brings forth what is already there, waiting to be born: the hidden splendors of self-knowledge. That is where a personalist education begins, in this Socratic conviction that our first and highest object of study resides within. All there. Given. Teachers may offer information, know-how, technique, example. But until the student's innate calling declares itself, we have nothing but mimicry, memory work, superficial performance. It is only after we have tapped an authentic incentive that true education happens. Then, everything that lends depth and distinction unfolds before us—from the inside out. We have a mind that will seek out, interpret, invent. We have a life that makes its own purposes and takes on its own interesting texture.

But how many of us, confronting our children and our students, can affirm that Socratic proposition? Our relations with children are political through and through: relations governed by power, by an invidious protocol of dominance and submission. Every encounter with a child is too tempting an opportunity to vindicate and edify ourselves, to assert the importance and the "rightness" which we have so little occasion to experience in the world. We confront these small, dependent humans in the full arrogance of our egotism: our chance to play God. And behind our ego, working through it to process the next generation into its proper allegiance and deference are the dominant forces of society: state and corporation, governing party and privileged class. They use our parental ego against the young as the conduit of their purposes. What do these powerless children learn first of all from their supposedly well-meaning parental authorities? That they are natural-born nothing: wax to be stamped, clay to be molded, the raw material of other, more competent people's designs.

Nothing could demand more of us than the personalist ideal of education: the most difficult thing in the world to ask of anyone. The renunciation of power, the one power that is most unquestionably within our "right" to exercise: our power over the young, to use them or abuse them in pursuit of a hundred secret, selfish goals. Everybody has an *interest* in the education of the young. And how easy it is for us to insist that *our* interest is the child's interest. For what could be more self-evident than that our desire to have hard-working, superbly trained, *successful* children—the sort of children who are produced by good schools—is all for the children's own good? What could be more in *their* interest than an education that will gain them jobs, status, rich rewards? Meaning an education that affirms *our* world.

Everybody has an interest in education, but what is the *child's* interest—independent of all adult intervention and influence? Does that seem an impossible question to answer? Very likely it does. As impossible as it once seemed to say what a woman's interest was in life independent of her husband or her father. As impossible as it once seemed to say what the interest of slaves might be in life independent of their masters. There are those who live in such ingrained, seemingly "natural" conditions of subjugation that we cannot begin to imagine what autonomous interest they have in the world. Children are in that category, more so than any other social dependent. Yet, they have their own interest; it is the interest that each of us discovers, if only in moments of unaccustomed exhilaration or strange absorption, when we become our own person, caught up in our own work, our own salvation. In such moments, we find an autonomy and an adventure that alone deserves to be called *life*. That is the child's interest, and it needs to be defended from nothing so much as the terrible "practicalities" that are always foremost in the adult mind.

The Limits of Deschooling

Most discussions of education in America have nothing to do with education; they have to do with schools. They revolve around problems of finance, discipline, community control, collective bargaining, busing . . . the countless, cliff-hanging emergencies that make it increasingly difficult merely to keep the educational system barely viable from year to year. Under the pressure of such crises, we easily forget that the schools, like all institutions, exist first of all to serve a collective vision of the good and the necessary. We allow that vision to sink below the threshold of critical reflection. It becomes an automatic assumption, rarely articulated in anything better than clichés. Our schools, we assume, exist for the benefit of the children. They are there to prepare their students "for life." Hard work and high grades in class are the first indispensable step on the road to success. Any child who cannot see things that way either needs to be adjusted or deserves to fail.

If I give no attention here to the immediate fiscal and social problems that besiege our schools, it is because I share the conviction of a growing body of discontented and dissenting educators that none of these assumptions deserves to go unchallenged. I confess that I have no idea how to save our schools; but then I am far from certain they should be saved if they are to remain the compulsory, competitive system of official certification they have become. In that form, the "life" for which they are preparing children throughout the world is lifelong subordination to the needs of an urban-industrial economy that threatens to grind the rights of the person and the planet to rubble. If we put first things first, then the question we must answer is not "How shall the schools survive?" but rather, "Can we find an ideal for the schools to serve that will make their survival worth caring about?"

Yet, as seriously as I believe that compulsory schooling betrays the personal rights of the young, I think it is unrealistic and—worse still—morally insensitive to demand, as Ivan Illich and John Holt have done, that we should undertake to "deschool" our society altogether—as if teaching might not be, in itself, a talent and vocation to be honored with its own institutional facilities. For all their problems, the schools are clearly going to be with us for a long while to come—limping, if not skipping. In part, this may be due to nothing more than the inertia of the social and professional interests that converge upon them. But we must bear in mind that those interests have come to include more than the white middle class and the mandarin elite, who might, in fact, increase their advantages in a deschooled society where private and parochial schools predominated. At the very minimum, we can credit the schools with providing the cheapest day-care and baby-sitting most working parents can find. In that circumstance alone, I daresay the deschoolers are up against one of their stubbornest obstacles. But, more significantly, the poor and excluded in our country have identified the schools as a central battleground in their struggle for self-respect and social justice. For better or worse, the schools are locked into the moral turmoil of our world, and perhaps that fact gives us just enough leverage within the system to divert this blundering institution into new paths.

For all the easy points one can score lambasting the "compulsory miseducation" that takes place in the schools, there exist wellsprings of idealism beneath the desolation of the system. They can be found in the urban minorities who assume (perhaps too wishfully) that public education has something to do with dignity and democratic values. They can be found in the hearts of teachers and parents who honestly want the young to be educated in some sense that goes beyond job training and competitive performance. Thanks to these restive social elements, we have seen the last ten years become one of the liveliest periods of humanistic and libertarian experimentation in the schools since the Progressive Education movement of the twenties and thirties. The energies of change are abundantly on the scene; what is still lacking is a commanding ideal that will give them shape by speaking to the deep need of the time. We have not yet confronted the full rights of the person in education.

The need is in the air. It can be felt in every theory and experiment that counsels us to trust the young with freedom and to prize their moments of original insight and creation above all else. But it may more often appear in the lives of young and sensitive teachers as a terrible frustration with the lies and limits of public education that finally forces them to quit the profession; or it may express itself among students in no more articulate ways than truancy, vandalism, dropping out, or sullen withdrawal—problems that have now reached epidemic proportions. Even among libertarian educators who have labored to create alternative schools, there is much confusion. They often interpret the search for personhood as a mere desire for escape—by nonwhites from white culture, by the poor from middle-class values, by children in general from adults in general. The result can be the sort of free school that becomes an enclave of stranded young resentment.

Or there are the efforts of those who take their lead from the Brazilian educator Paolo Freire, and who seek, like Jonathan Kozol, to use alternative schools for political consciousness-raising among the disadvantaged young and their parents, with a view to taking over the downtown administration rather as if it were the Czar's Winter Palace. But this is no better than to confuse education with agitprop, and it is bound to lose much creative energy to political factionalism. The victims of our schools include all the young, not only the poor. And, in any case, self-discovery needs more than agitational anger to grow on. It cannot be limited to identifying the people we will not obey and don't want to be like. It must include finding the person we would become. Besides freedom *from,* we must have freedom *for.*

There is another reason why I steer my way clear of discussing the school system here. To focus too much on the schools lends a certain misleading twist to the idea of education. Perhaps in spite of ourselves, we help confirm the assumption that education is for that special population of learners called "the young" who are housed in special institutions called "schools." As Ivan Illich has so well argued, this is the distortion that even free and alternative schools help to produce. They create a spreading social dependence on professionals and on all the restrictions that go with any kind of official institutionalization. Education, as I approach it here, is meant to be the essential gesture of human existence. It is the daily progress of our lives as we move through the adventure of experience, selecting, rejecting, shaping the moments into some workable meaning. Education is for everybody, anywhere, and for a lifetime. It may be an especially urgent part of childhood and youth, when curiosity is boundless and insistent, but it does not follow that there is ever a point where learning (especially if we speak of self-discovery) leaves off and we graduate into something called "life." Even death is a lesson, our final essay in human being.

So I cling here to the cliché of every university extension—that learning is a lifelong process. If that is so, then any philosophy of education whose ideals, methods, or institutions are too much limited to the young is bound to be inadequate. There are ailments of our school system—like its obsession with quick, competitive success, its infatuation with grades, degrees, certification—that can be cured only if we insist that education means continuing, lifelong access to learning. In this respect, I agree with the deschoolers. The practical right to *return* to one's education as an adult—meaning, the ability to take time out, to find instruction, to gain the use of necessary facilities—is even more important than the right to free schooling in childhood. There are choices that few people can sensibly make in their youth, least of all the choice of a life's work.

Why do we worry so anxiously about how promptly the young are learning to read, write, cipher, or perform useful jobs? Because we know they must learn these things *now,* in their early years, or most of them will have missed their only opportunity. This now-or-never pressure is one of the worst tyrannies of the system; it denies us the freedom to experiment, to fail, to turn back, to begin again—if necessary, to start a second career, to launch a new life. We must have an ideal of education which confronts our institutional life with the full force of that need.

If we conceive of education as self-discovery—rather than merely the mastery of skills or accumulation of knowledge—then we must regard every moment of life as equally pregnant with educational possibilities, and we see that there is no single institution, no one period of life where the whole task can be done. Very likely one lifetime will not be enough.

Two Streams of Educational Change

Two streams of contemporary thought meet in the personalist ideal of education. Both find their source in the Socratic dialogue and their more modern formulation in Rousseau's pedagogical novel *Émile*. There are many points where these two streams flow together. Both are nonauthoritarian and student-oriented—meaning, from the viewpoint of conventional education, they believe in "spoiling" children with "permissiveness." Both start from the assumption that the purpose of education is to make the student a free and autonomous member of a democratic society. If I segregate the one from the other in what follows, it is because I think there is a significant difference in their pedagogical psychology which allows us to see the one movement as a historical advance upon the other.

1. Let us call the first (and older) stream the *libertarian educators*. Here, I have in mind a family tree that looks roughly like this as it branches out from Rousseau:

> Johann Pestalozzi
> William Godwin
> Max Stirner
> Francisco Ferrer
> Leo Tolstoi
> John Dewey
> Maria Montessori
> A. S. Neill
> Paul Goodman
> Paolo Freire
> Ivan Illich

and all the contemporary free-schoolers and deschoolers (John Holt, Jonathan Kozol, Herbert Kohl, Edgar Friedenberg, George

Dennison, Neil Postman, etc.). From these figures, we gain a critical perspective upon the structure, governance, and politics of modern education. Here we find educators whose main project has been to resist the inordinate claims which public authorities have made upon the minds of the young since the advent of the modern state—especially in the form of compulsory public school systems. For them, education is not assigned knowledge, but the free growth of children; it is the earliest and most decisive expression in life of what Stirner called self-ownership. Tolstoi, one of the greatest of the libertarian teachers and among the first to organize an experimental free school (it was quartered on his country estate at Yasnaya Polyana and open to all the peasant children of the area) formulated the central question with absolute precision. *"Who has the right to educate?"* he asked. And his answer, "Nobody." Not the state, the church, the family.

> There are no rights of education. I do not acknowledge such, nor have they been acknowledged, nor will they ever be by the young generation under education. The right to educate is not vested in anybody.

Those who assume the right to educate, so Tolstoi argued, will educate in their own interest—at the expense of the child's autonomy. Hence, the coercion, the bribery, the authoritarianism of the systems created to enforce that presumed right.

Nobody has the right to educate, the libertarians insist, but children have the right to *be* educated. All rights in education belong to them and are meant to serve their needs, however they may experience them. Where that happens, learning unfolds as a spontaneous act that requires no official compulsion, no bureaucratic organizing, and minimal professional supervision. The pedagogical model from which the libertarians work is "incidental education" (as Paul Goodman called it)—the sort of totally informal, widely shared pattern of instruction which occurs naturally in all traditional communities, and which still prevails in the learning of a skill as basic as speech. Just as the young need not be *made* to speak, so they need not be forced to learn anything that is freely chosen and authentically necessary to their development. At its doctrinaire extreme (in the work of Ivan Illich) this conviction becomes open war declared upon all forms of professionalism in teaching. The schools are to be dismantled and replaced by passive facilities for self-education, such as libraries or workshops. Teaching continues, but not teachers.

2. The second stream of educational change is a more contemporary development—or better to say, a contemporary fascination with forms of psychic and spiritual instruction that may be as old as the most primitive rites of passage. Here the important connections are not directly political, but rather psychotherapeutic, artistic, religious. There is, as yet, no definitive inventory and no fixed name for this growing collection of philosophies and techniques which seek to educate below and beyond the verbal-cerebral level of the personality; it is most often called *affective education* or *human potentialities* or *personal growth*. Aldous Huxley once spoke of the field as "the non-verbal humanities." The leading figures that come to mind here are neither a genealogy nor a movement, but an emerging constellation of widely divergent disciplines. I think of:

> Wilhelm Reich (Bioenergetics)
> Abraham Maslow (Humanistic Psychology)
> Frederick Perls (Gestalt Therapy)
> Franz Alexander
> Charlotte Selver (Sensory Awareness)
> Ida Rolf (Structural Integration)
> Moishe Feldenkreis
> George Leonard ("Education and Ecstasy")
> George Isaac Brown (Confluent Education)

and the many therapies that have been invented at growth centers like Esalen Institute. The list of converging influences might be extended in a number of directions. We could include such spiritual leaders of the early twentieth century as Rudolph Steiner (anthroposophy and the Waldorf schools) and George Gurdjeiff, teachers who now attract growing attention for pioneering experiential disciplines of deep self-knowledge. Certainly the many yogas and sadhanas that are being adopted from the Eastern religions (especially Zen, Tantric Buddhism, and Sufism) belong somewhere near the center of the constellation. We might even include the vision of education we find in Carlos Casteneda's adventures with the Yaqui sorcerer Don Juan, for there are those who see such shamanic initiation rites as a significant model of personal growth.

A few of the libertarians I have mentioned (like Neill and Goodman) might take their place in both streams; for that matter, all the affective educators begin from the libertarian premise that instruction must be noncompulsory and free from competitive pressure. But, for all the overlap, there has been a significant division of labor between the two streams. We might think of it this way: The libertarians' task has been that of clearing the educational ground of official authority and social privilege. The tools they have used for the job are the familiar ideals of Western revolutionary politics: the rights of man, the appeal for liberty, equality, fraternity—here, all applied to the lives of children. Now, the affective educators appear, bearing a pack of long-forbidden and exotic seeds to sow in that liberated soil . . . or in as much of it as they can find along the margins of our society. For them, this hard-won ground is the opportunity to cultivate a limitless range of unsuspected talents in their students. They move from defending the rights of the individual to exploring the potentialities of the person, developing a curriculum of studies and a repertory of teaching techniques that represent the most dramatic departure in Western education since the work of the Renaissance humanists. With their efforts, we seem at last to have an educational ideal that is justly proportioned to the whole human being—body, mind, and spirit.

We are used to hearing our schools assailed by critics who want to know why "Johnny can't read, Johnny can't write," and who call for a return to "the basics," usually accompanied by a demand for strict discipline and hard competition. The affective educators have come up with a reply to that challenge which is an even deeper criticism of conventional schooling. They ask us to consider: Are we so sure we know what the basic skills of life are? Bad enough that Johnny can't read or write. But why do we stop worrying there? Why are we not every bit as concerned that Johnny is such a stranger to his organism and emotions that he will (like most of the rest of us) spend the rest of his life struggling under the burden of his ignorance? Why do we not worry that Johnny's body is gripped by thwarted anger and desire, that his metabolism is tormented by a diet of junk foods and nervous tension, that his dream life is barren, his imagination moribund, his social conscience darkened by competitive egotism? Why not worry that Johnny can't dance, can't paint, can't breathe, can't meditate, can't relax, can't cope with anxiety, aggression, envy, can't express trust and tenderness? Why do we not spare some concern that Johnny does not know who he is, or even that he has a self to find? If the basic skills have nothing to do with all this, then let us admit that they have nothing to do with Johnny's health, happiness, sanity, or survival, but only with his employability. Whose interest, then, is Johnny's education serving?

To my own way of thinking, the project of self-discovery must bring both of these streams—the libertarian and the affective— together in a single, graceful ideal. We must come to see that, at their core, each presupposes the other, and that neither by itself is sufficient. With Dewey, we must insist that no philosophy of education is complete until it combines the sociological and the psychological. We obviously need the libertarian educators' critical thrust and their political commitment to the defense of the young and oppressed, because the problem of education in our time is an *institutional* problem. The schools that control access to learning are embedded in our class structure and economic priorities; we must not lose sight of how that fact violates the natural rights of the young in their education. In the work of the libertarians, we can find all the fact and theory we could want to demonstrate how compulsory schooling destroys the spontaneity of learning and the free growth of the personality.

But if we give all our attention, as many libertarian educators do, to beating back the incursions of the state, the educational bureaucracy, the teaching profession, we may never get round to discovering the full dimensions of the students here before us. They may never have any other identity in our eyes than that of victims in need of consciousness-raising and a fair chance at the basic skills. We may allow their personalities to shrink down to nothing more than a thin political line to fight on. And then, for all our radical pretensions, we may by default endorse more of the dominant culture than we should permit to stand unquestioned, including a psychology of education which is repressively conservative.

This is the point at which I find myself growing almost claustrophobic with impatience as I read the libertarian educators, including the best among them, like Ivan Illich or John Holt. There is simply no *size* to the conception of mind that fills their pages. They sift through the injustices of the classroom in terrible detail; they offer brilliant insights into the hundred ways young minds are warped by class-ridden standards of literacy and scholastic achievement. But when I ask what, then, *should* be happening in the lives of these oppressed children if they are to be genuinely educated, the best answer that comes back is some more pliant way to teach the 3-Rs, or an eloquent, outrageously impractical plea for disbanding the schools forthwith. These are men who know that compulsory schooling is a prison; but the free school is an open door, and we want to know what they see beyond that inviting threshold.

The shortcoming of the libertarian educators is that they do not, by and large, inquire with enough curiosity into the self which is the object of self-ownership, neither into its secret tyrannies nor into its buried potentialities. Stirner, the nineteenth-century arch-anarchist whose analysis of human freedom could be acutely sensitive, spoke of how society installs "wheels in the heads" of its members, furtively robbing them of their autonomy. But neither he nor most other libertarians have recognized how subtle those wheels might be, or how well hidden. He did not suspect that they might be turning in our most fundamental assumptions about ourselves, nature, reality—that they might have to be plucked out of our tissues and organs, our sexual impulses and half-forgotten dream life. If education does not go that deep into the personality, it is apt to leave the roots of our alienation untouched.

I think, for example, of Francisco Ferrer, the brave and brilliant Spanish educator who was executed for crimes against the state in 1909. In his struggle with an oppressive social order, Ferrer imposed a strict anticlericalism upon his influential Modern School movement. But he went on to identify the "exact sciences" as the heart of his curriculum, convinced that only they provide a "secure and unshakeable foundation" for the life of reason. Thus, he restricted his schools to that narrow range of intellectual powers from which, in Lewis Mumford's apt phrase, the "mad rationality" of our technocratic society takes its strength. So, too, the Progressive Education for which John Dewey campaigned. It is perhaps the richest formulation of libertarian pedagogy. But for all its democratic and socialist values, the philosophy never questioned the essential rightness and rationality of urban industrial society. Rather, it took industrialism as its framework and sought to civilize the system. As a consequence, Dewey's emphasis on popular competence and pragmatic experimentation easily flowed into a curriculum that has integrated the schools all the more tightly into the lethal orthodoxies of the modern world.

The libertarian educators' image of human nature is still very much the Enlightenment conception of the free and rational citizen whose needs can be gratified by technological progress and whose anxieties can be stilled by science and sound logic. Even where the libertarians take the Marxist analysis of "false consciousness" and Freud's ideas about repression into their world view, they do not get much beyond the verbal-cerebral level of the personality. Both Marx and Freud remain committed to rational analysis and the intellectual mastery of the self. They both work from the assumption that we can *talk* our way to self-knowledge. It is only with free-schoolers like Neill and Goodman that the more problematical depths of the personality begin to enter the province of education for special attention. Early in his career, Neill came to agree with Wilhelm Reich that the freedom he sought in school and society required the liberation of the student's thwarted sexuality. There had to be a curriculum that comprehended the total organism, not simply the forebrain and voice box. His program then became "socialism . . . plus relaxed bodies." As for Goodman, his educational philosophy moved through Gestalt therapy toward an ever deeper trust in the wisdom of the body and the great Tao.

Affective education picks up from these beginnings, finding its source in the post-Freudian schools of psychiatry that assume the possibility of organic self-regulation and fulfilling growth. Where these developments cross paths with the spiritual disciplines of Eastern religions, as is now prominently the case with the humanistic and transpersonal therapies, we enter upon an educational prospect that seeks to take the whole of life into account, from prenatal experience to the moment of death, and which does not stop short of the promise of spiritual enlightenment. Wise silence takes its place as a sign of knowledge beside lots-of-clever-language-in-the-head; the sage comes to stand alongside the scientist and scholar as a pedagogical model.

If the affective educators fall short at any point, it is in their failure (as yet) to develop a well-conceived social program for their reforms, and in their general lack of political savvy. They surely cannot blink the fact that education is now the monopoly everywhere of institutions which are shot through with the wrongs and follies of the greater society. As long as children are processed through compulsory systems of indoctrination, there will be little that affective educators can do but offer small doses of remedial therapy in the later years, often to some very damaged human material; and that will never amount to a sufficient test of their methods. The growth center and private workshop are not an adequate response to the educational needs of entire societies; these are, at best, laboratories and showcases for new techniques. Nor is it necessarily a promising course to introduce minute amounts of affective education into the standard curriculum (as George Isaac Brown's program in Confluent Education seeks to do—though with commendable caution). We have before us the sad experience in this respect of Progressive Education as it was introduced into the school system two generations ago. Certainly it did something to ventilate a suffocatingly conservative curriculum and to liberalize the classroom. But once its principles became a matter of routine professional training and were patterned on the existing compulsory and competitive system, Progressive Education was distorted into many kinds of strange and unlovely hybrid. Its best libertarian intentions lost their plasticity and became a new set of pedagogical dogmas.

I recall the caricature of Progressive Education to which my younger brother was subjected when he began school in New York during the late 1940s, soon after a much corrupted Deweyan orthodoxy had swept the system. At the designated time each day, he was *required* to play with bean bags or finger paints, like it or not; and under no circumstances was he to read anything until the official lesson plan permitted it—and even then, he was never to do so phonetically. My parents were strictly warned against damaging his reading powers by allowing him to start too early and in the wrong way: best leave this great and mysterious matter wholly in his teachers' professional care. Such is the terrible logic of all big institutions and oversized systems. They poison spontaneity with routine, and petrify all intelligent flexibility. Think, then, what might happen to hatha-yoga, sensory awareness, and Zen tennis if they should be fed into the scholastic machinery of scheduled courses, requirements, lesson plans, grading systems. Imagine the counseling sessions that might find students protesting, "But do I *have* to take three units of kundalini?"

If the affective educators wish to avoid having their best contributions become the stuff of a Jules Feiffer cartoon, they have no choice but to take up the same political battle the libertarians have been fighting for so long. They must also break the hold of compulsion, competition, and bureaucratic professionalism upon the educational institutions of the world. Affective education has no proper home but in free schools.

Know Thyself, Trust Thyself, Be Thyself

Let us see if we can combine the two educational streams we have discussed here into a coherent personalist ideal.

There are three levels to the educational experience I have in mind. *First,* there is the spirit that governs the encounter of teacher and student; this we borrow from the libertarian educators, opting for the most voluntary form of association we can practically achieve, and at the very least a clear declaration by teachers to their students that they regard the existing compulsion of their system as wrong and unwholesome. *Then,* there is the range of experience we must seek to make accessible to the student; here, we borrow from the affective educators with the hope of displaying the full spectrum of human possibilities—from the skills of basic literacy to the higher powers of health and growth. *Finally,* within that range, we allow for the discovery of a unique vocation by each student, a center that is wholly one's own; this is the distinctly personal moment in education toward which both the libertarian and affective educators move.

If we were to fashion all this into a teacher's pact with his or her students, it might read like this:

OUR ENCOUNTER

You come before me as my fellow citizens born to the full rights and liberties of the community. I will respect that status even in the youngest among you, doing all I can to make your learning a free and spontaneous action. For only the experience of freedom teaches citizenly competence and convivial trust.

I am not here because I assume I have the right to educate you—whether in the name of the state, church, party, or people. Rather, I am here to honor your inalienable right to *be* educated—by everyone and everything in the community, in times, subjects, ways, and places of your own unpredictable choosing. I believe you will come to me asking to be taught of your own free will, in your own good time, because the appetite to learn and the desire to find adult models arise from your deep nature. That appetite and that desire need not be forced by law, shame, or fear to present themselves for instruction; nor, when they appear, need they be bribed with competitive rewards. I know that required attendance and invidious grading will corrupt your honest motivations, which are naturally grounded in wonder and curiosity. Where such coercion enters our relations, I will warn you that it can only be there because you are being educated against your own interests, and I will remind you of your natural rights of truancy.

My duty to my calling demands that I hold before you the best standard of accuracy and excellence I know, so that you may learn the discipline of truth. I will never mislead you into believing that your best efforts are easily attained; but I will never use the standards of my profession to belittle or intimidate, nor to keep you in a condition of dependence. And I will not expect you to endorse any truth or value until I have led you to discover its nobility and inherent necessity.

I will respect the importance of readiness in your education as an expression of your free growth. I will force nothing upon you that you do not invite me to teach. And since readiness knows no limit of age, I will work to give you practical access to knowledge for the length of your lives. You must be free and able to return to your education whenever life gives rise to the aspiration.

THE RANGE OF OUR WORK

You and I are members of a remarkable species possessed (perhaps) of limitless potentialities. I will help you explore the full size of your humanity, rejecting no talent or trouble we find there as outside the boundaries of true education. For *you* are my subject matter and constant study.

I will never regard the mere functional use of words and numbers as the paramount concern of your education, for there are many powers in us that soar beyond language and measurement. I will at all times keep you aware of the difference between those things that are merely of social usefulness and those that are humanly fulfilling. I will counsel you never to sacrifice the higher capacities of life for the sake of minimal practicality. I will never let you think the dancer is a lesser talent than the scholar, or the clown a poorer thing than the technician.

I will strive to preserve your childlike sense of kinship with all living things, for this is the basis of an intelligent reciprocity with nature. I will teach you the native competence of your body and the language of your senses, because in these you will find the inborn health of your organism. I will teach you how to propitiate the emotional furies within you so that you will not become the unknowing victim of secret fears and angers. I will introduce you to the ways of the imagination and to your visionary energies, so that you may know these as the richest source of the intellect.

I will do what I can to sound the spiritual dimensions of your being, not by divisive creeds or parochial doctrines, but by way of those high and fine experiences that make our loyalty universal. I will hold out the saints and prophets as examples of your own highest nature. I will acquaint you with the uses of solitude, believing that the closer I can bring you to the great stillness within you, the more wisely you will accept your mortal frailty. And in that lonely knowledge, I trust you will discover the compassion which is the one sure foundation for conviviality.

FINDING A CENTER

You (and now the "you" becomes singular, no longer plural) come to me as the person no one else can be, a unique event in the universe. Somewhere in you there is a special destiny waiting to be discovered. I will watch carefully for the moment of its awakening, because that is the crown and the summit of my calling.

I will always bear in mind as I teach you the inherited culture that it is a storehouse of uniquely created meanings, each the unexpected achievement of an inspired personality. I will regard you as one who may also have come into our lives to speak an original word. Perhaps it will sound strange to all who hear, and to me as well. But I will value that strangeness in you above all else and will allow no inhibiting authority to hold back its growth, because the life of our planet makes its way forward (if it does at all) by resourceful invention and bright surprise.

I will remember in the midst of all our studies that the one most important lesson that can pass between us is yours to teach, mine to learn. And that is the lesson of your essential identity.

> Know thyself
> Trust thyself
> Be thyself

Chapter 8

Work: The Right to Right Livelihood

> *Man needs work even more than he needs a wage; it imprints the form of man on matter and offers itself to him as a means of expression. Work, bodily work, is for nine-tenths of humanity their only chance to show their worth in this world.*
>
> *— Lanzo del Vasta*

> *A job is death without the dignity.*
> *— Brendan Behan*

When I think back to my earliest childhood perceptions of work, I come up with a primer of lessons which, I suspect, has been part of our society's conventional wisdom for several generations. It is the homely gospel of the American work ethic as I received it from family and neighbors, by universal example and unspoken assumption. It reads like this:

—Children play, grownups work. Work is what makes you officially grown-up. It is what grownups have to do, or they won't have money to buy things and have fun.

—Work is something you have to go looking for out there, in the world. You apply for it and compete for it. Other people have it to give. They are called bosses and they give you work as a reward for being the right kind of person. They don't *have* to give it to you, and any time they want to, they can take their job away. That's why you should want to be a good worker—so that you won't lose your job and be poor.

—Work is what fathers go away in the morning to do all day. It is very serious, because it is what the family lives by, and it is somewhat mysterious, because it happens far away—at some place called the office or the plant or the shop. Most mothers work at home, but that doesn't count as "real" work. "Real" work is a job you get paid for. The more you get paid, the more important you are. The best jobs of all go to "smart guys." Smart guys get jobs that pay lots of money for doing almost nothing—especially nothing hard or dirty. What smart guys do is called "working with your brains."

–Work is not something you are supposed to like. Mostly people complain about their jobs, just the way kids complain about school. That's what school is for—to get you ready for real life, which means working all day at something you don't like. While you're a kid, you get to play—when you're not in school. But when you're officially grown-up, you stop playing and get a job and have responsibilities. Having responsibilities means never having fun except on weekends and vacations . . . unless you are a smart guy. Smart guys find ways to "get ahead," so that someday they will be able to "take it easy" and have big fun all the time.

–People who don't work are either very poor or very rich. Poor people who don't work are lazy and contemptible. They are failures and freeloaders. You should despise them. On the other hand, rich people who don't work are "lucky." They might not be the sort of people you like, but at least they aren't freeloaders. They deserve not to have to work because they are successful. Smart guys grow up to be like them.

–Losing your job is one of the most shameful and terrible things that can happen, because then you have to ask for handouts and people will think you're a freeloader. That is why you must be hard-working and dependable, even if you hate your job.

Hard-working, Working Poor

Like most children, I absorbed these teachings by osmosis from the world around me. They were never raised for debate—because what was there to debate? Work was simply what people grew up to do with their lives; it was a built-in reality that came with being human. In my family, with its almost proverbial American immigrant background, nobody ever entertained the notion that there might be cultural styles of work, that our livelihood, like the food we eat, should be a material we shape and flavor to our taste. Nobody could have afforded to see things that way. My grandparents arrived from Eastern Europe with one fixed star in their universe: their willingness to work, without raising questions, without making trouble. Work was their one chance to prove themselves and to make good as Americans. They stepped off the boat straight into the mines and shops and factories of Wilkes Barre, West Wheeling, Akron, Chicago, grateful and glad for any employment they could find.

Eventually, by dint of steady toil and fanatical thrift, they raised themselves into the lower margins of that sprawling social conurbation called the American middle class. From first to last, work was the center and substance of their lives; it was their validation as useful citizens. Even more, the work ethic, as they honored it in their every waking moment, was the bedrock of their security and their self-respect. When all else failed or collapsed—as it did for them in the Great Depression—or whenever injustice or discrimination touched them, they could always fall back upon their willingness to work unstintingly and at anything until they dropped.

Yet it was a strange, contradictory pride they took in their work. I remember vividly how my father would rehearse the family litany whenever he had been bruised by insult or injustice. "I had to sweat for every nickel I ever earned . . . I never got something for nothing . . . nobody in this family ever asked for any handouts. . . ." It was pride mixed darkly with bitterness, because, for all he might say for himself as a hard worker, my father, like his father before him, never took satisfaction in the work he was hired to do. He loathed and cursed all his jobs. He was a gifted cabinetmaker, but—with the exception of a few failed business efforts of his own—he spent his entire working life as an underpaid carpenter, with never a good word for any job he held. He despised his bosses and the work they assigned him, which always had to be done on the quick and cheap, making no use of his best skills. Worst of all, he came to despise himself as one of the hundred million American nobodies who were stuck on the bottom rungs of the social ladder with no way up.

"Working poor" is the quaint social category we now have for families like mine, the sort of people who only get a little ahead of their debts by putting in ten or twenty hours a week of overtime. "OT" was like manna from heaven in our household; my father would announce its arrival like a portent of better days. But then he wound up working harder than ever, and it always showed. He would drag home dog-tired and short-tempered at night, leave bleary-eyed and unshaven the next morning, grumble as he ate warmed-over meals at how much less he was bringing home in his pay check than he deserved. And there was always the lament: The work wasn't worthy of him. It was slapdash and stupid and shoddy, none of it done with care or craftsmanship.

Hard work killed my father young—at forty-six. He died of heart failure and (I believe) of demoralization, with not enough money in the bank for a good funeral. My mother had to use up his life insurance to bury him.

My father was pugnaciously proud of being "hard-working." But his constant advice to me was, "Never work with your hands. Go to college. Become a professional man. If you work with your hands, you're not worth shit in this world." His pride, like that of all the working poor I have ever met, was the best face he could put upon his sense of helpless victimization. He had every right to the self-respect he claimed; he was the possessor of a noble and useful skill. He was a builder, a man who could make houses and fine furniture. He knew the true use of his tools. I have worked with executive paper shufflers and "decision makers" who will not contribute anything to the world as valuable as a single good table or chair my father made. In another age he would have been highly honored for his craft. But his pride could no longer be based on that, because he knew he was somebody's misused employee, the hireling of people who valued him only as a means to a fast dollar. So his self-esteem was infected with anger and envy; when he boasted of being "hard-working," he was making a slender virtue of a hated necessity. At last, his pride was an expression of belligerent and powerless resentment.

Whenever I hear politicians and labor leaders talk about "putting people to work," I wonder if they realize, as I suspect a great many working people do, what a pathetically minimal ideal that has become. What does "full employment" mean to men like my father whose daily work is an insult and a torment? Is it enough any longer for the economic index to measure how many people *have* jobs, without asking whether they take pride in the jobs they have? I wonder, when do we begin talking about the quality of employment, as well as its quantity? Another way of asking, when do we stop treating people like statistics and start treating them like persons?

There is one more thing I remember about my father's work life —something that always puzzled me in my youth. Every year my father got two meager weeks of paid vacation. When it came around, he swore he was going to lie out in the back yard and rot. And he would do just that . . . for perhaps the first two or three days he was off work. He would sit under a tree with some beer and a radio and do very nearly nothing. But soon enough, he would be banging away in some part of the house, remodeling a room; or he would be out in the garage, building a piece of furniture; or he would be clambering about under the floor boards, repairing the foundation. He would finish those long hours of work as tired and grimy as he ever came home from his job. But now he wasn't morose, he didn't complain. He would be talking about how well the job was going, or making sketches and puzzling out better ways to design the project.

One summer he used up his entire vacation working ten and twelve hours a day to help an incompetent neighbor put up a new porch. He finally took over the job, redesigned the porch, and pretty well did it all himself. All he got in payment was a bottle of whiskey. When my mother asked him why he was going to the trouble, he answered, "Because I can't sit out there and watch him do a half-assed job. It drives me nuts."

The True Dimensions of Alienation

If there was ever an example of alienation in the classic Marxist sense of the word, my father was it. He was the quintessential proletarian: totally vulnerable both economically and psychologically.

He never even found his way into an effective labor union to defend his interests. He was a man with nothing to sell for his livelihood but his labor; and at last even that was not enough. He had to surrender his self-respect as well. In that act of resignation, there is more than personal pathos. A noble tradition of craftsmanship is poisoned to death by such self-contempt, and the meaning of honest work is hideously distorted for all of us.

Yet, over the years, I have come to see, in large part through my own work experience at a variety of jobs, unskilled, white collar, and professional, that the problem of dehumanized labor barely begins with my father's example. His experience is really only the base line from which the further reaches of alienation may be measured. From the personalist viewpoint we adopt here, the hard core of the problem is not to be found among those who are, like my father, miserable and embittered, but among those who are exploited and acquiescent, alienated and yet complacent. It is only when we begin to appreciate how effectively people can be persuaded to will their own alienation from the work they do that we grasp the true dimensions of the problem.

One need not reach beyond a conventional left-wing analysis to recognize that a worker whose discontent is softened by a pay raise and shorter hours is still an exploited worker. Similarly, if working conditions are redesigned to make life on the job more relaxed and diverting (for example, the office is air-conditioned and carpeted, music is piped in, the day is strategically punctuated with coffee breaks in the handsome company lounge), we may still see this as alienated employment, even if those who work in this mellowed environment are unexceptionally cheerful. How so? Because their work still does not belong to them; it is still not an act of their own choosing done to their own standard. Instead, they remain dependent on the favor of employers and bosses; they are still powerless to determine the use to which their work is put; they own neither the means nor the fruits of their labor. They are still working as productive instruments at the disposal of forces they do not control and may not even understand.

In the years before I became a teacher and writer, I worked in factories that were unutterably dismal and hazardous. I worked in a chrome-plating plant where I was forever over shoes in muck and constantly breathing the fumes of boiling acid. I worked in a boiler factory where I was expected to sacrifice my eardrums to a hot and heavy riveting job that paid the dead minimum wage. The boss had to yell at the nearly deaf worker I was replacing (Dummy George, everyone called him) to tell him he was off the job. When I asked for a raise to do the work, I was fired. The plain wretchedness of work like this is obvious to all concerned; nobody needs to be persuaded that it is exploitive and humiliating.

But I have also worked at white-collar jobs—for both private and public organizations—where every effort was made to provide amenities. At one insurance company, the personnel department never let a week pass without announcing a busy agenda of activities and amusements: picnics and theater parties, baseball outings and amateur talent shows, tours and charter flights. There were company programs for everything: savings, mutual fund investments, discount purchasing, medical and dental care, retirement. Every pregnant typist was treated to a lunchtime baby shower by the firm; births, deaths, engagements, retirements were noted in the weekly bulletin, along with the company's generous contribution to the occasion. The corridors were carpeted; lunches in the well-upholstered cafeteria were kept cheap and nutritious; on one's birthday, everybody in one's department got a cupcake with a lighted candle on top.

There were people I worked with in that office who loved the company. They joined in on all the fun, subscribed to all the programs. It was the joy and mainstay of their lives. They *cared* whether "our" company caught up with Prudential or Mutual of Omaha in gross sales. From my work in the claims department, I could tell that the company sold some of the most dishonest health and accident insurance on the market. It also refused employment to Jews and blacks. But that, of course, was supposed to be none of *my* business. Nor were the totally reactionary politics which determined the company's influence in the city. There was no union; it was universally understood that there was no need for a union. And while the personnel office was always available to hear complaints or suggestions, there was no grievance procedure, no right of appeal upon dismissal. Without surrendering a fraction of its capitalist prerogatives, the company had found the secret of winning the hearts and minds of its employees.

Perhaps white-collar labor has always been the most coddled sector of the work force, but my guess is that, in the next generation, we will see ever more intensive efforts at morale-boosting of this sort in all areas of the economy. The literature documenting boredom, resentment, recalcitrance on the job grows by the year. Absenteeism, high turnover, industrial sabotage are prominently recognized as major obstacles to discipline and productivity. In response, "job enrichment" and "job restructuring" have become high priorities on the industrial agenda; academic study centers have been set up by government and the corporations to research the subjects, and imaginative experiments have been launched. No doubt there are tedious and dirty jobs which are very nearly intractable to any form of "enrichment": mining, waste collection, assembly-line and construction work, clerk-typing. But even here there are possibilities for blunting the edge of discontent: flextime scheduling, profit sharing, job sharing, work-gang assignments, more breaks, greater variety of job assignments. Recent contracts in the auto industry have stressed sabbatical leaves, paid time off, and more union participation in decision making, especially with respect to working conditions, quite as much as higher wages and overtime rates.

If we can take Japan as an example, there is room for a good deal of enrichment and amelioration within industrial capitalism. There, a suave paternalism has managed to co-opt most of the services of the Western welfare state and has thereby done much to capture the loyalty and enthusiasm of workers. It may well be that the next phase of advanced capitalist expansion will, ironically enough, hark back to Robert Owen's enlightened experiments at New Lanark in Scotland, which proved at the very beginning of the Industrial Revolution that a major investment in employee morale more than paid for itself in productivity. Owen was prophetically right, but, in the early nineteenth century, the compulsions of primitive accumulation blinded his fellow capitalists to his insight—with the result that capitalism came to be indelibly marked in the eyes of radical critics by physical degradation and brutality.

But that was never the essence of capitalist employment, as Marx, in his best analytical passages, recognized. The fundamental act of alienation during the Industrial Revolution was the subordination of work to money, so that work—any work and all work—came to be an abstract commodity valued only as a means of earning the wages that purchased subsistence and (perhaps) some leisured enjoyment. "Alienation," as Marx put it, "shows itself not merely in the result, but also in the process of production, within productive activity itself. . . . The work is *external* to the worker, . . . it is not part of his nature, . . . consequently, he does not fulfill himself in his work but denies himself. . . ."

At their most perceptive, both Marx and Engels noted that alienation in this deeper sense may be characteristic, not simply of capitalism, but of any high industrial system—especially one that serves the needs of a major economic power. But, convinced as they were (and, of course, Lenin and Stalin after them) that the medicine of revolution would somehow cure all the ills of society, they did not press the point or give it full theoretical scope. It was left to their despised radical opposition, the anarchists, to warn that such big systems, sunk as they are in a competitive nationalist ethos and the eternal arms race, are bound to overwhelm the human scale of life and so to subordinate work-as-personal-fulfillment to work-as-productivity. The sheer physical burden of work may then be ameliorated; but in its place, both in privatized and in collectivized economies, we discover that our work life has been infiltrated by clever strategies invented by planners and managers to seduce our allegiance and manipulate our energy for the greater glory of the system.

We may even progress then toward forms of workers' control and industrial democracy, but always with the understanding that our participation is constrained by certain abstract imperatives: efficiency, the rate of growth, the balance of world power, etc. "Participation" (by workers, consumers, investors, planners) has become a vogue word and prominent policy objective in many Western European governments; there, it is understood to be a major means of oiling away the discontent that inhibits planning on the scale of the Common Market. It may even be a sincere intention; but we should remember that every Nazi concentration camp was based on "participation," using inmates to police inmates in return for special favors.

Responsibility and Vocation

I want to argue that none of the enrichments and inducements mentioned here, not even the ingenious methods the Chinese have developed for collectivizing the altruism of the work force, goes to the root of alienation. I do not mean to say these reforms make no difference; they obviously render life on the job more pleasant and secure than it was in the worst days of wage slavery. But they do not make the *right kind* of difference. They may be necessary changes in many respects, but they are not sufficient. They alter the atmosphere and incentives of work, but they do not in themselves redeem work by any acceptable personalist standard, because they do not place the whole and unique person at the center of economic life. On the contrary, their clear purpose is to enhance productivity—either for private profit or for the national interest. The reforms I mention, including a high degree of industrial democracy, can be attached to work which is still done with total impersonality, to mass production and bureaucratic processing which casts things and services into the world carrying no one's name, invested with no one's honor, bearing no one's style. And that is still employment—work performed because others dictate, or because the system has decreed that it be done by somebody, by anybody.

There is an extensive range of amelioration and enrichment which is thoroughly compatible with industrial bigness, and indeed which increases the integration and efficiency of giant economies. Even the ideal of service (to the nation, the people, the state) has been co-opted in our time to serve the needs of despotic and dehumanized political forces. Some of the worst totalitarian regimes of the twentieth century have manipulated patriotic allegiance to grind Stakhanovite sacrifices from their people. That is precisely the danger in every form of collectivized morale. People are not asked to find themselves in their work, but to lose themselves in service to collective power. And to lose one's self in this sense—to surrender to an all-embracing and domineering collectivity—is to give up responsibility for one's work.

Responsibility—there we have the missing factor in both capitalist job enrichment and collectivist work morale, the crucial distinction that separates mere employment from true vocation. To have a vocation is to work with responsibility—not in any merely legal sense, nor in the sense of fearing that one will be pointed out as a slacker by one's workmates and reported to the party—but in the sense that our work is ourselves; we are at one with it because it grows from all that we have chosen to become in this life. It is our personal emblem and pledge of honor before the world. We *care* about our vocation, because if it is misused or proves inadequate, all that gives our life distinction and meaning is called into question.

It is a stubborn fact of human experience: Except in the most technical legal sense, I cannot hold myself responsible for work that is personally meaningless, let alone for work I despise. Meaningless work, despicable work, is work I blame on others; I treat it as a mere necessity, an imposed duty. I may even feel ashamed that I waste my life at such work. So I say to myself (and secretly to the world), "I am only doing this because I need the money, or I need the grade, or I need the credit, or reputation, or publicity. I am doing something my boss wants to have done, or the system needs to have done. I did not invent this job; I do not believe in it; I do not endorse it. If I had *my* way, I would be doing something else. So don't hold me responsible for its waste, its shoddiness, its criminality."

In this way, I seek to distance myself from the job. And that, essentially, is what alienation is: the withdrawal of self from action, the retreat of the person from the performance. Work then becomes a foreign object in one's life which is, at most, a means to an end, but no proper part of one's real identity. Alienation is not—as left-wing radicalism customarily contends—an estrangement merely from the means and fruits of production. It is also estrangement from the activity itself which allows us to deny our responsibility for what we do. And this is what surely follows when work has no *craft* to it: no challenge, no taste, no personal style. Work of that kind is a zero, a hole in the middle of one's life. It is life wasted, and nothing breeds more rebellion and resentment in us than the experience of having a precious piece of our life extorted from us, stolen away, used up. Confronted with work of this kind, we withdraw into fantasies of being elsewhere, doing other things . . . watching the clock, planning for the weekend. We are everywhere but right here, *at* work and *in* our work.

Responsibility, as I intend the word here, is double-edged. It means being responsible *to* and being responsible *for*. If we have a vocation, we are responsible *to* our work that it should be well done; we are responsible *for* our work that it should be well used. We want it to be intrinsically excellent by the highest standards of our craft or profession; we also want it to be of good and honorable service in the world. In our vocation, we wish to see *the good* achieved in both its senses: the well crafted and the ethically right. Only one force will provide this double-edged sense of responsibility—and that is love: the love we bear toward the work we do. Just as there is no way to talk about vocation without talking about responsibility, so there is no way to talk about responsibility without talking about love. To what and for what *can* we be responsible? (I do not say *ought* we to be responsible, but *can* we be responsible. I ask after the psychological fact, not the legal safeguard.) However law and public opinion may define our liability, we can hold ourselves responsible only to what we love and for what we love—just as, if we love a friend, a child, a community, we want to help them achieve the greatest possible beauty and nobility. And to the degree that we have entered into that project, we feel naturally implicated in what they become and what they do. We are at one with them in our love and would not part ourselves from their fate, even if we could.

The Buddha, in his wisdom, made "right livelihood" (another word, I think, for vocation) one of the steps to enlightenment. If we do not pitch our discussion that high, we have failed to give work its true dimension, and we will settle for far too little—perhaps for no more than a living wage. Responsible work is an embodiment of love, and love is the only discipline that will serve in shaping the personality, the only discipline that makes the mind whole and constant for a lifetime of effort. There hovers about a true vocation that paradox of all significant self-knowledge—our capacity to find ourselves by losing ourselves. We lose ourselves in our love of the task before us, and, in that moment, we learn an identity that lives both within and beyond us.

What else should the highest yoga be, after all, but the work we turn to each day?

"Take This Job and Shove It"

Each day I move through a world at work, an ocean of human activity as pervasively and as unobtrusively there as the ocean of air that surrounds me. I breathe in the labor of people around me; I live by it, yet I take it for granted like some free resource. People work, I work. That is what we are here to do; it is how we pass the time.

But our work is more than a pastime. It is our life. It takes up years of the portion we have been allotted on this Earth to work out our salvation. And not many of us work at a true vocation . . . sometimes I think very nearly none. Some, like my father, grind their substance away at hard and dirty work for too little pay and appreciation. Most are toiling at jobs whose worst burden is deadly and impersonal routine: typing, filing, checking groceries, selling across a counter, filling out forms, processing papers.

I have done such jobs myself. I still do them. A deal of what I do as a teacher in a colossal state college system is stale paper work and routine committee assignments that have nothing to do with education or scholarship, little enough to do with simple intelligence. Did any of us really have to read Studs Terkel's report *Working* to know what the daily deadly toll of alienated labor is? "I feel like a machine," "I feel like a robot," Terkel's interviewees complain. As I sit down to the task of revising this chapter, the record at the top of the American charts is Johnny Paycheck singing "Take This Job and Shove It." When we do not hear that lamentation from the people around us, it is only because we are not listening to what they say behind the heroic good humor that is the shield of their self-respect. Only look, and you can see their stifled personhood written in their faces; you can see it in the distraction that carries their thoughts to imaginary pleasures and leads to slip-ups and mistakes each day on the job; it is there in their surliness and bad temper. I have seen it in myself whenever I have felt the vital hours of my life being turned to dust by work that did not use the best I have to offer, whenever I have had to carry out the orders of employers who had no interest in the bright and extraordinary powers I could feel within me yearning to be hard-worked for all they were worth.

All of us have a gift, a calling of our own whose exercise is high delight, even if we must sweat and suffer to meet its demands. That calling reaches out to find a real and useful place in the world, a task that is not waste or pretense. If only that life-giving impulse might be liberated and made the whole energy of our daily work, if only we were given the chance to be *in* our work with the full force of our personality, mind and body, heart and soul . . . what a power would be released into the world! A force more richly transformative than all the might of industrial technology.

But *they*—the company, the system—rarely have any use for that calling. Our bosses do not even look for it in themselves. It makes no difference to the profit and loss; it does not show up (so the experts believe) in the economic indicators. So they sweep it out of sight and continue to work us as personnel, not persons. That is very nearly the prerequisite for being a successful boss in this warped economy: to blind oneself to the personhood of one's workers, to insist that business is business. That is treatment fewer workers will now accept; and the trend is by no means limited to middle-class, college-educated workers. In a recent statistical study, Daniel Yankelovich concludes that, in growing numbers through the seventies, "noncollege youth . . . take up the quest of their college peers for a new definition of success in which the emphasis is on self-fulfillment and quality of life, as well as on money and security." Thus, the Department of Labor reports that, even in a tight job market, twice as many people quit their jobs in disgust as did a decade ago; the number has gone from 200,000 per year to 400,000 and continues to rise.

Yet somehow we carry on. I am always astonished at how resourcefully most people find ways to stick at their jobs without becoming bitter or corrupt. Not everybody, of course. I meet enough people who abstractly and impersonally hate everyone they must deal with in the course of the working day, and even openly sabotage the job. And I meet those who are always posing like mannequins on display, getting by on a few knee-jerk courtesies the company has made them memorize . . . the telephone operators with their by-the-numbers cheerfulness . . . the airline stewardesses with their plastic smiles and public relations sex appeal. The kids who work for the fast-food chains are the saddest cases. Company policy is for them to make like living TV commercials, clean-cut and grinning for all they're worth, happy-happy-happy to be selling the world a billion bad hamburgers a day. Is somebody watching them all the time, checking their act . . . some Big Brother manager? They are so young, and here they are already faking their lives away to hold a nickel-and-dime job. Probably this is their first paid work, and what is it they are learning? How to be a conscientious stooge for the company.

But there are so many others I meet who miraculously manage to stay human on the job. They invent little strategies of self-encouragement and compensation to get them through the day. They decorate their work space with trinkets and placards of their own choosing. They smuggle a transistor radio into the shop to play "their" kind of music, though most of what they hear is idiotic commercials and payola disk jockeys. They divide the day's work into so many little contests and competitions that will pace them along. They secretly challenge themselves to absurdly high standards of neatness and precision to put some sport in the work. They organize games with workmates, they gossip, they flirt, they kid around, they kibbitz with the customers, they exchange jokes and novelties. Perhaps most of all, they gripe. Mutual griping always helps. It relieves the conscience to let someone know that *you* know this is a bitch of a job. That is a way to remind yourself and the world that you are bigger and smarter and better than this dumb job. And if you had *your* way . . .

When I worked as a teller for the Bank of America, I kept my head busy all day long repeating Greek declensions and memorizing poems. It kept my brain alive—and also made me a miserably bad teller. But even my mistakes were a secret gratification—a tiny way of obstructing B of A's smooth flow of high financial banditry. I imagine strategies like these have sustained people through all the most suffocating kinds of toil since the factory bells pealed in the first dawn of industrialism. They are symptoms of our vocational instinct fighting to survive: little sparks and flashes of our thwarted personhood. The pathos of the matter is that no private strategy of this kind will ever turn an empty or fraudulent job into a vocation—nor, for that matter, will any social reform. And far too many of us are entrammeled by just such work, struggling to avoid the embarrassment of acknowledging our entrapment. A phony job is a phony job; a wicked job is a wicked job. These are not matters of morale or social organization; not even revolutionary workers' control can change them. They are objective moral facts attached to certain forms of employment that have become the only jobs many industrial societies seem able to offer millions of workers.

Work that produces unnecessary consumer junk or weapons of war is wrong and wasteful. Work that is built upon false needs or unbecoming appetites is wrong and wasteful. Work that deceives or manipulates, that exploits or degrades is wrong and wasteful. Work that wounds the environment or makes the world ugly is wrong and wasteful. There is no way to redeem such work by enriching it or restructuring it, by socializing it or nationalizing it, by making it "small" or decentralized or democratic. It is a sow's ear that will yield no silk purses.

Here we have an absolute criterion that must enter any discussion of work. *Is the job honest and useful? Is it a real contribution to human need?* These are questions that can only be answered by a worker's own strong sense of responsibility. That is why the struggle for right livelihood is as important as the struggle for industrial democracy. For it does not matter how democratically controlled our work life is: If a job is inherently worthless, it cannot be a vocation. So, if we encourage people to search for responsible work—for work they can love as an image of their personal destiny—then we must not expect them to continue doing what is stupid or ugly. We must not expect them to go on working for the military-industrial complex or for Madison Avenue, to continue producing "people's bombs" or printing party propaganda. One cannot build a vocation on a lie.

The hard truth is that the world we live in, the high industrial world we presume to hold up as the standard of "development," is immensely committed to proliferating work that is wrong and wasteful. It does this in the name of growth, or the national security, or the standard of living; but at the bottom it all comes down to creating jobs that are unworthy of our best energies:

Huckstering jobs—inventing, advertising, selling expensive trash to gullible customers

Busywork jobs—sorting, recording, filing, computerizing, endless amounts of data, office memos, statistical figments

Mandarin-administrative jobs—co-ordinating, overseeing, supervising clerical battalions and bureaucratic hierarchies, many of which—especially in government operations—exist merely to spin their own wheels

Financial sleight-of-hand jobs—juggling cash and credit, sniffing out tax loopholes and quick speculative windfalls in real estate, arbitrage, stocks and bonds

Compensatory amusements jobs—marketing the vicarious glamour and escapist pleasures whose one use is to relieve the tedium and frustration of workaday life: spectator sports, mass media distractions, superstar entertainments, package tours, the pricey toys and accoutrements of "creative leisure"

Cop jobs—providing security against the theft and violence of society's have-nots, policing the streets, hassling the riffraff through the courts, guarding the prisons, snooping into credit ratings, school records, personnel evaluations

Welfare processing jobs—picking up the economy's casualties, keeping them on the public assistance treadmill, holding the social discontent below the boiling point

And at the dizzy top of the heap, we have the billion-dollar boondoggling—the cartel building, multinational maneuvering, military-industrial back scratching—which is the corrupted soul of our corporate economy. The list could go on indefinitely, a spreading network of waste and corruption that touches very nearly everybody's work life. How many of us could not finally be tied into it in at least some peripheral way—like it or not, know it or not? My own profession of university teaching has fattened enormously over the past generation by educating (or training) the personnel who have become the executive functionaries and white-collar rank and file in this flourishing surplus economy.

Many who are utterly dependent upon this dense congestion of socially useless getting and spending may never see the full context of the work they do. That is the peculiar moral dodge made available by our social complexity. It allows us to work in the blind at little, seemingly innocent fractions of big, dishonorable projects. The full extent of culpability may be nearly impossible to delineate; there are so many degrees and shadings. But the ethical issue is nevertheless there at the heart of our economy, and it must be addressed by any honest discussion of work. There is work that is good and useful; and there is work that is not. Work that is not good and useful is work that wastes the lives of people and the resources of the Earth—and industrial society generates a scandalous amount of that kind of work. Perhaps it is what our society does most. In our search for a true vocation, here is indeed a Himalayan obstacle. For it may mean there is a prodigious amount of work we are involved in which no healthy sense of responsibility should permit us to do at all.

Work in the Premodern World

It has not always been this way in the work life of the human race. In the past, work may often have been grueling and exploitive; but it was rarely so inherently mindless that it seemed designed for zombies, nor so wasteful that it was a sin against nature.

What are most people in premodern societies? They are peasant farmers, artisans, craftsmen, housewives—and children learning these livelihoods from their parents. In more primitive societies, they are hunters, fishermen, gatherers, nomads. Now, all of this is skilled work of an indisputably useful nature. It requires careful training, a mastery of cultural lore, the constant exercise of judgment and initiative. In doing the work, one experiences one's own competence and strives toward a standard of excellence that is respected by one's fellows. There is a difference between a good farmer and a bad one, between a good hunter and a bad one—a difference the community appreciates and cares about, because the work is a necessary value to all concerned. To become good at these things is an exercise of one's cunning, experience, inspiration —qualities that, in some measure, extend and define the personality.

Even under the bleakest conditions of social exploitation, working people in these societies, at least among themselves, can be a community of mutual appreciation and critical regard—not simply because they are being "nice" with one another on the job like bored office workers exchanging pleasantries and good humor, but because their work is a real measure of competence at a significant project in the world. This is an irreducible cultural and personal value, for there is, at last, such a thing in our nature as an instinct of workmanship that can tell an honest job from a fake, and cares about the difference. The women, too, in traditional societies are more than the "mere" housewives we might mistake them for. They are possessed of a remarkable repertory of domestic skills which might include midwifery, horticulture, cooking, baking, pottery, weaving, clothes making, tanning, butchery, medicine, ritual acts, artistic decoration, and, of course, child rearing. Even in their usual condition of subjugation, women in premodern societies—or at least nonaristocratic women—can be judged by real ability at respectable work.

Wherever men and women do work like this, there is apt to be enough know-how, challenge, and responsibility about their labor to contribute significantly to their maturity. Inherently, the work allows for at least that amount of growth which children experience in becoming adults who know a valuable skill; their experience is not that of "growing up absurd." And there is the assurance that what people do with their lives is worth doing; there is a clearly recognizable necessity to their labor; perhaps the very survival of the community depends upon it.

I have no wish to romanticize the condition of premodern people. I recognize full well how physically onerous their lives may be. I am also aware that in their civilized phase, traditional societies invariably fall under the domination of aristocratic elites which fiercely exploit the lower orders and denigrate their work as vulgar and brutish. In this way ruling castes impose their own corrupted priorities upon their society. Prestige, wealth, and refinement become prerogatives of the most parasitic social elements, while honest toil is made to seem degraded, vile, and burdensome; so its full vocational potentiality is hardly likely to be realized. Instead, a refined and prodigal idleness comes to be seen as the highest value in society, and cultural creativity is understood to be a leisure-time activity wholly incompatible with daily labor.

But all this is simply the mystification of the matter; the truth is that the work ordinary people do in traditional societies remains a thoroughly dignified and intrinsically engaging use of life. Its vocational meaning is still there, even if an exploitive social system obscures it. The all-important fact is: In premodern society there is no such thing as "unskilled" labor; there are no workers who exist simply as the routinized adjuncts of machines or assembly lines; there is no one, below the level of the privileged orders, whose life's work is a scam or a boondoggle.

"In Sorrowful Drudgery"

As we enter the modern period, an odd and ironic development takes place. The great revolutionary transformations that ushered urban-industrial society into history were essentially bourgeois movements, and to a major degree their guiding ideology was an ideology of work. Monarchy, priesthood, and aristocracy were condemned as parasitic and righteously swept aside. The moneyed middle class pressed forward to assume a new heroic identity as the indispensable productive agency in society. The world was to be remade, progress was to be launched, human dignity was to be vindicated by men of enterprise and invention: merchants, shopkeepers, entrepreneurs, technicians. Somewhere deeply mingled into the ideology of bourgeois revolution was a Calvinist ethic of diligence, frugality, and honest toil. The result might have been the liberation of work from its age-old degradation and the rediscovery of vocation.

But that is not what happened. For there was, after all, a strange twist to the middle-class work ethic. Calvinism did not regard labor as a redeeming joy, but as a curse and a penance to which the godly must resign themselves as a testing from on high. Work, like sexual shame, was a sign of human fallenness; its function was not to offer fulfillment, but to discipline the appetites and humble the will. It was an experience of self-denial, not of self-discovery. Max Weber speaks of the new work ethic as a "worldly asceticism"—the discipline of a taskmaster God that must be suffered for the good of one's soul. Even prosperity was not to be enjoyed, but humbly accepted as a sign of divine election. One might accumulate wealth, but must never admit to taking pleasure in it. It was an ethic that gave a certain somber dignity to worldly effort; yet it could only drain work of its aesthetic, sensual, and creative possibilities. It *wanted* work to be drudgery, for it relished the discipline of long-suffering patience.

Of course, capitalism was not wholly the creation of puritanical asceticism. There was room within it for the flamboyant robber baron, the crafty inventor, the world-beating captain of industry. The dour Calvinist ethic was also mixed through with a high-spirited cult of revolutionary progress that inspired many humane hopes. But progress can be measured by some very strange standards—and by some that have nothing to do with happiness and fulfillment. There can be a progress in efficiency and productivity which stands prepared to sacrifice every human value to its maniacal designs. This was the sort of taut rational order that appealed to the followers of Saint-Simon and to the Benthamites. Without any religious overtones whatever, this stringent brand of utilitarian rationality can become as life-denying as the most extreme forms of Calvinist austerity.

The economic thought that guided early industrialism is the

unlovely hybrid of these two cultural strains: Calvinism and utilitarianism. What comes of that blend is indeed a "dismal science" grounded in the firm expectation that misery, privation, and class oppression will only increase as time goes on. Classical economics was reconciled to suffering and degradation as necessities of economic law, ordained by the same high will that had established the laws of nature. This was like saying that life on Earth is doomed to be a kind of long-suffering perdition and that industrial progress is the devil's own crucible. William Blake shrewdly recognized the demonic thrust of the new economy. In his brooding prophetical epics, he saw the new industrial society rising and spreading before him like the landscape of hell, a fiery torment of mankind and the mothering Earth that was the terrible product of a twisted religious energy. Himself a gifted craftsman, he was especially appalled by the impact of industrialism upon work. Something had entered the experience of working people that had never been there before: *unskilled labor,* work in which there was—inherently—no character, no chance for even minimal judgment and style. The immediacy and integrity of labor were being ground away by an economic science which subordinated all human activity to abstract measures of efficiency. Work was being atomized by the machines: divided, subdivided, fragmented, and rendered mindless—so that, for the first time in human history, supposedly "free" workers in their place of work quite literally did not know what they were doing.

> *And all the Arts of Life* [Blake lamented] *they chang'd into*
>   *the Arts of Death in Albion.*
> *The hour-glass contemn'd because its simple workmanship*
> *Was like the workmanship of the plowman, & the water wheel*
> *That raises water into cisterns, broken & burned with fire . . .*
> *And in their stead, intricate wheels inverted, wheel without*
>   *wheel,*
> *To perplex youth in their outgoings & to bind to labours in*
>   *Albion*
> *Of day & night the myriads of eternity; that they may grind*
> *And polish brass & iron hour after hour, laborious task,*

Kept ignorant of its use: that they might spend the days of
wisdom
In sorrowful drudgery to obtain a scanty pittance of bread,
In ignorance to view a small portion & think that All,
And call it Demonstration, blind to all the simple rules of life.

Work of this kind, the "sorrowful drudgery" of factory hands who must "view a small portion and think that all," is the peculiar creation of industrial production. It derives from the rationalized division of labor and the strange standard of efficiency which that division generates. From the very beginning, the factory was a place for the unskilled—for minimally trained women and children whose only task was to assist a vast machinery which was understood to be doing the *real* work. In no traditional society did fragmented and mindless work of this kind exist as a permanent and essential economic institution. The only rough comparison we might make would be with the mining and quarrying that was assigned to slaves in the ancient world, or with the galley rowing that had long been used as punishment for convicts. That is the level of degradation we must descend to in seeking a precedent for factory labor. But it was just such work that came to be hailed as the secret of economic progress and the wave of the future.

". . . the simple rules of life." Perhaps we are sometimes too clever for our own moral good. There is such astonishing genius in our machines and productive systems; but we forget that the doing is as important as what gets done, the making as valuable as the made. Economics is a science not only of commodities but of the human need for self-respecting work.

Over the past century, many of the worst physical privations of early industrialism have been ameliorated. Classical economics has been challenged by socialist dissent and other humanistic schools of economic thought. The developed societies have moved from conditions of scarcity and primitive accumulation to high consumption economics and the welfare state. Much has changed. But work life in every modern society still bears the mark of the industrial brand. We have grown accustomed to minute divisions of labor and the top-down managerial hierarchies that exist to hold all the pieces together; unskilled and semiskilled labor has become an established category of employment; workers continue to regard work as a sorrowful human plight, but now without the spiritual support and bracing discipline of Calvinist belief. Instead, they set their hopes upon softening or escaping the burden, though they are, of course, tied to it by financial need.

Most important of all, we press forward with ever more ingenious forms of mechanization, making work, more than ever, the province of the machine. Such progress may often threaten workers with unemployment, but the dilemma is: Almost universally, people believe that a truly modern economy must be capital-intensive, because this alone promises them deliverance from work. Meanwhile, the daily grind goes on, with an increasing concentration of expensive machinery at the center of work life, defining jobs, setting the pace, generating most of the services and paper work, doing most of the managing and administering in the economy.

The element of capitalist exploitation in industrial history is obvious enough. But sooner or later, in any discussion of work, we must address ourselves to the machine as an independent factor in the degradation of work, one that continues to make itself felt even in the world's noncapitalist economies.

This is no easy criticism to raise without risking the charge of being "antitechnological." But it is no part of my argument to deny industrialism its great ingenuity and high promise. Rather, I submit that this promise was thwarted at the outset because the machine was not introduced into our society as a way of enhancing the work life of people. It was not, for example, discriminately grafted on to existing craft traditions with a view to easing their burdens and improving their technique. (That, incidentally, was what the much-maligned Luddites, the notorious machine wreckers of the early nineteenth century, wanted: a careful and gradual adaptation of industrial technology to the patterns of their craft. They only struck out at the new power looms when they were used as a weapon to destroy the rights of skilled labor.) Rather than growing gracefully into the work tradition of the society, the machine was aggressively forced into one area of economic life after another without any effort to salvage the wisdom of craft lore, without any concern for the dignity and integrity of people's labor.

Industrialism has not been a matter of workers selecting technologies that heighten their skills; it has been a matter of outsiders —entrepreneurs, financiers, political planners, professional technicians, and assorted high industrial experts who may know absolutely nothing about the vocational meaning of people's work— forcing their interests and ideas upon defenseless, usually disorganized working communities, often in a deliberate effort to displace whole craft traditions or to rebuild an entire economy. This is by no means a vice restricted to capitalist industrialism. The same high-handed methods were used by zealous Marxist revolutionaries to "modernize" Russian agriculture, with every intention of obliterating the old agrarian patterns. As in the Western economies, there was no interest in bolstering up a noble way of life by adapting the new technology to the needs and customs of farm families and communities. Mechanization was used to sweep the economic landscape clean of all resistance so that an entirely new urban-dominated order of production might take its place.

The justification for policies like these is always the same: the new technology will make for big numbers—*more* power, *more* profit, *more* productivity. Often enough the justification is valid; *more* is produced. Perhaps it is even fairly distributed . . . eventually. But fair shares and social security are not the only values at stake in the matter. There is another human need in question—the need for right livelihood. And I ask: What happens to that vocational need when industrial progress smashes the traditions and makes war upon the very sensibility in which the sense of vocation is rooted?

Mechanization Takes Command

It would be foolish to say that the machine *caused* the alienation of modern work life. It is not machines but people who cause things to happen in history. The machine was assimilated to a basically distorted work ethic, one which saw work as a just retribution visited upon a fallen humanity. By virtue of that assimilation, industrialism came to express a grim sensibility that subordinated work to abstract goals like profit and productivity. As work was more and more identified with vile drudgery, it was seen as something to be abandoned to machines—to unfeeling iron slaves that worked without joy or responsibility at whatever task they were assigned. Once again, as in the aristocratic past, work was associated with some lower order of existence—but now with something unalive, alien, no longer recognizably human. What could this be but a very special kind of humiliation for those whose work was most like what machines do, or for those whose work life was most dominated by the demands of mechanized systems? And what would we expect them to do, but seek to avoid that humiliation by having as little work and as much leisure in their lives as possible?

Anyone who has seen Charlie Chaplin trapped among the gears in *Modern Times* or watched HAL the computer wreak havoc aboard the spaceship in *2001* must surely be haunted by these portrayals of man as the enslaved adjunct of a vast, hostile machinery. It is a powerful image of our popular mythology. In it we see work being assimilated to the realm of the subhuman—and not muscle work only. Even brainwork—management, planning, decision making—comes to be the province of "smart machines" which (so untutored people begin to fear—with much help from the inventors and merchandisers of these machines) can think better, quicker, more reliably than people can. No, there will never come a time when the machines can do without us; that is a science-fiction fantasy. But we have already granted the machine its most crucial victory. We have convinced millions of toiling men and women that work ideally belongs to machines, that progress means "saving" labor by relinquishing it to machines, which will always do it better. So they begin to see leisure, not work, as the proper arena of creativity, freedom, growth. They dream that perhaps one day soon, when progress is complete, we shall all live in a workless world, a cybernated Utopia where society will finally be able to make a "human use of human beings"—to use the phrase coined by Norbert Wiener, the founding father of cybernetics.

I suspect there is enough skeptical common sense in most people for them to recognize such futuristic brainstorming as the pipe dream it is. But as notions like this infiltrate our journalism, literature, and even much serious economic thought, one toxic effect is surely achieved: *Work is steadily read out of the human condition.* It begins to look like some marginal part of a vast, alien realm called "the economy" which is dominated by machines and machine systems, by complex technicalities that can only be understood by those who draw upon data banks and computer networks. The only human involvement that matters significantly in this mammoth economic mechanism is not the lowly task of "working," but professional specialties like "managing," "planning," "consulting," "programming," "decision making"—highly refined skills whose prestige is predicated upon what mechanized systems cannot do . . . *yet.*

What does the ordinary person's meager daily labor count for beside these exalted forms of high industrial expertise? It is a cipher in an economist's esoteric formula—no more. All the more reason, then, to look elsewhere for significant meaning. Consequently, where work once stood at the center of life as an indispensable aspect of responsible adulthood, we have instead recreation . . . play . . . hobbies . . . the joy of sex . . . fun and games, all of which finally seem to come down to a sort of full-time, gourmet consumerism: cultivating extravagant wants, buying things, using them up, buying more.

The degradation of work and the economy of high consumption waste: the two are linked together by a misconceived machine technology that was brought into the world to replace work, not to enhance it. By the light of that misconception, official economic policy comes to regard the daily work of ordinary people as primarily a means of putting spending money into their hands so that they may become units of effective demand in the market place. It is not the content of their work that matters, only the pay check that comes at the end of the week. From the perspective of such an economic calculus, anything that will distribute purchasing power can take the place of work: a guaranteed annual wage, welfare, tax relief, a negative income tax. As far as the economic indicators are concerned, all these are interchangeable means of manipulating the economy. So presidents and their advisers gravely balance the benefits of public works against price stability, and finally make their choices—perhaps by applying some purely statistical device like the Phillip's curve, which relates unemployment to inflation in terms agreeable to business elites. And if the decision is to "make work," it does not matter whether people are employed building ballistic missiles or building hospitals. A job is a job, a dollar is a dollar.

An economics that cannot do justice to the meaning of vocation will never serve the needs of the person.

Our Work Is Our Life

The going style of industrial progress calls for the maximum amount of labor-saving technology. Where that progress is left to be made by private capital, the guiding criterion will surely be profit, and the result is apt to be technological unemployment. *But* the justification offered will be that "labor-saving" equals "leisure-making," and leisure is what life is all about.

Here, I adopt a radically different position, arguing that our personhood is realized in responsible work. Therefore, the true direction of progress is not to save labor, but to *preserve* it from indiscriminate technological advance: to preserve it, to make it whole, to make it real. If anything must be saved, it is the very concept that work is a necessity of the human condition—not a mere means of survival, but a paramount means of self-discovery. We have a need to work; we have a right to work; and neither the need nor the right has to be justified by proving its profitability or productivity, any more than our need to love, play, or grow should be made to present its cost-benefit credentials. Our work is our life, and we cannot exercise our right to self-discovery in a world that deprives us of our natural vocation.

Does this face us with a conflict that requires the world to turn away from all industrial technology and to "go primitive"? Not in the least. There is no incompatibility between craftsmen and their tools, and the right machine in the hands of a skilled and autonomous worker can only enhance the joy of the task and the beauty of the work. The inventing of better tools and machines is a natural action of craftsmanship and one of its highest expressions. But an honest concern for vocation is clearly incompatible with big system industrialism and the economic science that undergirds it. Where mechanization moves in massively from outside the working community and its traditions—as it has in Western society over the past two centuries, as it does today everywhere in the third world—the result is bound to be the destruction of craftsmanship, the displacement of responsible work. Then we are thrown into a vocational vacuum. This is "progress" that covets the inert product of labor, but neglects the living means; it wants the wealth of the selling, but forgets the value of the making.

Nor is it any solution to say that an expanding economy makes up for the work it destroys by generating new jobs. That it does, but at a very different economic level. Big systems take us into a new economic universe where work is keyed to another rhythm and character. There, work is fragmented, hierarchical, and minutely specialized; it is dependent on opening up massive new markets by stimulating wants and wasteful appetites; it becomes ever more embedded in promotion and merchandising, administration and co-ordination, paper work and personnel management; it citifies more and more of the population drawing people away from their ecological roots; it drifts steadily away from responsibility and personal engagement. It is altogether a different quality of work.

I cannot say this historical pattern, which has repeated itself in every high industrial economy, capitalist and collectivist alike, is inevitable. But I am sure it is inevitable where new technology is not respectfully grafted on to the pre-existing work tradition with a steady resolve to preserve work that possesses vocational integrity. I cannot say how big or small a factory or an economy must be to stay vocationally healthy; but certainly that vital balance will not be achieved where bigness is not disciplined by a standard outside itself. That standard is responsible work, and the most obvious way for it to be applied is by letting workers themselves assimilate to their craft the tools and machines and systems that facilitate their labor.

No worker is unwilling to see his or her work become useful to more people by being technologically amplified. But workers who love their work will not readily see it destroyed or cheapened by a technique whose only promise is to produce *more*—even before we ask how much *more* might be gained within the traditional pattern.

In recent years, the so-called Green Revolution techniques of high-yield agriculture have encountered such popular resistance in many poor countries. Peasant farmers have correctly sensed that the new approach, which derives from the American agrindustrial system, threatens the survival of small-scale farming. The methods are too technical, too expensive, too capital-intensive for peasant economies to assimilate. But in some quarters where that resistance has held firm, other cheaper and more adaptable ways of increasing production have been found—methods as simple as intercropping, introducing more annual plantings each with a shorter growing season, developing more secure storage facilities or better water collection methods. At least a few agrarian economists are coming to see that the resourcefulness of the world's two billion peasant farmers is one of our most undeveloped assets.

We are talking about a prospect here which, I realize, must sound to some like a prescription for indigence: the project of winning work back from the machines by scaling down the industrial establishment—an item that is nowhere on the agenda of government, business, or organized labor in the developed societies. What would it cost us in material terms to build such an alternative economy of modest means and high fulfillment? The question is impossible to answer because we have no rational idea of how much of anything we really need to be healthy, happy, and secure; there is no such word in our economics as "enough." Certainly poor countries need lots of everything, especially food. But how much of what they need is here and available, being used up by the self-indulgent habits of affluence? How much of the food and land that the poor need is being squandered on the unhealthy tastes of rich societies that must have their coffee, tea, and tobacco, and insist on eating only cattle who have eaten the world's most expensive feed grain?

We have no way whatever of knowing how much productivity the developed nations genuinely require. We are only beginning to come to grips with the colossal waste their affluence includes. When we decide we must keep people at work at mass-production levels to provide us with shoes, how many pairs of shoes per person do we think we have to own, and how long is each pair supposed to last? Certainly we need assembly lines to produce automobiles; but how many cars do we need to a family, how big and classy need they be, and how long can we make them to last, free of planned obsolescence? Ask the same questions of everything in sight from where you sit right now. How much of it really needed to be made, by any standard you would be willing to defend on your own moral responsibility?

If we could imagine cutting away the fat on which our middle and upper classes spend so freely (let us start there, but eventually we may include the junk the poor also waste their meager incomes upon), how much heavy production would still have to be done in our society? Of course, it is this fat which now employs most of our work force. But that is precisely the madness of the system, is it not? If we stop buying luxuries off the top, the corporate powers-that-be make sure the system stops producing bread and butter at the bottom, and nobody works. No waste, no essentials: the secret of the expanding economy.

Until we have some idea of what a rational and becoming standard of living demands, we have no way of knowing how much work needs to be done on a mechanized big scale. And we have no such idea. Our supposedly hardheaded economic science is the plaything of wild consumer fantasies and infantile prodigality. No one should be admitted into the profession who has not read Tolstoi's fable *How Much Land Does a Man Need?*

The Coming Liberation of Work

Considerations of rational need aside, one may still wonder if it is realistic to make the demands raised here of the world industrial economy. Is this not rather like butterflies making demands of dinosaurs?

I think the question is put wrong way around. We should rather ask: Is it realistic to go on scorning people's need for fulfilling work? Is it realistic to conduct ourselves as if we might continue to intensify the alienation of work life without producing a socially crippling epidemic of demoralization? The fact to hold firmly in mind is that, spiritually and ecologically, urban-industrialism is indeed a dinosaur whose days are numbered—a culture that is flirting with extinction. It is weighing that heavily upon the limits of human and environmental tolerance. Our planet will not much longer endure the spread of an economy that makes so many of us dependent for our life's work on wasteful and irresponsible employment. That is the deep reason why the ideal of vocation has begun to assert itself in our day. Once again, in a crucial area of life, the needs of the person vibrate sympathetically to the needs of the planet, and we see people spontaneously disaffiliating from the big Earth-tormenting systems in search of the human scale.

The disaffiliation begins at the fringes, of course, and it proceeds by fits and starts. But the signs of new growth are as vividly there as the symptoms of discontent. Let me turn some of my own random observations into a few predictions: an impressionistic survey of the future of work life in the industrial societies. In the coming generation, I would expect to see a sequence of reforms and experiments rapidly unfolding as people delve deeper and deeper into the root causes of alienation.

1. There will be more and more demands for job enrichment and restructuring in all areas of the economy, especially in clerical routine and assembly-line work. Experiments in flextime scheduling, mixed skills teams, job sharing, work-gang and "whole job" assignments, and a growing emphasis on variety and flexibility will become the new frontier of personnel management. Major organizations, both private and public, will proudly advertise their repertory of morale-boosting inducements. They will tell us how they have "personalized" and "custom-tailored" their jobs to the needs of their employees. Concurrently, unions will press for more paid holidays, sabbaticals, a shorter work week, and longer vacations as

independently desirable fringe benefits that may come to weigh more heavily in contract negotiations than wage and overtime demands. Soon these reforms will be hailed in the media as a "revolution" in industrial work life, though, in fact, they make no structural changes in the economy and are little more than temporary palliatives.

2. There will be increasing pressure for industrial democracy and self-management in the workplace. In the major industries, an aggressive new breed of union leaders will demand representation in top managerial decisions and more shop-floor democracy, perhaps taking their lead from the "co-determination" arrangements that the Scandinavian and West German trade unions have enjoyed for a generation or more, and which the French Government is now urgently promoting. The success of their efforts will vary and will probably be effectively stymied in the big corporations. But in smaller firms and newer industries we will hear about a new enlightened style of management which strives to take workers into responsible partnership and even shares the profits. The models for these experiments will be companies like the Scott-Bader Commonwealth in England, International Group Plans of Washington, D.C., Texas Instruments, and Bolivar Rearview Mirrors in Tennessee.

3. We will see more people dropping out of conventional employment to pursue livelihoods in the crafts and trades with a new spirit of self-discovery and ethical commitment. Many will be university-educated, even potential professionals, but they will be looking for a quality of work the professional world rarely offers. Perhaps they will have to rely on public assistance and food stamps to make the transition, and many may have to settle down to a simple, low-consumption living pattern, but that will be part of the autonomy and dignity they seek. We already have a crafts renaissance blossoming in America; its wares are in the streets and in many an urban bazaar. Craftsmanship has become one of the havens for the dropped-out young of the sixties who have rescued countless good old crafts from extinction. I think we will see more people turning to this alternative economy as they discover that they can find better value for their money in these new handicrafts

and services than they can find at Sears or Wards. The danger with the new crafts is that they will steadily drift out of the *People's Yellow Pages* into more opulent boutiques to become the next generation of gourmet merchandise.

4. We will see a growing number of work collectives and producer's co-operatives spring up in which people will band together to support one another's vocational needs. These may take the form of crafts co-ops, maintenance and repair collectives, or collectively owned shops and businesses. Some will be Community Development Corporations based in rural slums or urban ghettos modeled after experiments like the OEO-financed FIGHT organization in Rochester, New York, or HELP in New Mexico. Others may be worker-controlled industries reclaimed from the ruined businesses that many failed conglomerates of the sixties are leaving behind, an imaginative salvage operation which the Federation for Economic Democracy in Washington, D.C., is now pursuing. I suspect many of the new collectives will be women's groups organized by resourceful refugees from home and family in need of a liberating security and determined not to fall into conventionally masculine careers. Whatever the form or origin, the spirit of these enterprises will be the same. Because they will be worker-owned and managed, they will offer the most advanced forms of authentic job enrichment; the fulfillment of people in their work, rather than the size of earnings and output, will be part of their basic standard of efficiency and success. Above all, they will want an honest commerce with the daily needs of people: good value at a fair price, with maximum personal attention. That has certainly been my experience in dealing with such collectives. One is confronted with people of competence and conscience who take a simple delight in having at last found a useful purpose in life.

5. There will be an increasing number of dissenting professionals among us—in medicine, law, education, welfare, counseling, city planning, science, and engineering—who will strive to recapture the waning idealism of their callings. Many will assume "advocacy" or ombudsman positions outside their professions; they will become full-time troublemakers and boat-rockers, watchdogging the ethics of their colleagues—on the model of Ralph

Nader's "Raiders." They will project a new relaxed professional image that strives to set aside the defensive formalities and to undo the mystifications of their work. Many will finally band together to practice in legal collectives, free clinics, free schools, or radical think-tanks, placing their skills at the service of the vulnerable and the dispossessed. The economists among them will take an especially interesting turn as they become the champions of causes like land reform, community development, environmental defense. They will infuse their profession with a new ethical concern, as passionately principled as Marxism, but less rigidly scientistic, less ethnocentrically hostile to traditional ways and wisdom. Their research will do much to argue the viability of the work reforms listed here. They will set about inventing new criteria of efficiency, practicality, and economic reality that will be grounded in the vocational needs of people.

6. Finally, there will be more family farms and rural communes appearing in the wake of an aggressive national campaign for land reform and rural rehabilitation. These efforts will introduce a variety of organic techniques into the agricultural economy and will achieve astonishingly high levels of productivity with maximum economy. The open secret of their success will be the use of labor-intensive methods and small-scale technology. Unlike the agrindustrial combines that now blanket rural America, these will be people who came to the land to work in partnership with the soil, rather than to poison the land for profit. Perhaps they will begin to make the country look somewhat like a Jeffersonian democracy once again.

If I am right in believing that the central impetus behind contemporary dissent and disaffiliation is the need for self-discovery, then no reform that fails to bring a true spirit of vocation to our work life will prove satisfactory for more than a little while. One by one, we will see the layers of alienation stripped away as people try this reform and that. The real issue will not always be clearly articulated; at times, it will seem that a shorter work week or a little more say-so about working conditions is enough. But I suspect that phony job-enrichment ploys will rapidly prove inadequate; forms of managerial participation that simply implicate workers in the waste or folly of their employers will quickly be discarded. Gradually, it will become clear that what people are really seeking is the chance to create an identity through their work which rises to their highest personal aspiration. They will finally see that the discontentment of their work life can only be remedied by finding the responsibility of a true vocation. With that realization—a truth that validates itself in every working hour—we shall have a new economics which is grounded in the value of labor, not the price of commodities, and which will take its proper place among the moral sciences.

Chapter 9

In the Empire of Cities

The Mark of Cain

We talk a great deal these days about the problems of cities: financial insolvency, crime, welfare, housing, traffic. In every advanced, industrial society, each of these problems has its own small army of specialists to debate the policy alternatives, and all the debates reverberate up to the highest levels of government where they are likely to become the most urgent and expensive programs in modern political life.

But we rarely reflect upon the one problem that has no specialists and gives rise to no policy: the problem posed by the city as an imperialistic cultural force that carries the disease of colossalism in its most virulent form. The industrial metropolis is the biggest artifact humankind has ever built. In it, all the dilemmas of superscale which we have addressed in these pages reach their extreme. No other form of bigness—the bigness of modern nations, corporations, plants and factories, military-industrial complexes, bureaucratic institutions—would be conceivable without the city, and the city is taking over everywhere. In corners of the globe where industrialism is still only a hope and a dream, the city is already there, the ritual centerpiece of a worldwide cargo cult that waits for capital and know-how to arrive from distant lands of enchanted affluence. So they stand, a gleaming glass and metal skeleton of high-rise hotels and office buildings, freeways and airports rising out of tropic jungle and desert heat, embodying the highest hopes of forward-looking political elites bent upon ushering their nations into the twentieth century. Even the mass movements that are revolutionizing the lives of the world's peasant billions have been generaled by urban intellectuals who do not claim victory until they have captured the metropolitan centers of their country.

Megalopolis presides over the gargantuan expansion of contemporary society in all its aspects. It is not merely the container of big things; it is our collective commitment to bigness as a way of life. It is the daily pressure of city life that turns people into masses, crowds, personnel. Simply to make sure the traffic keeps moving and that the money changes hands, urban bureaucracy must reduce its subject millions to statistical abstractions and computer printouts. At the same time, the city is a compendium of our society's ecological bad habits. It is the most incorrigible of wasters and polluters; its economic style is the major burden weighing upon the planetary environment. Of all the hypertrophic institutions our society has inflicted upon both the person and the planet, the industrial city is the most oppressive.

Today, we take the city for granted. We regard its culture as—quite simply—"modern history"; we cling to its power and productivity as our very hope of survival. We forget what a newcomer the city is in the human story, and how unsavory its reputation has been throughout the past. The Bible, for example, reaches back to a time when the city was a new, strange, and dangerous thing in the world—the creation of a killer and outcast. It tells us that the first city was founded by Cain after the murder of his brother Abel. Having slain the gentle shepherd, Cain was cursed by God to become a vagabond and a fugitive. Wherever he turned, the Earth cried out against him for his crime, until at last he fled into the land of Nod to build the first city as his refuge and fortress.

We do not expect to learn our sociology from old myths, but the essential truth of urban society is there, not far below the surface. The legend reminds us how severely the city has wrenched the organic bonds that tie brother to brother, the person to the Earth. Within its walls, cunning and imperious talents were brought together outside the influence of custom and kinship—the merchant and the moneylender, the war lord and the priest: parasites who preyed upon the wealth of the surrounding countryside. From the beginning of its history in the ancient river valley civilizations, the city has presumed to use its control of weapons and brains to wring tribute from the land and has dignified its extortion as "government."

Even when cities have begun their career as obscure and humble towns—as they did in the early days of Western Europe—there has been an irrepressible dynamism in their nature that grows steadily more expansive until, as we finally see in our own time, they capture the economy of the planet. The city is inherently a powerhouse of rapacious energies. If those of us who belong to its culture and economy could see ourselves in the full perspective of urban history, we would recognize that we constitute the oldest imperial interest in the world—the empire of cities, incessantly forcing itself upon the traditional, the rural, the wilderness at large. If we do not acknowledge our habit of dominance, it is because we have so effectively flattened our opposition that there is no voice left to speak against us. Like all imperial powers, we fill the silence that follows our conquest with assumptions of historical necessity. Whatever holds out against us—the peasant, the nomad, the savage—we regard as so much cultural debris in our path. The mark of Cain is still on our brow, but we wear it as a crown called "civilization." *Civilization*—the world made "civil," made citified, swept up into the urban order of things.

I have lived out my life in the empire of cities. Yet, I have only recently come to see that my stance in the world as an urbanite is of far greater historical consequence than any other identity I bear. All the rest comes and goes in the rapid flux of contemporary events. My position in life as an American, as part of middle-class society, as a male, or as a member of the white race—I can imagine all these being radically transformed in the years ahead, perhaps even obliterated by the revolutionary currents of the modern world. But there is nothing on the scene that challenges my place as an urbanite, because there is no revolutionary movement afoot —not even in the third world—which is not a product of the city and which does not use the city as its arena and its instrument. Whether we are capitalist or socialist, white, black, or Asian, rich or poor, when we speak of "progress" and "development," we mean bringing more and more of the world under the governance of the city.

Today, all the decisions that are being made about the future of our planet are being made in cities by city brains. We take it for granted that this should be so. For must not every nation have its capital? And what else can a respectable capital be, but a metropolis of tall towers and busy streets, thronging shops and world commerce? At this moment, the optimum size of the European farm population is being debated in Brussels, Paris, and Bonn; the fate of the whales in their ocean home is being settled in Moscow and Tokyo; the future of the Amazon tribes and the Australian aboriginals is being decided in Brasilia, Rio, Sydney; the output of the rural communes of China is being deliberated in Peking; the shape of the world's deserts and rain forests is being determined by investments planned in New York, Zurich, Abu Dhabi. And all the bureaucrats and bankers, commissars and corporate economists who are making the decisions are men of the city. Reactionary and revolutionary alike, they are the triumphant bourgeoisie that has swept all before it—except perhaps the wrath of the planet itself.

Tacitus once said of another empire, they create a desert and call it "peace." Of ourselves we might say, we create a wasteland of cities and call it the "modern world."

I must make it clear at the outset that all I say here in criticism of the city, I say as a city dweller born and bred. New York, Chicago, London, Los Angeles, San Francisco, and Berkeley . . . I have never lived for more than a few months outside such metropolitan areas. They are my world. I cannot even say that I love the city or hate it. I simply belong to it. By what right, then, do I presume to know that rural or primitive ways are "better"?

The answer is I don't. The little experience I have had of farms and raw wilderness has taught me that the world beyond the city can be severely demanding; I would not choose that world for myself nor romanticize its virtues. But nothing I say here assumes the existence of some one better way of life outside the city; less still that the city might be replaced by rustic bliss. What I do contend is that there have always been *different* ways of life other than city ways, and that these have contributed to the sustaining variety of our species, for each has drawn out some measure of our beauty, nobility, and heroism. My argument is that these different ways should be allowed to continue as authentic options. It is not my right, either by default or decision, to let the city crowd all other cultural choices off the stage of history—especially not now, as we begin to realize that our culture is so impractically extravagant that we dare not let it monopolize the planet.

The Urban Margin

The legend of Cain can teach us still more about the nature of the city. We recall that Cain was a tiller of the soil before he committed murder. After the crime, the Earth he worked upon was cursed by God and would not bear fruit for him. Cain, the first urbanite, had so estranged himself from God and nature that the very ground beneath his feet became barren. He could no longer provide for his own needs.

We find the first principle of urban economics epitomized in this image of guilty sterility. It reminds us that the city comes into existence by withdrawing people from the primary production of their life needs—fuel, food, raw materials. Those who leave the land must draw upon the labor of others, who might, after all, keep for themselves what the mouths of the city must eat. It was Cain who asked, "Am I my brother's keeper?" But after he fled to the city, who were Cain's keepers? All his brothers, left behind to work the land he had abandoned.

If a society is to have cities, there must be some measure of fat in its economy—a decent surplus that will permit significant numbers to do as Cain did: to leave off tilling the soil and take up some secondary work. Let us call this the *urban margin*—the crucial factor in the survival of cities. Without it, no society passes beyond the agrarian or pastoral level; where that margin withers away—as it often has in the course of previous civilizations—even the most magnificent cities fall into rubble. Their towers crumble, their temples are abandoned to the bat and the rat, their names pass from human memory. The city must have its margin; but what shall it offer in return? How is it to earn its keep?

More and more as I live out my days in the empire of cities, I find that question in my mind, not as a matter of abstract economics, but as a matter of conscience that bites into the ethical tissue of my daily life. *What am I doing to earn my keep? What are all of us doing in these cities that will pay our way?*

For think how much it costs to keep us alive in this churning urban machinery simply at the level of basic daily necessities. Try, for a moment, to imagine the array of special services, the vast administrative superstructures that must surround every one of our economic needs, if only to guarantee minimal health and welfare. Think of the life-sustaining traffic that must come and go between the source and the use of the goods that feed us, warm us in our homes, clothe us. Think how costly it is merely to remove our daily wastes. In the midst of this busy apparatus, we who fill the cities begin to look like so many million astronauts, hermetically sealed into some strange science-fiction vehicle that is constantly dependent on life-support systems of enormous expense and complexity. At every point, those who mediate the necessities of our survival are surely earning *their* keep; they may well deserve more than we pay them. If a hundred people must process and pass along the bread I eat at my table, all of them are supremely important to me. They keep me alive; they deserve their wages. And, in their eyes, the work I do is justified because it helps pay that wage. So, it would seem, we are all earning our keep.

Yet, there is a distinction we must make here which our city-biased economics too often ignores. It is one thing to decide what each of us justly deserves from our society for the work we do; it is another thing entirely to decide how much the planet itself can afford. Our individual getting and spending belongs to the market place, where any foolish stunt or novelty may fetch its price; but the urban margin belongs to the global environment, and that ledger severely discriminates the essential from the nonessential, the useful from the wasteful.

Conventional economic thought (and this includes a great deal of socialist economics whose adherents should know better) does not concern itself with that difference. It translates everything into exchange values—abstract cash quantities that blithely lump wheat and jelly beans together in the same accounting. For its purposes, a commodity is a commodity—just as jobs are jobs, and profits are profits. In the market place, one does not ask the morally pertinent question: Do the goods and services, employment and investments before us use the Earth's resources well or usefully? All that matters is the price they sell for. Or, if we are socialists, all that matters is their equitable distribution. In such an accounting, the wealth of nations would be increased if we were all profitably at work as hairdressers, history teachers, and penny-whistle carvers.

An economic science based on such premises easily leads us to believe that the urban margin can be extended indefinitely. Which is exactly the aim of the empire of cities. It is modern society's effort to urbanize the world, on the assumption that the industrial power of cities generates unlimited wealth, and thereby abolishes the old distinction between an economy of production on the land and an economy of consumption in the towns. Instead, the industrial city aspires to absorb all the factors of production into its ownership and control, and perfects their economic rationalization. It takes over the land itself. Its agricultural commissars and agrindustrial conglomerates become the world's most productive farmers. So it would seem that the more urbanism, the better, until at last the city has transformed the whole Earth into one integrated industrial system.

That is the prospectus, for example, of Constantinos Doxiadis, one of the most influential European urbanologists.

> Man [he tells us] is moving from the era of farming and small isolated villages to the era of urban systems. One or two generations in high income countries and five or six generations in lower income countries will see the elimination of villages. Everybody, including farmers, will live in urban systems whose location, birth, and growth are defined by the laws of Nature and Man.

Doxiadis' only concern is that this inevitable movement should be rationally and fairly planned to avoid shantytowns, oversized architecture, excessive dislocation. He looks forward cheerfully to the creation of a benign and efficiently organized "Ecumenopolis," the global city, which he estimates will concentrate nearly all the world's population on 5 per cent of the land area. As Doxiadis develops the idea, it has the sound of science fiction about it. But he only extrapolates from the commanding facts of the day. In a recent study done for the Brookings Institute, James Sundquist predicts that, by the end of this century, 60 per cent of the population in the United States will be concentrated in three massive conurbations, one embracing a T-shaped sector of the Midwest and Northeast from Chicago to Boston to Washington (117 million), one running from Sacramento to San Diego in California (34 million), one stretching from Jacksonville to Miami in Florida (13 million)—with the rest of the society living in only slightly less impacted metropolitan areas.

Somewhere at the core of this Faustian vision of a totally urbanized world, there is a solid and important truth. The industrial city *is* something new under the sun. It is not, like the cities of the non-European past, simply a ceremonial center, or market place, or seat of government. It may be all of these, but it is primarily a center of production; it expands the social wealth. It has been doing so ever since the weaving towns of medieval Flanders and northern Italy came into existence as places of specialized manufacturing. Even if, throughout the capitalist phase of their history, the urban-industrial societies have failed to distribute their riches fairly, the wealth has nevertheless been there. It is still there, and more of it than ever. That abundance, and the knowledge that has brought it into existence, are the bright promise of our age. They hold forth the prospect of unprecedented personal freedom, good health, and fulfillment for our entire species. But already, as we move through the second century of the urban-industrial process, we begin to see that there are liabilities which burden the urban promise. We are learning that there are, after all, limits to the urban margin. Two of these are now as familiar to us as the news of the day.

First, there is the maze of economic irresponsibility and social bad habits we call "pollution." Though our economic science has never adequately reckoned the cost, we now see that environmental deterioration has dogged every city in history—and all the more so the industrial cities of the past. Pestilence and subtle poisons accumulate in urban areas, taking a heavy toll in life and vitality—to the extent (so some historians speculate) of bringing down empires as mighty as those of the Romans and Mayans. In the past, however, when cities were small and vastly insulated by rural and wilderness areas, and when the general social pace of life was tied to an agrarian rhythm, it could be left to the Earth's natural systems to recycle the pollutants and buffer their global impact. Now, increasingly, the cities are running out of room to hide their garbage, and they cannot wait for natural processes to clean away the toxins. Some of our new atomic wastes require time of astronomical proportions for their safe disposal. No responsible economics any longer pretends that the price of cleaning up and protecting the environment can be ignored. But once that long hidden expense is taken into account, the urban margin is cut drastically. We begin to see that we are not quite as rich as we once thought—not if we continue to measure "progress" by the number of people a society can pack into an urban-industrial environment.

The second liability of urban expansion that now presses in upon us is the cost of organizational impaction, a factor that eventually catches up with all oversized institutions. There comes a point in their growth where administrative superstructure must sag of its own excessive weight. The mere problem of keeping track and keeping in touch ("data retrieval" and "information flow," as the systems engineers call it) begins to consume more time and personnel than does the direct provision of goods and services. Cities, as our biggest and most multifaceted organizations, now suffer this kind of bureaucratic obesity in the extreme. Too many people . . . too much area . . . too many responsibilities . . . at last, there are more supervisors and co-ordinators and overseers on the urban scene than productive workers.

In our cities today, municipal employees make up one of the largest categories of the work force—and still they must struggle to keep the social machinery in decent repair. How many more would it take to do the job adequately? In New York City, until the recent fiscal austerities of the mid-seventies began to pare their numbers back, municipal workers totaled well above 400,000—a veritable city within a city, three times the size of ancient Athens. Transport workers alone in New York total 33,000. Some of those on the urban payroll may make a direct contribution to the unique cultural qualities of the city, but they are a definite minority—a handful of librarians, museum curators, zoo keepers. Even if we were to include in this category New York's 60,000 schoolteachers (on the dubious assumption that they are doing something more culturally valuable than compulsory day-care and literacy training) it would still be the case that one out of every twelve working people in the largest American city is employed at nothing more creative or economically productive than transporting people, policing people, taxing people, licensing people, picking up the social casualties, and carting away the garbage. Yet, to finance this expanding universe of services and facilities, cities must cannibalize more and more of their resources, usually beginning with the moneys that would otherwise go toward culture, education, and the refinement of taste—the values that supposedly redeem the harshness of city life. It is the old paradox of the toll bridge. The more tolltakers there are, the higher the tolls . . . until finally the main reason for collecting the toll is to pay the tolltakers, and so the productive commerce on the bridge dwindles away. Meanwhile, on the other side of the desks and counters in the thousand offices where municipal services are so haltingly performed, the urban public may now be using more collective time waiting in line and filling out forms than it spends in front of symphony orchestras or great paintings.

Can the Earth Afford Us?

These liabilities of urban bigness are becoming more painfully vivid to us by the day, though, for the most part, our leaders and economists (and I daresay most urban intellectuals) are still at the stage of regarding them not as the absolute limits they are, but only as "problems" that can be solved by some clever financial maneuver or quick technological fix. But there is a third and deeper vice we have not yet fully recognized, one that lies at the heart of urban economics. The city has a peculiar way of corrupting the appetites of people. It awakens cravings that inevitably swell beyond anything the urban margin can support for more than a minority.

The way in which the city does this is intimately connected with some of the most precious qualities of urban culture. It is the unique cultural role of the city as a cosmopolitan center to open people to the variety of human possibilities. The city stimulates the desire to experience what others have known, to enjoy what others have created. It encourages people to *want* things—out of curiosity or envy. It fills their imaginations with fads and fashions that may change by the day, leaving much waste behind them. At the same time, even as it heightens the fantasy life of people, the city isolates them from the basic ecological facts of life in such a way that they cannot clearly judge the difference between wants and needs, necessities and luxuries. Their tastes may become refined to the point of absurd self-indulgence, if not neurotic obsession. Witness, for example, the passion we have cultivated in our society for phonographic precision—for exact accuracy of sound reproduction. From high fidelity to stereophonic to quadrophonic sound systems . . . an immense, specialized technology whose products now reach a dizzy level of extravagance. All of us could easily name a hundred more such bizarre, but widespread fascinations whose costs cannot help but to burden the urban margin. Yet, they have become commonplace expectations for those of us whose appetites no longer have any sensible relationship to land, labor, or resources. By the very fact that they are locked away from the Earth in an artificial environment, urbanites lose sight of the planet as a living entity with whom they must maintain an organic reciprocity. This is not a loss that can be made good by the brainpower of experts, because their experience is also bounded by the empire of cities. And even if some few among them fight their way free of that bias, they will never be a match for the sheer ecological ignorance of whole urbanized nations that live with no inner sense of ethical obligation to the Earth.

I think of this each day as I drive to work past a dismal industrial landscape of factories and plants that sully the sky and the waters of San Francisco Bay with their exhaust. In all these buildings there are people hard at work, earning their keep. Somewhere in the midst of their making and doing, the necessities of my daily life are being provided. But where? One must look closely, because the essential work they do is all but swallowed up by the smothering excess.

I pass a factory that employs hundreds of men and women. From its pipes and drains an oily film trails off across the bay. What are they making there? Pet food: chemically embalmed garbage in high-priced cans. Beside it there is another plant . . . it packages lipstick and eyeshadow. Further along are warehouses crammed with sporting goods, air conditioners, power mowers . . . and beyond these, open lots filled with "recreational vehicles" and "pleasure craft."

A truck thunders by me with two drivers aboard—a costly monster of a machine that leaves a cloud of expensive exhaust behind. Where is it going? To Denver, to deliver a ton of Kleenex and to bring back two tons of cupcakes.

Who are the people driving on all sides of me, one to a car, burning thousands of barrels of oil this morning to clock in at their jobs? Secretaries who shuffle papers for advertising firms that lay out millions of dollars to sell us perfumed bath oils in elegant jars . . . assembly-line workers who will spend the day putting tiny screws in the world's fastest selling four-speed hair drier . . . the assistant vice-president in charge of sales for a billion-dollar defense contractor that produces a line of plastic gadgets that go inside a sealed unit that makes up the central module of a machine that stamps out the printed circuits of a guidance system that will enable a missile to incinerate a city.

And here I am, racing along beside them, burning up as much gasoline as any. On my way where? To teach Tudor and Stuart history to students whose goal in life is to join the ranks of these secretaries and assembly workers—or, if they are very lucky, to become the assistant vice-president in charge of sales—so that they too may earn the money to buy the pet food and hair driers and sporting goods.

One morning of one day on one freeway in one city . . . how long can the Earth afford us?

Of course, the city I am driving through is an *American* city, and that makes it exceptional—but only to the extent that America's middle and upper classes can (with the help of heavy debt-financing) buy the frivolities that people in other societies can only gaze at longingly in the movies and television shows we export to them. Wherever in the world the magic industrial emporium opens its doors, people flock to its counters. Why should they not have everything I can have . . . and why should I not have everything David Rockefeller can have? The cult of competitive consumption seems to be the universal solvent of the modern world. Only the Chinese, the Albanians, and some of the new people's republics of Asia seem determined to hold out against the ethos of high consumption with some sense of responsible social discipline. But I think their virtue may be improvised out of stringent necessity and will last only as long as it is enforced by strict censorship. Certainly, the socialist nations of Eastern Europe (including the Soviet Union) have proved as susceptible to the lure of affluence as any capitalist society. Throughout the area, popular discontent with the shoddiness and paucity of Russian merchandise has created a lively black market in Western consumer luxuries. If anything threatens the Russian sphere of influence in its European satellites, it is not foreign espionage, but the subversive charms of American blue denim and Japanese transistor radios.

People do not cultivate these prodigal habits because they are perverse or incurably greedy. It is simply that, once they have been drawn into the orbit of the city, they lose touch with the limits and reciprocities that come naturally to a life lived close to primary production. How are they to judge the social value of food, water, energy, when they know these things only as commodities that wait in the stores to be bought, or which magically appear at the turn of a faucet, the flick of a switch? How are they to know what environmental burdens their waste creates, when the forces that govern their economy all but command them to consume, and then pack their waste out of sight before they can reckon its amount or damage? Of course, in the Western economies, commercial huckstering exploits that ignorance cruelly; but the ignorance was there in the first place as a condition of urban life.

The city has always generated extravagant appetites. Its economics, like its culture, is a fabric of abstractions and free fantasy that has less and less connection with ecological reality. That might be an affordable vice within the urban margin, provided the city remained what it has always been: a minority culture. On that scale, its industrial power might significantly enrich the human race, while its ecological costs could be easily absorbed. But when that power reaches out to take the entire planet into its economic designs, then we confront one of those stubborn historical snags Marx liked to call "contradictions." As the cities become bigger, the sum total of practical ecological sensitivity in the population diminishes, until we are at last asking what is economically impossible of the planet. Then, instead of increasing the wealth of the world, the urban-industrial establishment, by virtue of its administrative and organizational overhead, its environmental damage, its incorrigible voracity, begins to waste more than it produces.

The economy and the culture of the world need the city, but only in small doses. In turn, what the city needs, if its promise is not to be blighted, is to be surrounded by vital alternatives to itself, alternatives that can resist its extravagance and save it from overexpansion. Some of us in the city may just barely be able to see that need; but we cannot meet it out of our own capacities. City brains simply cannot gauge and guard the urban margin. There has to be another social interest in the world to do that, an independent rural and traditional alternative which we in the city must now deliberately re-create—not because we expect those alternative ways of life to be wiser than ours, but only because we know they will be *different* from ours, able to bring a contrasting perspective into the counsels of nations. We must free the land from the control of urban priorities and place it in the trust of those who wish to live outside the empire of cities as the human voice of our planet's organic discipline.

Deurbanizing the World

There would be little chance of deurbanizing the modern world if the millions that now flock to the cities *wanted* to be there. But we have more than enough evidence that urban life remains as much a minority taste as ever. And if that is so, then deurbanization is not something that need be *made* to happen; it need only be *allowed* to happen, as if by a natural gravity.

The very shape of megalopolis tells us the desires of our urban millions. It *sprawls*. It sprawls to cover whole seacoasts and continents. That structure is the social trajectory of people struggling to escape, to get "farther out" from the crime, congestion, dirt, and disease of the inner city. The slurb and the conurbation exist because there are so many who only come to the city for the work or the welfare they cannot find elsewhere. Given the least option, they will put as much distance between their homes and downtown as possible. Suburbia, with its dream of rustic ease, is as old as the industrial city; now in America, it makes up most of the people we count as "urban"—80 million of the country's 150 million greater metropolitan population; and it continues to grow faster than the central city. The suburb has never been a simple *addition* to the city, as in medieval times, when people would poke through the walls to extend the town. It has always represented the search for an entirely different quality of life. It seeks to be everything the inner city cannot be—a place of sunlight, clean air, grass, trees, peace and quiet. Above all, it promises a human scale of life, with friendly neighbors, privacy, security. Suburbia's favorite models are the village, the hamlet, the small town, even the farm and the ranch.

In most suburbs, of course, this bucolic imagery is little more than a deceptive promotional illusion. Too often, it comes down to a fake thatched roof and a fast-food franchise done up to look like a big red barn. Behind that thin veil of wishful thinking lies the same abrasive reality that fills every urban area. I have visited residential subdivisions called "Country Crossroads" and "Green Acres" built next to an international airport where the jets roar over every ninety seconds. I have walked through plush suburban shopping centers called "Old Orchard" where every store was a chain outlet and the mall was incessantly perfumed by the Mantovani strings. The pathos of all this is obvious. But illusions have their own significance. What suburban escapism represents is a vote *against* the city by people who remain economically bound to the city. It is a failed jail break on the part of a massive antiur-

ban constituency. And we can add other populations to its numbers: the inner-city residents who would be in suburbia if they
could afford the prices; the welfare families that have been
squeezed off the land by agricultural combines, or who came to
town only because their farms declined into rural slums; the alien
(often illegal) immigrants who have also come to the cities to escape the deepening rural poverty of their homelands. All these
are *in* the city, but they are not *of* the city. Just as the millions
who fill the cities of the third world are hardly authentic urbanites;
they are refugees from a decaying countryside which their governments now believe must be farmed for big cash crops by advanced,
Western techniques that are far too costly for small holders. Yet,
so poorly has this new agricultural technology kept up with the
rate of urbanization in the third world that nations everywhere in
Asia, Africa, Latin America (and for that matter in Western
Europe and the Soviet Union) have become progressively more
dependent by the year on food imported from North America,
most of which goes to feeding their hungry cities.

In a public opinion poll taken by the Federal Council on Environmental Quality in 1974, only 20 per cent of city dwellers said
they preferred to live in cities. Thirty-two per cent would choose
small towns, 31 per cent suburbs, and 20 per cent farms. Similarly,
in a poll taken in London by Research Surveys Ltd., no less than
three quarters of those polled in the central city declared that they
would prefer to live in suburban and rural areas. Their list of
grievances against the city would surprise no one; I imagine
it could be duplicated by surveys in every quarter of the world:
too much dirt, crime, traffic, noise, loneliness; too little security,
companionship, play space for children, fresh air.

We might add one more fact that suggests the frailty of the
city's grip on its people. In the United States, where the trend toward urbanization has been among the most pronounced in modern times, the most recent census figures (1976) show that there
has finally been a marked shift away from metropolitan areas toward small towns. Significantly, much of the movement has been
on the part of senior citizens who have gone off to spend their retirement in Florida, Arizona, or Colorado. It would seem that

when people in their later years finally have an open choice, many elect to leave the city. This is the same senior population whose less affluent members are apt to exchange their lives in the city for a mobile home and a continuing tour of rural areas and wilderness. Perhaps all they find in their belated exodus is a succession of crowded National Park campsites or a land developer's plastic Shangri-la in the sun. But clearly the city does not hold them.

We may be building Constantinos Doxiadis' Ecumenopolis, but I believe that we are building it against the human grain. The city has never been a way of life that appealed to more than a strict minority, nor should we expect it to be. It is a harsh, acquired taste. Until they are forced to it by economic necessity, most people will not become urbanites. If at last they are driven from the land, they come to the city as people first came to the factory towns two centuries ago—in defeat and desperation. And what do they find there when they arrive? Rescue, if they are lucky. Private charity, public assistance . . . perhaps in time a menial job. But very few are even that minimally fortunate. In America those who arrive in the city from Appalachia, from the Mississippi delta, from Puerto Rico, Mexico, Korea, and the Philippines are apt to become the first generation of a permanent welfare family.

Even more so, in the third world cities, only a bare fraction of urban emigrants ever enter the industrial work force. Venezuela is typical in this respect. There, more than half the population has now, very rapidly, become urban; but much less than 10 per cent of the urban migrants hold jobs. The rest beg and scramble in the streets for whatever they can get. The figures are as dismal every place else in the underdeveloped world. Across the globe, the word "city" is becoming synonymous with "slum," "ghetto," "shanty-town." Nor is there much hope that economic development European-American style can undo the social deterioration of forced urbanization. As Colin Norman has pointed out, it now costs $20,000 of investment to create one modern, capital-intensive job in an industrial economy. That is a cure the urban margin cannot afford. If the Chinese, as they claim, are uniquely avoiding the worst forms of urban wretchedness, it is because they have made a maximum effort to keep people on the land by bolstering the rural

economy. That is the policy Gandhi wanted for India, but his peas-
ant-centered economics, like his concern for labor-intensive technology, was (with much encouragement from Western experts)
quickly cast aside by the country's postliberation leadership.

For the few that have the wit, education, and initiative, the city
may offer promising careers. But for the rest, it offers only one
identity—that of the urban masses. That has never been an identity
people have voluntarily chosen. Yet, ironically enough, urbanization is very likely the most expensive social process ever developed
for keeping people poor and miserable. Even at the bare minimum
level, city living costs dearly. The industrial city is surely the most
exorbitant combination poorhouse, madhouse, and morgue in
human history.

How many of these discontented urban millions would return to
the land if they were given the realistic option? Suppose, in our
own country, in place of suburban illusions of farm and village, we
were to experiment with making the real thing available as a viable
choice, in the form of small-scale, but technologically well conceived family farming. Suppose as a matter of high public policy,
we were to offer people all the training, technical assistance,
loans, and subsidies they need to make the transition from urban
to rural life. What might the result be? We need not expect that
everyone would choose to till the soil, but we might see enough
people make that choice to provide the basis for an autonomous
rural economy where others would find their work in the villages
and towns that served the land. A farming population must also
have its doctors and dentists, its teachers and merchants, perhaps
even its theater company and orchestra, if it is to overcome the
isolation which has always been the bane of rural life in the past.
Here, I suspect, would be the sort of humanly scaled and secure
life people now seek in the suburbs, but it would have the reality
and independence that a mere dormitory community can never
claim.

We might then see a spectrum of choices open out which gave
us a far more varied world than we are now building within the
empire of cities. There would still be those who would elect to live
in the inner city. But outside that superheated industrial core,

there would be the open organic textures of small towns, rural hamlets, agrarian co-operatives, and family homesteads, where we would have what our world so desperately needs: a growing population in touch with the realities of primary production and the practical limits of the urban margin. As their numbers expanded, we might finally see the megalopolitan sphere of influence shrink back from the land and, in so doing, become what the true city has always been at its most humane—not a demographic monstrosity swarming with alienated masses, but the way of an often creative, sometimes zany, and always mercurial minority—a fascinating human energy constantly in need of cultural ballast from the rural world beyond its boundaries.

Who Owns the Land?

The trouble with most discussions of the city and its problems is their tendency to isolate the urban from the rural as if these were two separate spheres of discourse. Even worse, we often find urban and rural divided from one another in people's thought as if they were two historical epochs—one (the rural) belonging to the dying past, the other (the urban) representing modernity for as far as they can see. To think this way is to deprive the city of the only context within which its ailments can be healed. That hard separation creates the illusion that there is no longer any realistic place for people to be but in cities or suburbs; these are the deck, all else is the cruel sea. The whole project of saving cities then becomes a matter of ingeniously redesigning urban space to absorb more and more millions, and of finding ways to stretch the urban margin to infinity.

At the extreme, we come upon Paolo Soleri's schemes for repackaging urban sprawl into neat, megastructural ant heaps called "Arcologies." Or we have Gerard O'Neill's maniacally well researched proposal for orbiting cylinder cities in outer space where life will be free forever from the law of gravity. Or Nigel Calder's plans for city-sized geodesic domes floated out to sea on icebergs, enjoying a perfumed air supply and year-round springtime. Like Doxiadis' predictions, these too sound like sheer science fiction.

But they are not so intended. They are only meant to give some precise, imaginative shape to the forces that are now unfolding all about us in the empire of cities. What we have in these ambitious projections is simply the root assumption of all contemporary city planning writ large—namely, that the city must inherit the Earth, and that all its problems are problems of design and finance. But that is fundamentally wrong, because cities are not buildings or traffic patterns or municipal budgets. Cities are people. The problems of cities are the problems of people. And the basic problem of all cities today is that most people who live in them do not want to be there; they are not citified, they do not wish to be. That is why all the other ills of the city prove to be so intractable—because there is no way to save cities that are inhabited by people who hate cities and do not value their culture. Nor should any sane person want to solve such a pseudo-problem. Rather, we should say, "Those who wish to escape, let them escape. Let these people go."

The greatest contribution anyone can make to defending cities from their suicidal habits is to liberate those who wish to leave them. But we will find no way to do that unless we face the political issue of the land—its ownership, control, and use. The land is the vital context of all urban problems; it holds all our living alternatives to the empire of cities. Any urban policy, any city planning that does not begin with the politics of land reform misleads or deceives. Deurbanizing the world means freeing people from cities where they do not wish to live. But that, in turn, means freeing the land as a real economic and cultural option.

There are not more than a few areas of the globe—like Java or Belgium or Bangla Desh—where urbanism has been forced upon people by sheer overcrowding. In most parts of the world, the flight to the city leaves behind open land and deserted villages. The urban migration is a fact of politics, not a fact of population. The big city is a facet of the gargantuan style of industrialization; it exists as an emblem of modernization and as an instrument of centralized political control. If any economic force stands behind it, it is not demographic necessity, but the pressure of big agricultural technology, together with the tyrannical social planning that accompanies it. In our own country, one might add to these forces the concentrated, private ownership of land which acts deliberately to restrict rural alternatives. In America the land has not been used up; it has been *bought* up. It has not vanished under excessive population densities; it has simply gotten to be owned by fewer and fewer people. It is there, but it is fenced off and barricaded by law.

In America today, 70 per cent of our population lives on 2 per cent of the land. Those who live in our two hundred largest cities take up only .7 per cent of the land area. What lies outside that tiny urban island is hardly the wastes of Alaska and Death Valley. Rather, as any casual drive through open country will show, there are millions of tillable acres behind the fences often lying idle, doing nothing but being *owned* by absentee landlords—oil, timber, and mining companies, railways, realtors, land speculators. The main economic function of that land is to accumulate unearned increment, while paying notoriously little in the way of taxes as its value steadily increases. Millions of acres more is deliberately underused or misused by wealthy "tax-loss farmers" who have no serious interest in producing food, raw materials, or livestock, but only in harvesting some strategic tax write-offs, or in attracting government subsidies for land *not* being planted—a form of anti-agriculture that has become one of the most expensive "welfare" systems in our society. In the course of the 1960s alone, such generously subsidized nonproductivity transferred nearly $30 billion from the public treasury to firms like United Fruit.

All together, the congested condition in which we live in the United States has been brought about over the past fifty years by systematically squeezing 40 per cent of the farm population out of its livelihood. From 1940 to 1960, 22 million people left rural America for the cities, one of the largest migrations in modern times. The result is that some two thirds of all privately owned land in the country has come to rest in the hands of only 5 per cent of the population. As for our public lands—they have become an even more lucrative target for opportunistic interests: a honeycomb of franchises and concessions in logging, coal, oil shale, and uranium whose leases cover millions of acres.

Land reform is rarely thought of as an aspect of city planning and urban policy. Most Americans think of it as a cause associated with backward third world countries. Of course, it is a cause there. In the sense I write of it here—as a plea for an autonomous and decentralized rural society—it is a cause everywhere, even in many socialist nations whose politics is every bit as citified as our own. But land reform—taken as a catchall phrase for a vast array of social, fiscal, and tax policies—is also the undiscovered revolution in American politics. Its invisibility has everything to do with the negligence and ignorance of urban intellectuals where all things rural are concerned.

By and large, most urbanites, including the best educated, have swallowed all the propaganda they have been served about the efficiency of agrindustrial farming—just as they are more than willing to believe that if our farm population has been declining so rapidly, it must be because all these people have eagerly elected to enjoy the excitement and cultural rewards of the city. (*"How are you gonna keep 'em down on the farm after they've seen Par-ee . . ."* or New York . . . or Los Angeles . . . ?) They believe what the oil, energy, and timber companies tell them about the necessity of large-scale operations and the enlightened use big conglomerates make of their gigantic franchises. Finally, they are convinced that we have become an urban society because there simply isn't anyplace else for people to be but in cities; the land is completely taken up with the needs of our survival.

But, in truth, they know nothing about the land; they have no idea who owns it or in what quantities; they are totally ignorant of how land development (or deliberate nondevelopment) is financed and taxed (or not taxed). They know nothing of the criminal interests that have gone into land speculation, recognizing it as one of the choicest plums in our economy precisely because it is protected by such a depth of public ignorance. When it comes to the economics of land, it is our urban millions who are the gullible rubes and hayseeds. For the land is still the basic wealth of the world; agriculture remains one of our country's biggest businesses, one of our largest earners of foreign exchange in the world market; real estate speculation continues to be what it was in George

Washington's day—one of the nation's crookedest and most profitable games.

Exploring this expertly constructed labyrinth of corruption and special privilege might require the attention of a small army of specialists. But, at last, it all comes down to a single social fact: The land has been stolen from the people as outrageously in America as in any banana republic. It has been stolen from them at their own expense, and they are paying the price for that theft every day in a thousand different ways. They pay for it in the price of their food, in their rent, in their property and income taxes. They pay for it in soil erosion and pollution, in rural slums and welfare. But they are paying for it in one major and economically incalculable way that is shaping the entire course of modern history. The vast agglomeration of private landownership is one of the major reasons why we have become a society of big, dehumanized urban areas; it is one of the main forces that has built the empire of cities. People did not leave the land willingly or under the pressure of abstract economic necessity. They were bribed, cajoled, muscled, duped, and driven off the land. And they are still being driven off. As of the mid-seventies, the American farm population is down to a mere 8 million people, less than 4 per cent of the population, and still dropping; since 1970 alone, the net loss has been 1.5 million, each year another 2,000 families joining the fateful migration. They are not always replaced by some supposedly more efficient form of agriculture that comes forward to feed the hungry world. Often, their place is taken by sterile land speculation or mere urban sprawl. Every day in America, the cities eat up another three thousand acres of land. That much tillable soil—easily enough for at least a dozen family farms—disappears under suburban subdivisions, highways, parking lots, urban flood control projects, and airports. There are some knowledgeable students of the subject I have talked to who estimate that that much land, if it is reasonably fertile, and if methods of intensive cultivation are used, could support between sixty and a hundred families and leave eggs and extras to sell.

Even where big agriculture moves in to take over, it is the world's most expensive, most ecologically ruinous form of farming.

Since the end of World War II, big American agriculture has increased its use of high-polluting petrochemical fertilizer by nearly 700 per cent, while the amount of land under cultivation has actually shrunk by 16 per cent. It is estimated that it costs Americans ten to twelve petrocalories to produce one food calorie. In China, where more traditional methods survive, the investment is two petrocalories. To raise one acre of corn, American farmers currently use eighty gallons of oil. Given the rising costs of petroleum, this is luxury farming indeed. Yet, this is the style of agriculture which American oil and chemical companies are now exporting to the underdeveloped nations through the World Bank as the "Green Revolution," the solution to world famine. Wherever that "revolution" is introduced, it has the same effect as in our own country. Big farms replace small ones, and the peasants are driven into the cities to become urban masses, many of them starving squatters.

And here is the special irony. In many cases, giant conglomerates and combines like the American Tenneco, which farms 1.8 million acres in California and Arizona with publicly subsidized irrigation water, report heavy losses for their farm income. Their profits do not come from farming but from tax write-offs, vertical consolidation of food processing and distribution, or from the speculative increase in land values.

It is true that the heavily mechanized techniques such firms use have enormously enhanced the amount of production per capita of farm labor. But per capita production is the *only* criterion by which they qualify as more "efficient" than small-scale farming, and that is obviously an irrelevant criterion in a world where people go begging for employment. We do not need to "save" labor on the land. On the contrary, we can grow more food per acre, of a higher quality, with less use of chemical fertilizers, pesticides, and expensive machinery, by simply returning people to decently sized family farms.

A century ago, the robber barons of the railway industry swindled our society out of millions of acres of public land. Today, after one hundred years of litigation, railroads still hold over 20 million acres of some of the best land in the country. Standard Oil of Indiana alone holds another 20 million acres. The major paper corporations own another 100 million acres in the southern states. Here in our own country, just this handful of corporations owns a land area larger than nations the size of Spain or Japan. There is nothing technically or economically unrealistic about land reform, in either the developed or the underdeveloped countries. If this issue is not normally addressed by urban policy or city planning, it is only because—as these astonishing figures make clear—it is politically explosive. It is no less so in socialist societies where agriculture is under the control of commissars who are addicted to the same oversized and overcentralized style of farming as are America's corporate managers. All of us who live in megalopolis are the prisoners of fetishistic bigness—on the land and in the city. Big profits, big power, big technique, big markets. The walls that surround the modern city are invisible barriers of selfish interest and pathological economics.

Farming the Cities

And in the meantime . . . until those walls crumble, until the policies arrive that will liberate the land from the empire of cities . . . what are we to do?

Here and now, we who live in the cities must begin to loosen our parasitic grip upon the planet. We must find ways to earn our keep, even before deurbanization restores an authentic rural economy to the land.

It is an odd fact that concerned ecologists who worry about the future of the world food supply tend to write off the cities as barren space inhabited by incorrigibly extravagant people who can be nothing but consumers and wasters. That, of course, is the current fashion, especially in the United States, where according to one estimate, the acreage our cities squander on lawns, golf courses, and cemeteries could raise enough food to guarantee a nation the size of India against famine. In an automobile-dependent city like Los Angeles, about half the land area has been given over to the automobile in the form of freeways, streets, and parking lots. It is estimated by the British Civic Trust that there are a quarter million acres of arable land in the cities of Great Britain, enough to grow

25 million tons of potatoes each year; but it is lying unused, fenced off, derelict. If we grant that urban space *must* become barren land, then the figures are astonishingly bleak for the future of the world food supply. In America, for example, over the last two centuries, nearly a quarter of a billion acres of cropland has been "lost" from cultivation to the growth of cities. And, as we have noted, the urban invasion continues to advance at the cost of three thousand acres per day. But if I think no further back than World War II, I can recall an ephemeral urban folkway called the victory garden. In the neighborhoods where I lived during the war years in central Chicago, back yards and open lots everywhere were under cultivation even at a time when working people were fully employed and putting in a great deal of overtime, or working on swing shifts and graveyard shifts. Still, they found time for their gardening and (in my experience) regarded it as a rewarding occupation. At the peak of the war effort, in 1943, there were over 20 million home gardens in American cities. For the four-year period 1942 to 1946, such urban farming produced 24 million tons of food valued at over $4 billion.

There is something else I remember from that period which represented a significant difference from the prodigal ways cityfolk have lately taken up: the scrap drives of the day. Every block in town had its red-white-and-blue depositories for the collection of metal, paper, rubber, light bulbs, and even kitchen grease. Once each week, my schoolmates and I would be dismissed from classes early to take our wagons through the streets and alleys to pick up the scrap that people would put out for us. There were prizes for the kids who brought in the biggest haul, and their pictures might be run in the neighborhood shopping news.

All this was called the war effort, and it was undertaken as a patriotic duty—probably much the way the Chinese today practice a heroic national thrift. But then, soon after the war ended (the last strong government appeal for home gardening came in 1947), the scrap drives and the victory gardens faded away as quickly as if somebody had pushed a button. Somebody had. In the board rooms of the major corporations, in the offices of Madison Avenue, it had been decided that the age of "affluence" had arrived and that America (or at least middle- and upper-class America) would now set the world standard for high industrial consumption. Wartime thrift would be submerged in the ethos of the giveaway quiz show; the victory gardens would be displaced by the supermarket; the scrap drive would yield to Cadillac tailfins and disposable everything. For the next twenty-five years, the whole science of professional economics in the United States was devoted to proving that waste was virtue, thrift was evil, and that the urban margin was without limit because the world could never possibly run out of anything.

It was not really exceptional that people found the time and space to carry on urban horticulture during the war. The exceptional circumstance is how quickly the practice ended afterward. For as long as there have been cities, people have carried on at least some marginal kind of husbandry in whatever space they could set aside. In English cities the kitchen garden is as old as London. In Paris roof farming is a venerable working-class custom. The vacant lot, the back yard, the roof, the window box, the shed have long been taken by urbanites as the opportunity to plant a few fruit trees or a small vegetable crop, to keep chickens or pigeons, rabbits or bees, to raise snails or shellfish, to cultivate some herbs or spices, perhaps even to graze a goat on the family garbage. In the nineteenth century English milltowns were using hogs as street cleaners; they were fattened on the municipal waste and then slaughtered for food.

Customs of this kind have been an ancient and integral part of the urban tradition—until now. Now, certainly to most Americans and Europeans, it must all seem odd and faintly barbarous to put urban space to such organic uses. The fashion that has been set by the most advanced industrial nations is to make the city wholly sterile and as remote from its sources of food and fuel as possible— as if what high industrial efficiency required was the utmost circumvention of obvious economic connections. Everything must now pass through the cash nexus and be mediated by special services and lines of supply. All we live by must come to us packaged; it must be wrapped, tinned, foiled, bottled, boxed, cartoned, canned, cellophaned, sealed by package within package within package . . . a practice that has made packaging the fourth largest industry in the economy and the largest part of our solid wastes.

As if by divine fiat, our cities seem to have been forbidden to raise any part of their own food. Rather, they must cover their soil with concrete, asphalt, or lawn (preferably lawn that needs the attention of power mowers and chemical fertilizers). If there are parks, let them be landscaped, but never cultivated. If animals are kept, let them be pets that live off special, highly expensive, canned diets. At the same time, all that the city consumes must become garbage to be collected, burned, or buried at enormous expense. None of the nonorganic waste is to be recycled—a word that has only lately entered our industrial vocabulary under pressure from the environmentalists. On the other hand, if the environmental "lobby" (as it is called . . . but for *whom* is it lobbying?) wins its point and we elect to salvage this waste, the task must be done by an elaborate technology invented to do the sorting and saving that could be done by hand in every kitchen. As for the organic wastes—these are to be run through the garbage disposal and washed into the nearest river or lake where, in time, they will produce costly problems of eutrophication. Under no circumstances must they be composted into soil and fertilizer, for then who would buy all the high-priced chemical substitutes Dow and Du Pont have concocted for us?

One need only list these practices to recognize their patent absurdity. They are the rules of a mad economics whose purpose is to turn the city into a completely artificial and dependent environment. More so than the simple demographic fact of increased urbanization, it is this unwholesome style of modern city life that makes us so ecologically vulnerable. For we come more and more to live as if the concrete beneath our feet separated us from the Earth by a thousand barren miles. It doesn't. The soil is still there, available for us in our yards, parks, vacant lots. It is only a few inches away under the asphalt, just as the water and fertilizer for an urban husbandry is no further off than the garbage dump and the sewers. The only real barrier that stands between our cities and the soil is the economic style of societies that have identified "modernization" with urban sterility.

The Internal Frontier

But now, there are signs of change—small but significant signs. Today, in a number of American cities, a resourceful contingent of urban ecologists is trying to break through that barrier. I have in mind groups like the Community Environmental Council of Santa Barbara, California; the Institute for Local Self-reliance in Washington, D.C.; the Briarpatch Network on the San Francisco peninsula; the Urban Farmers of Berkeley—to name only the most visible and best-organized efforts I have come upon. Here are people who are rediscovering the farm and the village in the midst of the city. They have developed systems of back yard composting and intensive cultivation that will allow a family to grow most of its own fruit and vegetables on an average-sized city lot. They have found ways to farm the rooftops and are experimenting with aquacultures and hydroponics that allow food to be raised in a nearly self-contained ecological cycle. They have discovered that a supplementary diet of sprouted beans and grain, which can be raised in basements and kitchen containers, will provide more nutritional sustenance than most of the embalmed food we bring home from the supermarket. They are working out networks of neighborhood barter in goods, tools, and know-how that can make communities out of otherwise isolated strangers.

At this point, there is no telling how far these experiments can extend the urban margin; in the densest part of the inner city their role may be limited—unless we can imagine banning the automobile from our streets and taking up the pavements and parking lots to plant the land beneath as neighborhood commons. But I think those who dismiss such efforts to farm the city are victims of treacherous corporate propaganda. For the city does not destroy the soil; it only covers it over, often in ways that are plainly less valuable than it would be to use the land for horticulture and husbandry.

If we do not recognize that fact, it is mainly because we now see urban land through a thick haze of speculative property values which can make it more profitable for the owners to let land lie idle as open lots than to sell it off or put it to use. But profit is not the same as social value. That is what enlightened city planners are coming to recognize as they recommend policies of "planned shrinkage" and "urban intensification" within our cities. Their objective is to check the urban sprawl by concentrating residential areas and their costly social services within more economical units, while allowing the land to become attractive open space. Even in cities as densely populated as New York, there are areas like the South Bronx which have become deserts of burned-out housing and abandoned streets. In cities all over the world, there are such waste spaces and blighted enclaves where no one will live or go walking. They ordinarily fall to the most marginal uses—dumping grounds, warehouses, automobile graveyards. . . . In reality, their main economic value is simply to be *owned* by interests, who hope, in time, to reclaim their unearned increment if the area is ever renewed.

Within a program of planned urban compaction, how nicely these areas would dovetail into the designs of our urban farmers. They could feed the poorest thousands on organically grown foods that would need no fertilizer more expensive than composted garbage and no transport whatever to reach the tables of consumers. They are an internal frontier that promises us a way to deurbanize our world without first requiring people to leave the city. Instead, we work our way *through* the city and out the other side, bringing people an experience of the Earth and its ways that begins no further away than the nearest soil they can find or liberate.

The Responsibility of Intellectuals: A Postscript on Urban Imperialism and the Planetary Emergency

As I look back over what I have written in the preceding chapter, I realize how Utopian my proposals may seem to many in the intellectual and academic community. I am arguing that, at the highest level of historical endeavor, defending the rights of the person and the planet demands that we repeal the urban-industrial dominance. And that means scaling back our cities, liberating the land from their imperial grip, re-creating a vital rural life and autonomous wilderness. But what have I come up with as a way forward toward that goal? An appeal for an esoteric cause called "land reform" *in America* . . . a few fledgling efforts at urban horticulture and neighborhood self-reliance . . .

Needless to say, if causes and activities like this are to have any effect, they must be placed within a full context of fiscal and economic policies that involve nothing less (in the Western capitalist societies) than a massive transfer of landed wealth that is now in the hands of major corporate interests whose selfishness and benightedness know no limit. I fully recognize that necessity; it is exactly what my appeal for land reform assumes. But this great campaign will do nothing to roll back the empire of cities if it is not grounded in a new sense of our organic reciprocity with the land and a firm determination to rebuild the nonurban cultures of the world. I am convinced that creating that guiding sensibility must begin to make itself felt here and now in practical, accessible ways that will wean the urban millions from the culture and economy of cities. What our city masses need—and perhaps their intellectual leaders and political spokesmen still more—is the vivid, daily experience of alternatives to the urban artificiality and dependency that have for so long shaped them to the urban-industrial dominance. They need a discipline and a work that will put them in touch with an intelligent ecology. It was Gandhi's wise approach always to keep his followers and himself close to the spinning wheel and the ashram, in order that they might keep a sense of community and their powers of self-sufficiency steadily in mind; otherwise, what would their campaign for independence make of them but another nation of urban masses?

So, here, I turn to these homely experiments—better ways to use our back yards and rooftops, better things to do with our garbage —knowing that my critical opposition includes something even more formidable than the business and governing elites of our society. It includes the very intellectual community in which these words must find their readers. For, at last, the fact must be confronted that we—those of us who write books and read them—*we* are the most militant defenders of the urban-industrial dominance. Even more than cities serve the interests of corporate elites, they serve *our* peculiar interests. That sociological fact has everything to do with how "practical" and "realistic" any proposal for scaling down the cities will ever be *allowed* to seem as it passes through the critical filter of our minds and out into the general public awareness.

Many class interests converge upon the wealth and power of the city, but there is one interest which has buried itself so deeply in the city that it has made itself invisible to all criticism: the interest of intellectuals as the aboriginal urban class. The culture of cities is so peculiarly *theirs*—their creation, their addiction—that the drive of the city to expand and govern dissolves for them into a supposition of the conventional wisdom. Whatever other powers and privileges it may further, the empire of the city is the empire of the intellectuals.

The city as a class interest—that much has always been implied by the very word "bourgeoisie"—the burghers, the people of the towns. Within the framework of medieval society, the towns stood as an estate of the realm, a discrete social interest so embattled by rival forces that they had to raise walls to protect themselves. But then, from the point at which the cities grew wealthy and independent enough to break the power of the old aristocracy, modern sociology has more and more exclusively concerned itself with probing the internal divisions of the city itself. From here forward, the once unified townsfolk are discriminated into haves and have-nots, and the word "bourgeoisie" comes to mean the owning and ruling class *within* the cities, the capitalist guild masters and entrepreneurs. The age-old division between town and country, rural and urban, comes to be seen as a receding and atavistic social fact. The landed interest becomes the rear-guard action of a waning aristocracy or the mere inertia of stubborn peasants resisting the tide of modernization. In time, the land is bought up by city money and turned into another factor of production, and so, like all other forms of industrial capital, it is assimilated to the class struggle of urban worker against urban owner. Thus, it goes unnoticed that beneath the classes that come and go, at one time or another dominating the economy of the land, there is *the land itself* and all the life it has always supported. Besides the sociology of class relations in the countryside, there is the ecology of human relations with the land—an intercourse that cannot be treated as people treat machines or factories or cash. For the Earth is not merely a factor of production; she is a living thing that makes an ethical claim upon our loyalty. Our identity is organically woven into her history; she has generated us out of herself, nurtured, shaped, and sustained us. And she will be heard.

All this is what people forget when they cut themselves off from the soil and take to the city. It is what has been wholly neglected by the dominant radical ideologies, all of which stick fast to the conflict of industrial classes within urban society. To that narrow focus they assimilate all other social tensions like so many vibrations circling out from one center. But while this familiar and by now classic antagonism holds our attention, another, no less consequential class division opens out in every quarter of the modern world: the division that pits all urbanites, rich and poor alike, against everything and everybody that stands outside the boundaries of urban culture and economy. The rural, the traditional, the primitive, the natural environment as a whole—all these have become the exploited proletariat of urban society. The city lives off their life's blood, in many cases confronting them not simply with oppression but with absolute extinction.

As things now stand, the chances are that, by the end of this century, every premodern culture, every remaining stretch of untainted wilderness will have fallen before the arrogance and ignorance of the city. The Pygmies and Bedouins will be gone, the tigers and the eagles . . . gone forever, along with countless other cultures and species. We are living through the most rapid and massive extermination of life-forms and cultural traditions in history. It is happening to provide the cities with their food, their fuel, their luxuries and raw materials: the leopard skin coat on the celebrity's back, the coffee in every working man's cup. We have no word like "racism" or "sexism" for this form of exploitation. Perhaps, from now on when we hear the bland sociological term "urbanism," we should listen for its imperialistic overtones.

I am reminded of a passage in *The Communist Manifesto* that speaks volumes about the subliminal class interest of intellectuals. Like all the major ideologues of their time, Marx and Engels were intensely citified minds. In their eyes, only two significant classes existed: the bourgeoisie and its work force, making ready for the revolutionary apocalypse. The rest—including all the world's peasants and primitives—were mere cultural relics with no role to play except to be swept along behind the vanguard of the urban proletariat, "the class that holds the future in its hands." As for "nature"—the word appears in the Marxist corpus only as an abstraction meaning economic necessity or material reality. What else could it mean to men who could have only seen a tree or a bird on a Sunday walk through Hyde Park? So, in the *Manifesto,* it stands as an indisputable contribution to social progress that

the bourgeoisie, by the rapid improvement of all instruments of production, by the immensely facilitated means of communication, draws all, even the most barbarian nations into civilization. . . . The bourgeoisie has subjected the country to the rule of the towns. It has created enormous cities, has increased the urban population as compared with the rural, and has thus rescued a considerable part of the population from the idiocy of rural life. Just as it has made the country dependent on the towns, so it has made barbarian and semibarbarian countries dependent on the civilized ones, nations of peasants on nations of bourgeois.

". . . the idiocy of rural life." There we have the world as seen from the reading room of the British Museum. The cool arrogance of the words reminds us how completely the dominant radical movements of our time have been overshadowed by the sensibility of urban intellectuals. Even the figures we accept as great spokesmen of peasant revolution—Mao, Castro, Che Guevara, Fanon, Ho Chi Minh—have been urban intellectuals, wholly committed to the culture of the cities. Is that not why they have been so widely granted the right to speak for the peasant billions of the third world? Because they speak *our* language—the language of the city, the language of social theory and ideological analysis. They confront us with that certain commanding authority—meaning the mark of the university classroom, the sidewalk café, and the morning newspaper. They are men who speak from books and through books. That is the certification they bring to their revolutionary mission: They come to the people bearing the revolutionary word —in print. Yes, they take the rural masses into their ideological designs, but only as a necessary and strictly preliminary instrument of power, an organizational base for national power and "the great leap forward" into urban-industrial development. Like every progressive intellectual (and, indeed, like every capitalist technocrat) they know that the traditional, the primitive, the nonhuman things of the Earth are so much grist for the mills of modernization. Their cause may be that of the wretched of the Earth; but their world view is that of the industrial city. When their revolutions have succeeded, when the forces of European imperialism have withdrawn their last soldier and their last dollar of controlling capital from their conquered colonies, the cities of the old imperial powers will remain—and more will be built in their image.

There have been only a few radical intellectuals who have shown the willingness to defend the dignity of traditional ways and to lay a critical edge against the empire of the cities. Significantly, they are the voices that belong to the Third Tradition—to the cause of the person. Kropotkin, Tolstoi, Gandhi, Danilo Dolci—these and a scattered handful of anarchist philosophers have summoned up the humility to question their own intellectual foundations.

Now, what I write here is an appeal for just that kind of humility addressed to all of us who thrive on the culture of cities, because the problem of urban imperialism is peculiarly the problem of intellectuals. It is *our* problem, the people who deal in ideas. For us, the city enriches the life of the mind as no other social form ever has. We *need* the city and *use* the city for what it most distinctly offers: limitless inquiry, creative experimentation, the rapid exchange of issues and information. Yet, even as we toil to augment these indisputable values, we automatically transform our cities into the brain trusts of the world. We give them a monopoly over the means of cultural production and distribution—the press, the media, the educational institutions, the sources of information and research. Literacy itself is, after all, an urban invention, as are science, scholarship, the very notion of professional intellect.

Inevitably, then, it is the mind of the city—this mind that has spent so little time in dialogue with the rhythm of the seasons, the ways of the soil, the language of wild things—that comes to interpret history, nature, society. The facts, the news, the issues—all must be what urban intellectuals say they are. The studied powers of articulation and persuasion are more and more concentrated in their control until everything beyond the city comes to seem mute, pathetic, stupid. It cannot speak for itself . . . or rather, it cannot make itself heard. How can it even enter the arena of debate when that arena is the very city which menaces the survival of all that is nonurban? History—meaning history as the city records it—saves only a small, quaint corner for the unlettered and unbookish who have risen to protest the cause of the nonurban world. How do we remember John Ball, Guillaume Cale, Chief Crazy Horse, Nestor Makhno, José María Morelos, Emiliano Zapata, and all the other Jacques Bonhommes and John Namelesses of the past? Examples of inarticulate and futile violence . . . sad, backward eddies in the running stream of history. As Eric Wolf has put it, voicing the orthodox radical view: "peasants in rebellion are natural anarchists" and, as such, they are "anachronistic."

Even if, from time to time, a few of our artists and thinkers abscond to some rustic enclave of the world or an appealing patch of wilderness, their work is still tied to the city for public attention and critical appraisal. If they took up residence in caves and trees, they would, in their very persons, in the needs of their life's work, still be outposts of citified intellect. Many intellectuals have genuinely or condescendingly praised natural ways and simple folk. But the charms intellectuals find outside the city have always become talking points in an urban discourse: something to report upon or analyze before an audience of fellow intellectuals. Virgil composed his *Bucolics* for Roman patricians; Rousseau rhapsodized the noble savage in the most fashionable Paris salons. Even Tolstoi, who fervently longed for an anonymous life among the muzhiks, remained, in spite of himself, the world's greatest novelist, bound to an international reading public that adored him all the more for his homely virtues. As an urbanite, everything I know about traditional society, I have learned from anthropologists who taught me to see the limits of my own culture and the dignity of primitive folk. But I have never heard of a single anthropologist who decided to go native. The cultural wind never blows in that direction; the admiring observers all come back to the university to write their monographs and hone their methodologies to a keener edge—just as all the nature poets and landscape painters send their work back to the metropolis to be appreciated.

Tolerance, breadth of vision, catholicity of taste—these are the cosmopolitan virtues. That is what cities are all about. But to study is not to *be;* to appreciate is not to belong. No question but that study and appreciation are worthy pursuits. But what happens when the city, which is the peculiar culture of intellectuals, begins to diminish the human and natural variety? At that point, the city, which rewards its people with so many rare intellectual prizes, becomes a lethal force that takes more than it gives.

It is a central thesis of Marxism that, when the class struggle reaches "the decisive hour," a small contingent of the bourgeoisie will "cut itself adrift and join the revolutionary class." Marx identifies these renegades as "a portion of the bourgeois ideologists, who have raised themselves to the level of comprehending theoretically the historical movement as a whole." That dramatic transfer of allegiance has happened often enough; almost all the revolutionary movements of modern times have been generaled by middle-class leaders. But from the viewpoint of a "historical movement" Marx himself never comprehended, the leadership of the bourgeois ideologists has had calamitous results. It has imposed upon every form of revolutionary discontent the values and sensibilities of intellectuals who have never reflected critically upon their own deeper class interest. With the exception of Gandhi, we have yet to see a major revolutionary leader who has been prepared to dissociate from the cultural imperialism of the city. That, at last, is where the class loyalty of the intellectuals sticks fast. As ardently as they may believe in justice, they believe even more tenaciously in the city—to the point of assuming it must surely be the means of achieving all good things. After all, the city is the repository of knowledge; and that, as the modern world has learned, is the key to power—the only power most intellectuals can ever expect to wield.

We live in a world where cities grow bigger and bigger, and where urban intellectuals grow smarter and smarter. Nothing could be more difficult for any intellectual to believe than that there could be something seriously and radically wrong with a cultural style that allows intellectuals to become so very smart. Does not the very possibility of criticizing the city for its liabilities imply the knowledge of something more, something beyond the city? The page through which I speak to you—the bound and printed word before your eyes—is a product of urban culture, as am I, who now presume to recriminate the city for its vices. The city has brought us a vast knowledge of other times, other places. We overflow with ideas and issues. But with every passing generation, there is less that anybody can *be*—except a subject or satellite of urban culture. The Eskimos cannot be Eskimos any longer, the forests cannot be forests, the whales cannot be whales. Everything succumbs to the empire of the cities, and all the alternatives we study become merely academic.

My appeal here has been for vital options beyond the city. But that is not all I speak for. I also appeal for the city itself as only an intellectual can. The colossalism of the city does not simply spell the end of traditional society and free wilderness; it is the death knell of true urban culture as well. As sincerely as they may believe that the culture of the cities is the essence of civilized life, intellectuals must come to see that, when all the world is urbanized, there will be no real cities left. Already we see our finest cities oozing away into the amorphous demographic swamps we call urban areas.

In the introductory history courses I teach, I make a point of pausing in my discussions of the great cities of the past: ancient Athens, medieval Paris, Renaissance Florence. I ask my students how big they think these cities were. Invariably, those who have not been told otherwise will guess that they must have numbered millions. In fact, the three cities together may not have made up a population of more than a half-million, give or take Athens' few score thousand slaves. By our standards, they were small towns; yet, the culture they created is immortal, as astonishing an achievement as any artist or intellectual could ask of a city.

There is a lesson in this fact that has much to do with redeeming the city from its imperialistic sins. Clearly, cities do not need to be big in order to be vital. On the contrary, they can swell to gargantuan size and yet have no culture whatever, beyond what they import ready-made from New York and Europe, or glean from the mass media. All that the culture of cities has ever required is a small nucleus of authentically citified minds—meaning, people who nurse a peculiar hunger for incessant intellectual action, the clash of ideas, the fast turnover of tastes and values. These are the people who make full use of the city's potentialities, and there need not be many of them to produce a living culture. A few hundred thinkers, artists, and students will do, along with a few thousand people more to provide patronage, criticism, appreciation. We can find such types today in some corner of almost every city that is not merely a real estate speculator's façade. They crop up in the Bohemian quarter or around the local university. They haunt the bookshops, the libraries, the theaters, the art galleries. They may not take up more than a few streets where they find some hospitable cafés or public houses; but wherever they gather, they create a fertile space in the midst of the daily commerce. And that is where the culture of the cities blossoms, if it blossoms at all.

Intellectuals and artists are never more than a relative handful in the urban populace, but it is their kind, along with the merchant, the moneylender, and the artisan, who invented the city. All these joined forces because they thrive upon a lively commerce of goods, cash, ideas. They are a special, somewhat frenetic breed who relish living in a speeding traffic of mental and monetary abstractions. They generate enormous nervous energy and, all too frequently, they burn out fast. The world they create around them in the city is endlessly exhilarating, but it is no place to look for models of sane and healthy balance. It attempts too much and moves too quickly; its inhabitants easily lose their way in the constant blizzard of possibilities and distractions.

That is the other and darker side of the culture of cities. In return for its intellectual stimulation, city life exacts a high price of its people. Its freedom encourages every kind of eccentricity and psychotic license. Precisely because its citizens live in artificial environments filled with their own abstractions and exaggerated concerns, the city is easily consumed by collective hallucinations. It gets carried away with its own fantasy life and weakens toward erratic fluctuations of temperament. Extremism is the peculiar vice of urban culture: the cannibalism of ideas by ideas.

We must add to this inherent instability the troubling fact that there has never been a city that did not have its underworld and its tenderloin—its lawless fringe where the lunatic, the criminal, the charlatan, and sometimes the genius congregate. The cutthroats come to the city to find victims and the shelter of anonymity. The scoundrels and madmen come to find a gullible public in the turbulence of the market place; they may even rise overnight to become celebrities and messianic leaders preaching great causes, great hatreds. And then, for certain, blood will run in the streets. In the history of cities, riot, war, witch hunts, persecution, blood vengeance, savage factionalism take up as much space as the city's contribution to rationality and civilized good manners. There have been few cities that were not hotbeds of paranoia, prepared to massacre their enemies on all sides and tormented within by vicious dissension. If the nation-governing cities of our own day are less often torn apart by political violence than those of Renaissance Italy, it is because they now store their furies up for wars of a global scale.

The city has always been a mad and murderous place to live—hardly a place we should expect to see chosen by more than an eccentric minority. Its volatile combination of creative forces and destructive passion suggests an image that may help us understand the proper role of that minority in the history of our planet. We may borrow a metaphor from the sciences and say that the city is a *laboratory* where our race experiments with its most powerful form of energy—the human imagination. In the city, imagination is given the free play it can enjoy no place else. It has more raw experience to work with and can mix it with nearly arbitrary abandon to produce the most ingenious or monstrous concoctions. That is why the city is no fit judge of its own actions. From the urban intellectual's viewpoint, every latest idea, every scintillating new inspiration that flashes through the journals or takes the academies by storm may look like the secret of limitless progress, the one sure way to steer the course of history. But for every wise and durable contribution it has made to the human repertory, the culture of cities is strewn with a hundred castoff fashions, each the passion of a decade . . . or of an hour. The city lives by the thrill of the moment, the book of the month, the man of the year.

Like every dangerous experiment, the city needs to be tightly contained; it simply cannot be trusted with the entire planet as its laboratory. Its sensibilities are too unstable, its perspectives too short. Our cities need to become once again what they have traditionally been: small centers of inventive intensity safely buffered by a larger, nonurban culture that will balance their extremes. We have reached a point in our history where no one can any longer dispute the world-shattering power of organized urban intellect. What urban intellectuals must now do is to impose upon themselves a planetary sense of conscience that binds their loyalty to the living variety of the planet. In that act of renunciation, they may not only make their peace with the planet; they may also discover the true and essential city that now lies suffocating beneath the dead weight of megalopolis.

III

THE SUBTLE ART OF CREATIVE DISINTEGRATION

Chapter 10

When Empires Fall

The Desert Experience

> Everyone is called to be a monk today; everyone undergoes the desert experience, like it or not. The call is general. The Western world is undergoing a deep spiritual experience, and, so far, not doing too well.
>
> It is this climate of chaos, this desert scene, this time of disintegration, that can be a grace.
>
> The ancient monks who went out into the desert found just this experience. Everything they had known, believed in, had confidence in, fell apart in that wilderness. Faced with the onslaught of chaos, they were tempted to despair, for they found the faith they had was too weak to sustain so great a demonic upsurge. Yet, in their distress, they prayed for faith and faith was given them.
>
> If anything is needed in this hour, it is men who know their way around in the desert, men who can understand what is going on there, can interpret it, manage with it. To be a monk in this time, then, is really to be the man of the hour. No man in the Church is more necessary, more useful. The desert is the monk's world, and today the world is a desert.

The words are those of a Trappist monk, now living in New Guinea, with whom I have been corresponding for the past four or five years, exchanging views on the moral and spiritual turmoil of the modern world. Our letters pass back and forth at about six-month intervals. He prefers to send his by sea mail—to maintain a civilized pace to the dialogue.

The passage I quote has been haunting me since I first read it in one of his early letters. I think the insight it offers has been growing at the back of my mind all the while I have been at work on this book . . . a seed blown to me from distant parts. We have all heard the modern world referred to as a "wasteland"; in other books, I have myself made heavy use of that despairing symbol. But my Trappist friend, drawing upon a tradition far older than the anxieties of the industrial metropolis, reminds me that wastelands have, at times, been places of refuge and renewal. Or at least they can be used that way by courageous spirits, precisely because they throw us back upon the last and richest of human resources— the fertile solitude of the deep self.

For those of us who feel the inherited mass and class identities of our age crumbling away, it is indeed as if a desert gathered about us. We ask who we are, what we are, where we are to turn . . . and there is no one who can answer for us. We must make our own path. We must, and we do. In an era that has sent astronauts to scale the mountains of the moon, it is tempting to entertain Promethean images of ourselves, to see ourselves as space pioneers and star voyagers. But my letters from far-off New Guinea suggest another image that may be better suited to our condition— something humbler, more somber, yet no less heroic: that of the first desert fathers making their way beyond the walls of a failing empire, searching for their salvation in the trackless waste. "Called to be monks . . ." Or let us say, we are called to ponder the example of the monks, as we encounter our "desert experience"—losing the world to find ourselves, putting off the assigned identities of our culture in order to gain our personhood.

But there is more than a pregnant metaphor in my friend's words. Listening with my historian's ear, I hear in them also the recollection of a great communitarian adventure, one that reaches back in the Western world nearly two thousand years to another time of troubles. Then, too, a great empire had fallen on evil days, as I believe the empire of the industrial city has now. In the disorder that ensued, the monasteries were by far the most imaginative, popular response to the protracted social crisis. They spread through the countryside and dilapidating provinces, bringing cultural vitality and convivial order to a chaotic world. The achievements of that movement—its durability as an anarchist economic form, its wise eye for the spiritual needs of the person—are everything that the leadership of our very secular, very practical world forgets or ignores when it begins casting about for realistic lines of policy. And, no doubt, to most of us who look back from this historical distance, the monastic communities of Rome's imperial twilight cannot help but look quaint and exotic. Yet, each of them was the trial-and-error invention of very ordinary men and women, grappling experimentally with the dilemmas of advancing social disintegration, making do from day to day against all the odds, piecing their survival and sanity together in the midst of shameful official incompetence.

Before this century is out, I doubt that their experience will seem quite so alien to us. For, if there is any hope of saving the rights of the person and planet in the years ahead, we—by which I mean the ordinary, chronically powerless people who live in the belly of the urban-industrial leviathan—*we* are going to have to find our way back to a comparable sense of mutual aid, a comparable capacity to live self-reliantly within more local and domestic economies, a comparable appreciation of the wealth that lies in modest means and simplicity of need. We are going to have to rethink some of our most firmly held assumptions about property and privacy, security and success, recognizing that there is simply no livable future for the competitive, self-regarding, high-consumption, middle-class way of life which we have been taught to regard as the culmination of industrial progress. And we are going to have to undertake that reappraisal from the bottom up, expecting no encouragement from leaders and experts who are the chief products and principal beneficiaries of our high industrial compulsions. It will be up to us to begin coming together, talking together, working together. We are going to have to stop keeping our cares and material goods, our troubles and our talents, our wealth and our psychic wounds to ourselves and begin sharing our lives like mature, convivial animals.

But how are we to get together? In what spirit, in pursuit of what guiding vision? The modern world is littered with unhappy experiments in collectivism, large and small—failed Utopian communities, authoritarian cults, soul-destroying mass movements. Brook Farm in nineteenth-century New England was a way of getting together; it lasted five years and then the philosophers and writers who were its too-fastidious residents tired of the hard work. The totalitarian people's republics of Asia and Eastern Europe are ways of getting together; but how long would they last in the absence of nationalist propaganda and state censorship? The Manson Family, B. F. Skinner's Walden II, Huxley's Brave New World, Orwell's nightmare of 1984 . . . they are all ways of getting together. Where do we look for a model of common life and work that is competent, humane, and liberating?

The Monastic Paradigm

I think it is a kind of new monasticism we will need to carry us through the coming generation of social uncertainty and economic dislocation; I suspect that is the general style of life to which more and more people will find themselves turning spontaneously at the grass-roots level where we meet one another as friends, family, neighbors. What does such an admittedly odd conjecture call to mind, I wonder. Medieval chapels, robes and bells, hair shirts and incense? No, that is not what I mean. I will make no case here for the mortification of the flesh or the celibate life; less still is it my intention to encourage any form of sectarian retrenchment or doctrinal exclusiveness. I take it for granted that the planetary culture which it is our task to build will have to be universal and eclectic—*pan*clusive, even in its professions of faith. It can learn from the past, but it must be open to the present moment and to our species-wide experience.

I want to be careful how I develop my thoughts at this point—careful not to sound anachronistic or parochial, because the word "monastic" is hard to work with, precisely because it belongs to an ancient, well-defined tradition that has endured long enough to leave its distinctive mark on history. Let me make it clear, then, that my interest is in monasticism as a model, a tested, historical paradigm of creative social disintegration. I turn to it because it illuminates the way in which the top-heavy and toxic institutions of an exhausted empire were sifted down into civilized, durable communities where a vital, new sense of human identity and destiny could take root. The spirit in which I approach monasticism is somewhat that in which E. F. Schumacher once wrote of "Buddhist economics"—with the intention of evaluating the hidden ethical assumptions that guide our lives, and perhaps with an eye to extrapolating a viable, contemporary alternative from an old and exotic idea. But in this case, the exercise is not merely hypothetical. There *was* a monastic economics, as well as a monastic politics and sociology; the tradition is still with us, lingering at the fringes of the modern world. The achievement is a real one, there to be examined as a significant social institution which, as a matter of historical fact, managed to embody many of the values Schumacher credited theoretically to Buddhism.

I suppose it is a historian's habit, when confronted with a problem, to go rummaging about in the past for precedent and tradition. Perhaps that is the peculiar contribution I can draw from my work and training—to salvage a few of the human possibilities that existed before history making became the monopoly of industrial cities. Certainly, I take heart in knowing that a social form containing so much that our time cries out for—an economy of simple yet ingenious means, a communitarian culture of nonviolence and spiritual growth—has been tried in the past during times of extreme disorder and has worked, not as a marginal oddity, but as a cultural force that in time became so deeply implicated by its success in the political, economic, and intellectual mainstream of its society that it was constantly in danger of being co-opted and corrupted, constantly in need of being reformed.

The achievement which I would hope the monastic tradition might especially model for us is its remarkable capacity to synthesize qualities of life that have become fiercely polarized in our world. I have in mind the tragic way in which industrial society has pitted the personal against the convivial, the practical against the spiritual. As we live today, these values make war upon one another like deadly enemies. Yet, the task of saving the person and the planet demands that we make peace among them. And here we have a tradition reaching back more than a thousand and a half years in Western history which gives us reason to hope that such a harmony of opposites does exist, can be *made* to exist. Specifically, it presents us with two significant facts:

First, the tradition began in the seclusion of the private cell, in the depths of the lonely soul struggling toward personal salvation. Yet, soon enough, these solitary cells were surrounded by supportive communities which still hold their place in history as a standard for convivial sharing and principled egalitarianism.

Second, the tradition began as a desperate search for spiritual purity on the part of men and women who had abandoned the world and all concern for success, wealth, power, even bare physical survival. Yet, soon enough, these unworldly exiles had created a network of independent domestic economies that were the most stable, orderly, and productive in their society, with more than enough surplus to provide charitable care for the needy, the aged, the indigent.

In these two facts there is much to be pondered by those who assume that the need for personal solitude and spiritual growth must necessarily lead to a narcissistic dead end devoid of social conscience and historical influence. For what are we to make of the seeming paradox that people who did not put social obligation "first" or make it the monopolistic concern of their lives, nevertheless achieved one of the most culturally vital forms of egalitarian fellowship? And further: that people who did not allow practicality to dominate their lives nevertheless developed an economic style of astonishing inventiveness and productivity? I suggest that the key to the paradox lies in recognizing how much can be achieved if we once allow the social and economic necessities to become "secondary" considerations, trusting that they will draw their best motivations from a psychology of wise indirection. Then we allow other energies to rise within us—energies that are born of personal need, but which unfold naturally into the surrounding world. It is perhaps somewhat like the paradox involved in recognizing that feats of great physical exertion are often best achieved by *relaxing* into them; the muscles give up their distracting strain, the breath regains its even rhythm, and we achieve a smooth flow of easy effort. Similarly, we may become more authentically convivial, more resourcefully practical by relaxing the bullying anxieties that insist we *must* be socially engaged, and so discovering that we *need* to be, we *want* to be. *Of course,* we are social animals who must fulfill a social responsibility; *of course,* we must feed, clothe, and shelter ourselves in order to survive. But is it not possible that these things fall most gracefully into place in our lives if we do not let them become our constant obsession, but instead trust that they will emerge with just the right urgency and ingenuity from the process of self-discovery?

In the case of monastic communitarianism, we have a way of life in which, both historically and psychologically, the claims of the person have always been given an unquestioned priority. At the very outset, as people come forward to announce their vocation, each is granted a place of personal sanctuary and much time for solitary withdrawal. From the beginning and as a matter of unconditional right, there is the guarantee of absolute privacy, inviolable solitude; the disciplines of contemplation are taken up in a spirit of principled detachment from the pressures of material necessity. Yet, inevitably, both sociability and practicality come to surround the inner quest, because their sources have been tapped within the person; they grow *out* of, instead of being imposed *upon*. If the socialist and communist ideologies of our time had not opted to become so fanatically antireligious in orientation, they might have learned a great truth from the communitarian experience of the monasteries. They might have come to see conviviality, not as a difficult social duty that must be strenuously inculcated upon us as a matter of class consciousness (an approach that only produces mass movements), but as a culminating relationship between free and unique persons. They might have come to respect the existence of a personal reference which supports, but also delimits, the claims of the collective will.

At first sight, it may seem an unlikely comparison to make, but in many respects Maoist communism may be the nearest, large-scale equivalent we have in the modern world to the monastic tradition—the nearest, and yet how far off. So much that Mao wished to achieve—the social ethic of self-sacrificial service, the tight agrarian communalism, the integration of manual work and intellect, even the economic development he hoped to see spring from collectivized labor and folk technology—all this is part of monastic history. The monks also committed themselves to "going among the people," voluntarily assuming the social role of serfs and peasants; they preached and taught in their localities; they became the best farmers and craftsmen of their age, the inventors and disseminators of many new technologies. From their contemplative commitment, they reached out to share knowledge and resources with the surrounding society. They traded goods, kept school, distributed alms, transmitted the culture. Often, at their Christian finest, they sought to bring "the peace of God" to their neighbors, or at least to offer shelter from the endemic violence of the times. With the world around them, they practiced an economics of charitable sharing and hospitality that might almost be seen as the earliest anticipation of the modern welfare state. But what did this impressive range of social interaction and neighborly responsibility finally rest upon? Again, we come back to the private cell, the soul in search of personal salvation. That first of all . . . then the rest.

But with Mao's communism, every effort is made to subtract the personal and spiritual elements of the monastic tradition; the ideal is totally secularized. And then what motivation is there left to tap? We fall back upon the familiar repertory of modern political propaganda: the belligerence of patriotic pride, the appetite for vicarious collective power, competitive material standards of national production, constant agitational appeals to comradely duty that draw their force from people's guilt and fear. Finally, everything is subordinated to the collective project of building still another "Great Power" in the world, still another urban-industrial colossus, where—as now seems likely in the People's Republic—policy making after Mao will rapidly gravitate toward technocratic methods and conventional industrial values.

Admittedly, the conviviality that grows from personalist sources will never serve to build societies on such a giant scale. Its natural focus is the small community, or, at largest, an anarchist network of communities—the form which most monastic orders finally assumed as each house, having reached an optimum size, sent out its members to find new land and to make a new, small beginning. For those whose measure of "society" is pegged at the level of nation-states, social classes, mass political movements, multinational corporations, megalopolitan cities, this is bound to seem a negligible scale of human association that falls shamefully below the horizon of politically realistic discussion. But, then, my interest here is precisely in those social forms that disintegrate such bigness, seeking to replace it with socially durable, economically viable alternatives. The question I address myself to is: Where do the little people of the world turn when the big structures crumble or grow humanly intolerable? At that point, it becomes important for us to know what a political and intellectual leadership devoted to the big system orthodoxies will never tell us: that there are small alternatives that have managed to bring person and society, spiritual need and practical work together in a supportive and symbiotic relationship.

An Economics of Permanence

There is one more feature of the monastic paradigm which deserves to be mentioned—another instructive synthesis that follows from the personalist approach to the social and economic necessities. This has to do with the highly sensitive way in which the monastic economy has generally managed to balance technical innovation and ecological intelligence.

A strong argument could be made (as has been done by Lewis Mumford) that the monks played an indispensable role in laying the agricultural and technological foundations for later European industrial development. Their contribution in this respect might almost be seen as medieval Europe's "great leap forward." Many of the most hostile wilderness areas of Europe were pioneered by the monks; many of the Western world's most basic techniques and machines were either invented or perfected in the monasteries: the water mill and windmill, the animal-powered treadmill, the clock, rational accounting, new methods of farming and grazing, fulling and tanning, brewing and wine making, stockbreeding and metallurgy. These were indeed crafty and assiduous communities of work. Yet, their relations with the land remained frugal and gentle, their technology was always kept to a moderate scale. This was because the monasteries never regarded economic activity as an end in itself, never idolized productivity, never measured their success by profit or by any criterion of competitive national power. Instead, their economics sprang from a work ethic that regarded manual labor as a spiritual discipline. *Ora et labora*—and one worked as one prayed, in the pursuit of personal sanctification. In this respect, Mumford credits the monks with having found the secret of true leisure—"not as freedom *from* work . . . but as freedom *within* work; and along with that, time to converse, to ruminate, to contemplate the meaning of life."

The economic style of the monastic communities assumes that, with sufficient ingenuity and hard work, one can reach a point of balance with the land and the life upon it that will, dependably, yield enough. The challenge is to zero in upon that point of ecological "climax," to adjust and revise and reassess, to make one's way forward, not by force, but by finesse, until one arrives at what E. F. Schumacher has called "an economics of permanence." There, the community finds itself firmly centered amid a grand series of natural rhythms and cosmic reciprocities that can support it indefinitely at a moderate, but substantially secure, standard of life. It is this finely tuned steady state of existence the monks were after, where each day is much like the last—another welcome chance to stand in the presence of the ordinary and eternal splendor. Such idyllic images have doubtless always been represented in the human cultural repertory as part of an age-old Utopian yearning. What the monastic tradition contributes to that dream is the disciplined conviviality and the work ethic that can alone make Utopian gardens flourish. It offers us a philosophy of work that dignifies and democratizes labor, instead of making it a dehumanizing tyranny we would prefer to give over to machines or impose upon a subordinate class. And it adds one more vital ingredient: the inner spiritual dimension of the dream. For this is no way of life that can be evaluated by purely external criteria or achieved by purely economic means. There is an *inside* to this economics which teaches us that we cannot set our sights on material plenitude or permanence without a proper culture of the person.

One might say that the monasteries created a healthy economic style because they simply had *no* economics—not as a body of abstract theory that stood apart from the daily round of work and worship. Rather, their economics was left to take shape from the prerequisites of personal growth. This clearly did not preclude the possibility of prodigious technical innovation; a machine, a more efficient technique might still be valued as a way of relieving drudgery. But the economics of the monasteries was kept "labor-intensive" because it was clearly understood that work is a necessary attribute of the personality, while limitless affluence is not.

Out of their commitment to the sanctity of the person, monastic communities have tended to find their way to an economic order that respects the rights of the planet. As a matter of spontaneous experience, if not of doctrine, they achieve a wise and harmonious rapport with the Earth. This is most marked in the Taoist, Tantric, and Zen communities of the East, where the traditions have blended into a mature nature mysticism. But even in the West, where Christian dogma forbids the adulation of nature, the monks have generally been drawn into comradely, if not reverent, relations with the natural setting in which they make their home. The *Opus Dei* is tied to the daily and seasonal rhythms, and the manuscript illuminations done in the monasteries have always celebrated organic form. My Trappist friend in New Guinea conveys something of this sensibility in one of his letters.

If a monastery is a little world, it is a world in which matter and spirit are wed. They are not divorced. The natural setting— generally one of great loveliness—and everything put into it speak of God. The buildings, the clothes, the food, the work, the style of living. There is the relation to day and night, to the passing seasons. There is manual labor close to the Earth and to growing things, to animals. One is aware of wind and of rain, of heat, of cold. There is silence as there is sound. There is the constant reliving of the mysteries of Christ's birth and life and death and rising, contact with the whole drama of God's relation to man all through history. Most of the above picture is not Christian, of course, but simply human: men of all times and places have found the divine in the world around them.

Silence

Reading over words like these, I realize once again how vastly we distort both economics and ecology when we reduce them to matters of quantity and technique. There is always a moral and psychological dimension to be accounted for: motives, values, needs, aspirations. In the monastic paradigm, the economic tempo of life is radically different from anything we are used to in the modern world. There is less productivity, less consumption, a slower rate of innovation, a lower intensity of economic action and concern. Things move slower; they stabilize at a simpler level. But none of this is experienced as a loss or a sacrifice. Instead, it is seen as a liberation from waste and busywork, from excessive appetite and anxious competition that allows one to get on with the essential business of life, which is to work out one's salvation with diligence. And in that project, we discover things of surpassing value that will never be calibrated in the economic index.

Like silence, for example, which commands no price whatever in the market place.

I sometimes think there could be no keener criterion to measure our readiness for an economics of permanence than silence. How much do we need? How much can we use?

In the conventional economics of our society, silence, of course, had no existence at all. It is not a commodity, a utility, a resource, a service . . . except perhaps in the form of soundproofing. But I have in mind the raw, original stuff of silence, as we would know it in the state of nature. Not sound blocked out, including wind and rain and bird song, but ourselves keeping quiet, subtracting our human clamor from the world, listening.

Notice how noisy the world becomes as it is "developed." If silence is the measure of permanence, noise is surely the measure of progress. The roar of the city, the rumble of traffic and of ceaseless machinery, the thunder of aircraft overhead even in the wilderness . . . piped-in music, amplified rock concerts, transistor radios yammering away along the streets, on the beaches, in the parks. How far must we travel nowadays to escape the cacophony? Societies, as they modernize, seem to acquire an infinite tolerance for noise, if not an appetite for it . . . as if nobody dared to be caught alone in the silence.

Until very recently, there have not been many people in the industrial societies who knew what to do with silence, except to fill it up with racket. We have feared the silence because it throws us back upon ourselves—*into* ourselves. And for too many of us, that is like being pitched into a bottomless pit. It is loneliness and abandonment, it is the cold hand of the grave closing around us. "Let's have a little *life* around here," we call out in a quiet moment, knowing what the quiet represents, dreading it.

But now, remarkably, we have a growing number of people among us who know something of meditation, retreat, solitude. They begin to value silence, hunt for it, will even pay money to buy a few quiet hours away from the noise. They are an important new population . . . the quiet people. It is only people who cherish the silence of the inner life, people who will defend the silence of deserts and deep woods, who are ready for an economics of permanence. Only they will be willing to slow down, scale down, quiet down. As with all those who belong to the monastic paradigm, there must first be that much intuitive sense of an interior world waiting to be explored. There must be such a willingness to see all things for what they are worth against the silent advance of our mortality.

No economics of permanence for us, then, until we regain our love of the silence, until we win back the grace of quiet attention.

I began these reflections on the monastic tradition by quoting from one Trappist monk. I will round them off by quoting from another who is better known to the outside world: Thomas Merton, writing in the quiet of his Kentucky hermitage.

I am alien to the noises of the cities, of people, to the greed of machinery that does not sleep, the hum of power that eats up the night. . . . One who is not alone has not discovered his identity, he has to be awake and aware. But to be awake, he has to accept vulnerability and death. Not for their own sake: not out of stoicism or despair—only for the sake of the invulnerable inner reality which we cannot recognize (which we can only *be*) but to which we awaken only when we see the unreality of our vulnerable shell. The discovery of this inner self is an act and affirmation of solitude.

Simplicity and Justice

The history and culture of monasticism are neither widely nor well enough known for the tradition to be of any direct influence in our day. Nevertheless, I suspect that the synthesis it achieved of the personal and the convivial, the spiritual and the practical, the technological and the ecological is the destination toward which many counter cultural experiments are feeling their way: the shared households, the work collectives, the urban and rural homesteads, the situational networks, all the awkward and inspired forms in which we see people coming together in the hope of finding a finer, more authentic and durable way of life. Some, like the Jesus People in their communes or the disciples of the Eastern religions in their zendos, ashrams, and lamaseries, are already familiar elements of the current scene. But perhaps more widely significant is the lively, if still diffuse, dialogue on "simple living" that has sprung up in the Christian churches, mainly among restless middle-class families, and which naturally gravitates toward thoughts of banding together, sharing labor and resources, creating a useful life's work in affectionate, self-determining fellowship. In recent years, this concern for justice, ecology, and the quality of spiritual life has shown up in a number of places:

1. In the early seventies, the American Friends Service Committee brought together two programs: a macroanalysis seminar in economics designed by the Movement for a New Society in Philadelphia, and a Simple Living project created in its Northern California office. The focus of both programs is a radical critique of

the morality and ecology of the American corporate economy and its attendent standard of middle-class consumption. This joint effort has inspired numerous workshops and seminars across the country and from it has emerged an excellent handbook, *Taking Charge,* an examination of "personal and political change through simple living," which has been widely distributed by Bantam Books.

2. At about the same time (1973–74) the Shakertown Pledge was drafted by a group of clergy and lay people as a commitment to world citizenship and ecological living. The pledge has also been given wide circulation, mainly through church social action groups, and has served to draw several congregations into continuing discussion of "creative simplicity" and global justice.

3. A politically sophisticated movement of "New Evangelicals" has made its presence known through journals like *Sojourners* (Washington, D.C.) and *Radix* (Berkeley, California), and through the organization Evangelicals for Social Action. Once again, the focus of concern is "the materialism of our culture and the maldistribution of the nation's wealth and services."

In fledgling efforts like these, one finds much that has always been part of the Christian social gospel: There is the same ethical disgust with corporate corruption and profiteering, with the capitalist rat race for cash and status, with oppression in the workplace, with imperialist exploitation, racism, sexism. But the analysis has been deepened by a vivid recognition of ecological limits which calls into question the viability of urban-industrialism as a whole, not only its capitalist variation. One is forced at the outset to confront the unprecedented possibility that the empire of cities may be at an end, that we have entered a period when the cause of justice can no longer be grounded in the myth of progress, in the expectation of indefinite economic expansion, in the smug ethnocentric conviction that the modern bourgeois standard of life is indisputably right. From this planetary perspective, something more than high institutional changes in ownership, management, and planning must enter the political prospectus. Accompanying the struggle against unjust enrichment, there must be a distinctly postindustrial revisioning of what wealth and well-being mean.

The economics of limitless growth yields to the economics of permanence, and to the concern for spiritual fulfillment that rests at its core. Here, then, we may have the emergence of a vital center where many currents of change flow together: the traditional ideals of decentralist socialism, the anarchist economics of Paul Goodman, E. F. Schumacher, and Leopold Kohr, the goals of the ecological activists, and the quest for personal growth in its myriad forms.

I would like to think that there is one more factor that will make its contribution to this gathering of energies—something that has only lately appeared on the scene. This is the dialogue that is quietly making itself felt within Roman Catholic monasticism, largely under the influence of Thomas Merton's work, and, to some degree, due to the feminist concerns of women in the church, especially radical nuns. There are at least a few among the monks and the cloistered nuns who have come to see the relevance of their tradition, and of world monasticism as a whole, to the needs of the age, and who have begun to search for ways to share their experience. The conference of monks, nuns, and lay people held at Petersham, Massachusetts, in June 1977 was a sign of this ferment. The event, one in a continuing series of meetings on what Merton called the role of "contemplation in a world of action," raised the possibility of a fruitful interaction between monastic tradition and those outside the orders who are working toward a postindustrial vision of personal well-being and ecological citizenship.

Perhaps the things I mention here are no more than straws in the wind; I list them more to recommend their example than to inflate their current influence. But, in any case, some very hardheaded commercial interests seem to be charting the course of such straws. At Stanford Research Institute, one of the country's leading military-industrial think tanks, there are already opportunistic brains at work devising ways to cash in on what SRI's Business Intelligence Program interprets as a spreading public taste for "voluntary simplicity." SRI defines voluntary simplicity as "human scale, self-determination, ecological awareness, personal growth," and, most worrisome of all, "a non-consumerist lifestyle based upon being and becoming, not having"—almost exactly the economic style of the monastic paradigm.

Straws in the wind . . . signs of the times . . . I watch the experiments I see about me, I browse through the reports of publications that monitor the fertile margins and interstices (*The Mother Earth News,* the newsletter of the Institute for Local Self-reliance, *Manas, Resurgence, The Co-evolution Quarterly, Rain, The Green Revolution* . . .) and I ask: What would all the healthiest, best-conceived innovations look like if they coalesced into a new cultural synthesis? Where do the most sensitive personalist spirits seem to be tending? And the most promising aspect I see before us is a sort of freewheeling, postindustrial monasticism —communitarian forms that delicately combine the need for personal growth with an economy of simple means and fulfilling work. Again, let me emphasize that I am not thinking of monastic culture and economy as anything more than a model, a theme from the past in search of timely variations. Imagine the model, then, as I do, expanding to embrace any number of spiritual and therapeutic commitments. Think of it, especially, as a new foundation for family life, as we see it becoming in religious communities like the Bruderhofs, the Hare Krishna movement, or Yogi Bhajan's Healthy-Happy-Holy Organization, or in more secular experiments like the Synanon communities or Stephen Gaskin's Farm in Summertown, Tennessee. Imagine that it might be practiced in urban neighborhoods and warehouse communities, in condominiums and revitalized suburbs and public housing projects. Imagine that it might become the social framework for honorable small businesses, for labor-barter co-ops, for craft and professional collectives, for community development co-operatives, for workers-controlled shops and plants, and that, in these contexts, it might assimilate the most ingeniously appropriate forms of modern technology. Even if there must occasionally be robes and bells and mantras in the picture, think of them surrounded by solar collectors, pocket calculators, methane digesters, the full repertory of "people's technology" which seeks to dignify and facilitate the work of human hands, not to eliminate it as a curse.

I would not expect any one effort or sect or movement of this kind to sweep the scene in the years ahead. Rather, I suspect we will witness a proliferation of designs for shared and simplified living that may, in concert, approximate the centrifugal role once played by early monasticism. Some efforts may be as tightly structured as the regimen of a religious ashram, some may be as loose as co-operative groupings of nonresidential urban families, similar to those being organized through the Interpersonal Support Network in California. And some may take strange and dubious twists. My pacifist instincts bridle at the connection, but even the guerrilla revolutionaries of our day seem to resemble nothing so much as the warrior fraternities of the medieval past—like the Poor Knights of Christ, closely knit, ascetically stern, utterly fanatical communities of monastic comrades-in-arms, serving self-sacrificially in the cause of the Church Militant . . . only now, it would be the Church of Marx, the Church of Mao. Diverse as the efforts may be and as short-lived as many are bound to prove, they will have this much in common: They will be the work of people who recognize that we must invent a future that presents us with something more than an endless succession of problems to be solved, struggles to be waged. We need to find a way of life that is whole enough to contain crises without being consumed by them. In the midst of the countless daily emergencies and injustices that tear our attention this way and that, there must be an abidingly normal place where we can be together as our frail and unheroic selves, a place we go out from to remake society and return to in order to renew ourselves: a center, a shelter, a home that can domesticate our responsibilities to the world.

There may never be more than a minority of our society who finally achieve some promising contemporary adaptation of the monastic paradigm. But then, cultural creativity is always the province of minorities. My conviction is that those who contribute to the process of creative disintegration have diagnosed the ills of the age more keenly than the official experts or the professional planners or the heavy revolutionaries. They are in touch with something contagiously and constructively idealistic. But their impact on our future, on the tastes and values of our society, will never be adequately gauged by a mere nose-counting sociology.

Nor can they expect their efforts to be acknowledged or encouraged in the cultural mainstream, any more than we could have expected even the keenest political minds of dying Rome to recognize in their day that the next chapter in Western history would be written by the scruffy and uncivil likes of a St. Anthony, ruminating in the wilderness, working, praying, building a new society out of sweat and rubble beyond the horizons of their age.

Chapter 11

The Size of Our Lives: On the General Problem of Scale

Small Means Personal

It has been the central thesis of this book that bigness destroys the rights of the person and the planet, and that, therefore, in defending themselves against the urban-industrial dominance, both person and planet reach out toward social forms and cultural values that work to disintegrate the colossalism of our institutions. In the previous chapter, we considered the sort of grass-roots, communitarian experiments that might serve to disenthrall us from the oversized structures of our political and economic life, rather in the humane and competent way that the monasticism of the late Roman Empire helped to divert the allegiance and energy of people toward new cultural possibilities. That is one task before us which begins no further away than those we meet each day as family, friends, neighbors. But the challenge we face is not only a matter of revitalizing the convivial cell structure of society from the bottom up; there is also the task of discriminately scaling down the gargantuan institutions that surround us before they collapse of their own weight or harden under the pressure of crisis into an implacable technocratic dictatorship. The project of creative disintegration also includes salvaging what is worth saving from the overbearing industrial bigness, as we make our transition to a personalist social order.

But what does it mean to "scale down"? What are the criteria of healthy scale? Certainly we need more to guide us than a slogan like "Small is beautiful." As evocative as the phrase may be, "small," like "big," is still a quantitative and external measure; but what we are after is a change in the quality of our lives that will lead us to see the adventure of self-discovery as our paramount cultural value. We must approach the problem of scale recognizing that the opposite of big is not small, but *personal*. Therefore, no alternatives we invent to take the place of our present institutions will bind the loyalties of people unless we can be certain that small is also personal.

And that is nothing we can take for granted. Though there is, as I will observe later, a significant relationship between smallness and personhood, the connection is by no means guaranteed. We need only think of the more obvious historical examples of small societies and institutions that have been inhumanly oppressive to register this important cautionary fact. The tribal and peasant cultures of the world have been small, but for the most part they have also been severely tradition-bound, often clinging to assigned social identities with a conservatism that has stifled self-expression and originality. The city-states of the ancient world and of Renaissance Italy may also have been small societies, but their politics was as vicious as anything we have known in the modern world, and there was ample room within their walls for slavery, class injustice, the oppression of women, children, aliens, and minorities. Similarly, before America became an urban-industrial giant, it was also a small-scaled society. But the New England witch hunts were carried out in town meetings among citizens who knew one another as neighbors; and the slave economy of the American South was mainly based on small and medium-sized farms where the relations between masters and field hands might be almost intimate; but no personal recognition passed between the social ranks. We must remember, too, that much of the worst industrial exploitation has taken place in one-owner sweatshops whose technology might now be viewed as almost ideally "intermediate" and where the boss was personally on hand to drive the pace of the daily grind.

There is a tendency to regard the current interest for small-scale enterprise as a matter of "turning back the clock." Some approve of such a return to the supposedly better days of the past, and others dismiss the proposal as wishful thinking. But I would argue that, insofar as we look to the past to discover models of smallness, we will almost invariably find them entangled in cultures that provided no greater, and perhaps even less, hospitality for the rights of the person than we enjoy in our own time. That is why my use of the monastic paradigm in the last chapter was carefully selected as one of the few precedents for personalist community. Even so, it comes attached to a sectarian commitment that could find no appropriate place in a planetary culture. If our concern, then, is to achieve a personalist order of society, we are discussing a distinctly contemporary project, one that requires us to look for our resources and inspiration primarily to ourselves and to the future.

But, of course, we need not reach for the evidence of history to learn how often small can be anything but beautiful. Our own experience will do. Surely all of us have at some point in our lives belonged to clubs or political groups, worked in offices or shops which may have been small, but which were shot through with nasty intrigue and spiteful human relations. In his play *No Exit,* Jean-Paul Sartre amply demonstrates that all the miseries of eternal damnation can be experienced among three people, face to face in one room. "Hell is other people," he reminds us, and there need not be as many as three. How many marriages have become a living hell created by two?

Obviously, there is a great deal that needs to be clarified about the problem of scale. Even E. F. Schumacher, who did so much to heighten the public appreciation of small-scale operations, never seemed to get the matter sharply in focus. He brought to our attention many small efforts that have worked brilliantly at finding a solution to some technical or economic difficulty; but he left out of account the small enterprises and institutions that have been far from humane, or even minimally efficient. In one of his late essays dealing with "The Critical Question of Size," he finally declares that "right size is a difficult concept. . . . What, precisely, is the right scale I cannot say. We should experiment to find out." But he never did get around to describing what a small telephone system or irrigation network or hydroelectric project might look like.

Does opting for smallness mean the abolition of such inherently big structures? Or does it mean that, allowing them to grow to their optimum technological size, we work for their managerial decentralization among smaller, more local groups of decision makers? The latter seems, for the most part, to have been Schumacher's recommendation. "The fundamental task," he believed, "is to achieve smallness *within* large organization." But even so, once big systems have been broken down into many small units (assuming that turns out to be compatible with their continued functioning), how do we make certain that what we have will be beautiful small units, not ugly ones filled with animosity, envy, and intrigue? Or do we forget about the quality of human relations and settle for the minimal consolation that, once power has been so effectively diffused, it will at least not come to be despotically concentrated in one place? That is the traditional anarchist safeguard, but it is a purely negative justification for smallness and decentralism. If we leave the matter at that, we have dealt with the problem of power, but not with the question of personhood.

Let me offer an example that may illustrate some of these dilemmas of scale. Anyone who has spent time in a large, busy hospital knows how crushingly impersonal the treatment can be. The procedural routine and co-ordinative superstructure, the heavy reliance on overbearing medical technology may defeat the best intentions of the most concerned doctors and nurses. Amid the organizational rigidities, nobody finds much time to provide tender, loving care, and the patients are apt to get lost among the paper work. On the other hand, when we visit a single doctor in a private office, that is medicine practiced on the smallest, most intimate scale. And what does that guarantee about the human relations we will now encounter? Does it assure us of warm, sensitive, and humane treatment? Not at all. We may find ourselves being bossed about, intimidated, even humiliated by a doctor who regards his patients as incompetent children and ignorant nuisances, and who may not be able to see them as anything more than a bill-paying assemblage of symptoms. We may be on the receiving end of a medical science that conceives of us as so much unfeeling biological machinery; or we may discover that, without being asked or warned, we are serving as guinea pigs on whom our doctor has decided to test a new cure. If no one has taught doctors to experience their patients as whole persons who come to them in need of emotional support as well as medicine, or to see themselves as fallible people providing a delicate human service that is ethical and psychological as well as physical, then it does not matter how small the system becomes; it will still be callous and authoritarian in the extreme.

In the essay I have mentioned, Schumacher confesses, "I do not know how to define what, in any particular instance, is the 'human scale.' . . . there is no easy, generalized answer." But in one chapter of *Small Is Beautiful,* he does try his hand at prescribing some theoretical principles of large-scale organization. The rules he suggests are wise enough as ways of countering the tendency of big systems toward bureaucratic aggrandizement; they require a specific justification for every increase in scale and centralization, which is bound to be a healthy discipline. But, again, at the end, Schumacher hesitates, cautioning us to remember that the best principles do not come from theory, but from "observation and practical understanding"—as if he still were not certain about formulating any general rules of appropriate scale. At one point, he even warns us about the possibility of creating an "idolatry of smallness" which could mislead us as much as the prevailing "idolatry of giantism"; and in that case, "one would have to try and exercise influence in the opposite direction."

The Experience of Mystification

If smallness, then, cannot guarantee the quality of life and of human relations in any institution, it becomes futile, or at least premature, to begin developing general principles of scale. We must start somewhere else, and that can only be in the motivations and sensibilities of people. This is, after all, where "practical understanding" is grounded. The problem of scale is finally not in our institutions, but in ourselves. Or rather, it is in our institutions because it is first of all in us—in the amount of alienation, in the degree of impersonal interaction we are able to tolerate. If we ignore this basic experiential dimension of the problem, there is no hope of solving it at some higher institutional level or in the realm of pure theory.

At the level of human relations, then, what we are concerned with is not, in the first instance, the experience of size, but the experience of *mystification*. That is the heart of the matter. The greater the amount or intensity of mystification, the greater the violation of our personhood. For mystification is, essentially, an imposition of false identity. It is the act of maneuvering people into somebody else's conception of who they are, what they are, the roles they are expected to play, the feelings they must feel, the limits of ability, allegiance, personal worth they must respect. Mystification is aggression upon the spiritual autonomy of others; it is inevitably a depersonalizing assertion of hierarchical status based on the assumption that there is an authority somewhere in the world that has the right to assign and to enforce identities. This violation of personhood can take place on a vast social scale —as in the case of a governing elite imposing its privileged political position upon the subservient populace of an entire empire; or it may happen on a scale as intimate as the relations between husband and wife, parent and child. Wherever people are intimidated or manipulated into an assigned identity, they are being mystified. They are being tricked into forgettting that they are persons born to the right of self-discovery.

The possibilities of mystification are many and subtle, so subtle at times that the parties on both sides of the transaction—both the privileged top dog and the submissive underdog—may be wholly unaware of the fundamentally exploitive nature of their relationship. They may have so deeply endorsed one another's assigned identities that they cannot see beyond the one-dimensional social surface that each has become. Thus, underdogs may actually will their own subjugation, and top dogs may, in the spirit of *noblesse oblige,* take on paternalistic duties that cost them handsomely in material goods and peace of mind. There are even forms of mystification that spring from the noblest intentions, as when a dedicated revolutionary leadership seeks to raise the consciousness and strengthen the solidarity of its following. So it unfurls a ready-made, collective identity—that of the "working class," the "masses," the "people"—and with it an entire world view, an ethic, a supreme allegiance, a stereotypic character. The intention is justice and liberation; but first of all everyone must take on one face, one name, one social destiny—that of the victimized millions. And there the revolution, even after its victory, may come to a halt, officially institutionalizing that one identity in a national culture and in a political mystique that remain adamantly closed to personal recognition.

Once we focus on the process of mystification, we can more clearly recognize the danger that lies in superscale operations. The bigger the institution, the enterprise, the movement, the greater the opportunity for people to mystify one another and themselves. On this point, I would raise no question with Schumacher's contention that bigness does inevitably breed problems of alienation and oppression. There is no easy way around that fact. By definition, big institutions exist to mass-process big numbers of things and people; they are inexorably drawn toward insensitive bureaucratic procedures. They become obsessed with strict order and accounting; so there must be precise regulations and much paper work, with ornate chains of command to check and double-check everything. As those who work in the system are screened off from the results of their action, their human sympathy and ethical sensitivity are deadened; their sense of personal responsibility fades into an infinite regression of delegated authority. Bigness encourages me (even forces me) to treat you like a cipher, an inconsequential fraction of the masses I must deal with. It licenses me to impose an abstract policy upon your flesh-and-blood particularity, and then to hide from the consequences behind a wall of red tape and procedural protocol. So we become unreal to one another, mere phantoms moving through a maze of impersonal rules and statistical formulas.

All this is familiar enough. It is the commonplace, Kafkaesque nightmare of modern industrial life which fills so much of our literature and art. Thus far, history has given us no reason to hope that even in societies where the profit motive has been socialized out of existence, big industrial operations and public bureaucracies will give up their habits of massifying and classifying. So it is unquestionably right that we should learn to distrust bigness and look for alternatives. But my argument would be that, while bigness is bound to be antipersonal, smallness *may* also be. Although the small scale is *necessary* to preserving the rights of the person, in itself, it is not *sufficient*.

A Dialogue Between Persons

What more do we need? Something that can arise only from within us as the outgrowth of intimate instruction and disciplined inner development: a sense of identity which makes each of us a unique event in the universe, a once-created-never-to-be-repeated center of originality. Only such a culture of the person will teach us that we are not mere fractions of an anonymous mass whose every need and response can be collectively anticipated. From that sense of uniqueness we draw the sensitivity to detect, and the strength to resist the insistent pressures of mystification.

This, I think, is the most challenging political proposition we derive from the personalist perspective: that there is no way to build the good society from the top down, no way to mass-produce humane values from the blueprints of some grand institutional design. Rather, we are asked to see our social·life as a dialogue among persons, each of whom stands before us as, in Buber's phrase, a "treasure of eternal possibility" that waits to be unearthed. Ideally, in a proper culture of the person, that experience of radical uniqueness would be every child's birthright and would carry forward through a lifetime of free growth—out of the home and the school and into one's vocation. But that ideal is still a long way off; and in the meanwhile we are left to improvise and make do, offering every opportunity possible for people to discover their powers of initiative and creativity, their depth and strangeness. We open spaces for self-expression and participation, for solitude and retreat. We care and we counsel; we take the time and go to the trouble necessary to affirm the reality of personal experience, the sanctity of personal destiny. Institutions have their role to play in the project, but only as the enablers and releasers of an aspiration that has been raised to the level of awareness. Thus, we may look to small institutions for a significant contribution to a culture of the person. They can provide the fertile conditions of intimacy, openness, and transparency that allow personal recognition to grow among us. They can bring us face to face with one another in convivial dialogue and so give us the chance to speak and be heard in our own voice. But to know that we *have* a voice of our own—that is something we must learn outside the institutional framework, from sources that can only exist unofficially, moving elusively about and between the formal structures of society as a fluid medium of Socratic inquiry and therapeutic work. For this we turn to teachers and healers, counselors and situational companions. Here is where we acquire the surest defense of our personal rights, which is the knowledge that our identity is born from within, not imposed from outside.

I realize that such a conclusion runs the risk of sounding like a truism—that only good people can make a good society. But I mean to put a special twist on the observation, one that draws upon our distinctly contemporary recognition of the degree to which institutions, policies, programs, public authorities—all the verbal and symbolic surfaces that claim our obedience—stand before us as mystifications of social reality. Over the past century, many political and intellectual movements have contributed to this stripping away of the lies and illusions that envelop the relations of people in a cloud of false consciousness. Marxism and the left-wing ideologies have exposed the hidden class interests that manipulate the cultural superstructure of society. From Freud and the psychiatrists we have learned the strange and secret power of the unconscious over our private life and public affairs. The existentialist philosophers have taught us how cleverly people use bad faith to evade their responsibilities and obscure their true motivations. All this has brought us to a critical and uniquely decisive moment in history. Never before has social power and cultural authority been as radically and widely demystified as in the advanced industrial societies of our day. Never before has human identity been so problematical. Yes, this makes our time an "age of anxiety," and there is no guarantee that the anxiety that results from the collapse of inherited orthodoxies will not turn people ugly and drive them toward the easy security of totalitarian collectivism. But there is also the creative possibility with which this book has been concerned—that they will turn inward to discover the whole human personality which now at last stands revealed as the institutions and assigned identities that have screened it from sight begin to disintegrate.

Inward—and yet this inwardness may become a significant political direction. For as we draw into ourselves in search of solid ground, a fissure opens between us and the authorities we are expected to endorse and obey. A gap appears where there is supposed to be automatic and immediate acquiescence. And in that space an act of life-affirming rebellion breaks out. Herbert Marcuse has called it "the great refusal"—the refusal of people to will their own alienation and to serve the tyranny of the economic performance principle. It is striking that Marcuse, in his analysis of that protest, links it with the very narcissism that is so often identified as the damning vice of personal withdrawal. But Marcuse wisely recognizes that there is a mature narcissism that lies beyond "egotistic withdrawal from reality" and which "may contain the germ of a different reality principle." The myth of Narcissus, he observes, can be read as a "revolt against culture based on toil, domination, and renunciation." It can recall "the experience of a world that is not to be mastered and controlled, but to be liberated—a freedom that will release the powers of Eros now bound in the repressed and petrified forms of man and nature."

There would be little point in raising such hopeful prospects if the ethos of self-discovery were not now before us as a pervasive part of the popular culture. But that is what happens as the process of demystification surrounds our identity with a tormenting void. The therapists, gurus, counselors, psychic facilitators, consciousness impresarios, growth centers, situational networks that have become so prominent in the course of the last few decades— all these step forward to fill the vacuum created by the demystification of our inherited institutions and appointed identities. Much of what they offer as self-discovery may still be shallow and amateurish; but their efforts nevertheless represent the birth pangs of a heightened sense of personhood. The hunger for authentic identity is there, waiting to be nourished. If we allow only the most opportunistic to minister to the need, then nothing creative will come of this unique moment; it will decay into the frivolous and pathetic self-indulgence that so many cynical critics insist it must be. But that will not happen because charlatans rushed forward to exploit the occasion; it will happen because capable minds and gifted teachers who might have educated the spiritual need of their time could not recognize the search for self-knowledge when it came to them in vulgar clothes, lacking academic preparation, bookish tastes, proper intellectual tone.

The approach to the problem of scale I recommend here begins with recognizing that the choice before us is not essentially between big and small, but between a society dominated by mystification and a society open to self-discovery. Rather than brainstorming institutional blueprints, therefore, we would do better to concentrate on the living experience of personhood, searching for ways to instruct the rising ethos of self-discovery, to permeate the world around us with opportunities for significant personal growth, in the confidence that people who have become persons will pragmatically find their own way to invent institutions that bear a human face. They will insist upon their right to exercise responsibility and express their originality. They will expect a pace and rhythm of life that allows for intervals of privacy and quiet self-examination, play and free creativity. They will demand full recognition of their unique needs and special talents. These rights of the person will become as essential to the self-respect of people as the traditional civil rights; they will inspire a new style of political agitation and action; and, as they are worked into the fabric of any institution, the pattern they assume will be the human scale of things.

I grant that this is a remarkable cultural transformation to contemplate for the compulsively dynamic industrial societies of the world whose people have become so used to pouring their labor and cunning into aggressive physical action—into conquest, invention, productivity, and the willful domination of nature. Yet, in a larger, planetary perspective, such a shift of consciousness may only be the compensatory swing of a cultural and ecological cycle whose time has come round and which carries us from the outer to the inner, from the active to the contemplative, from alienation to reintegration. The general experience of this rebalancing, as it enters the lives of more and more people, may be one of relief and relaxation—the welcome end of a long, unnatural strain. In effect, it is a movement that would have us internalize the concepts of growth and development, reclaiming them from economics and making them qualities of the inner life. That is exactly what we see happening in the psychotherapeutic thought of our generation, which begins to conceive of psychic health as experiential growth just as we sight the limits of economic growth.

In the eyes of those who still champion the urban-industrial dominance—and I have no doubt about the fact that they speak for a vast public consensus—such a redisposition of attention toward the inner self is bound to seem not only unappealing, but positively threatening. It undeniably strikes at the technological and entrepreneurial dynamism which they regard as our one best hope for achieving universal freedom and decency. From their point of view, there is no way to bring a full life to every human being except to press forward unstintingly along the steep road of economic progress until we have won our way to a dependable abundance for all. No one can deny the high humanitarian intention which stands behind this vision of a world where poverty and oppression have been replaced forever by industrial plenty. But economics is a far more paradoxical science than we have cared to recognize in the past—especially when we take into account the ecological reciprocities that surround urban-industrialism. Only now do we begin to see that the very forces which have produced the astonishing middle-class affluence of the Western world—unrestrained economic growth, the unfettered ingenuity of technicians and entrepreneurs—can overshoot their promise and bring down upon us a new dark age of privation and barbarism more devastating than anything mankind has yet experienced. Having found the secret of the expanding economy, we must now learn that the drive for limitless expansion can only bring us back around full circle to the regime of scarcity.

As long as we remain locked into the orthodox urban-industrial vision of human purpose, there is no hope that poverty, and the injustice it brings with it, can be more than temporarily and partially mitigated for a fortunate nation here, a privileged class there. As long as the industrial city, with its need to dominate and exploit the Earth, holds the planet in its imperial grip, all the social evils we would reform are bound to cling on. For soon enough the resources of the planet must run short before the exorbitant demands of urban extravagance, and then even the richest societies will be faced with the threat of squalor that has driven every civilization in history toward war, slavery, imperialism, and class oppression. Until we can respect the personhood of the Earth, we will never have a world in which the personhood of all people is safe. There is no way to treat the planet and the nonhuman things upon it as our disenfranchised proletariat without perpetuating the exploited human proletariat as well. An underclass of oppressed humanity will always be there—if not within the boundaries of the rich nations, then beyond them in a hungry third world that sinks steadily toward a condition of permanent poverty as its labor and resources are drained off to feed the insatiable appetite of the advanced industrial societies.

The alternative to this grim prospect is to find a new kind of bigness in which to invest our best energies: an inner bigness that does not oppress the person or the planet, but which liberates both from the alienation and exploitation that have always dogged our hopes for progress. And that search begins in the heartland of urban-industrial culture—with those of us in the empire of cities whose habits of waste and excess are the heaviest burden the global ecology must bear. We must recognize that the rights of the person which call out in us for vindication are the beginning of an economics of permanence that can provide enough for all. It must no longer be the size of cities, of factories, of the technological apparatus or the economic product that matters most to us, but the size of our lives—of our capacity for self-understanding. What yearns to be big in us, to be vast beyond reckoning, is the adventure of self-discovery. The larger that grows, the more lightly human society will rest upon the Earth.

The Politics of Personal Growth

Much of what I have written in this book has been in the way of projecting the social transformations which personalist values demand. I have sought to draw out what is politically implicit in the project of self-discovery: a world less urbanized, less dominated by the compulsions of industrial productivity, more characterized by small-scale, localized operations, by personal and participative relationships in government and the economy. I have said enough in argument with those who fail to see this bright potentiality in the rights of the person and who call for an intensity of social engagement that would leave no space for spiritual growth. But I cannot close without directing a clear appeal to those who share my interest in championing the personalist ethos. At last, it must be plainly stated that nothing about urban-industrial society will be *automatically* changed for the better by the mere diffusion of the psychological and spiritual needs I have discussed in these pages. We may indeed see the major urban-industrial institutions falter and deteriorate as their supporting human and environmental systems erode; the Earth may finally strike them down in wrath. But that will not be a creative disintegration; it will be a global calamity in whose wake the highest promise of self-discovery will be obliterated.

If personal distress and the ecological crisis of the planet grow severe enough, they may drive whole societies into chaos; and the frenzied human response to that combination of ecospasm and psychic disorder could be some version of the totalitarian dark age which Orwell predicted in *1984*—a technocracy of the ruins, grounded in terror and political superstition. There are already enough omens of that dire possibility on the scene. We see them in the authoritarian cults to which people now turn when the agonies of identity crisis and economic insecurity grow too extreme to bear. To be stripped of one's assigned station in life can be as frightening as it is liberating; it brings a demanding freedom which does not lead everyone toward autonomous self-realization. There are those for whom the experience ends in willing submission to some form of spiritual or therapeutic fascism. Let us be frank to admit that there is a worrisome amount of this evil in our midst: phony messiahs, exploitive gurus, psychiatric entrepreneurs who pervert the susceptibilities of troubled souls in order to gain big followings, big organizations, big money. Such crimes against the human spirit are the mirror image of all the big, bullying structures of our modern world that now menace personal and planetary well-being. Where human identity is thrown into radical doubt, we walk the razor's edge between the full freedom of realized personhood and the treacherous security of a new collective enslavement.

If the ethos of self-discovery is to create a true personalist order of life, it will have to undertake the project deliberately, resourcefully, bravely. It will have to find a distinctive political style that respects its special sensibilities and yet which can summon up the power to resist, to challenge, to initiate radical change, to assume responsibility for the revolutionary implications of liberated personhood. There are not many existing political instruments that will serve that purpose; those we inherit from the past—electoral politics, parties, legislative maneuvering, conspiratorial and terrorist tactics, mass movements, propagandistic manipulation—are deeply imbued with individualist or collectivist values. They will not easily adapt to the politics of the person, nor have they much of a record for answering the needs of planetary ecology.

Thus far, the personalist instincts of the day have had limited and sporadic political impact, mainly in the form of situational groups gathering in successful protest here and there, now and then. The results have not been negligible. Significant issues have been raised by women, ethnic minorities, homosexuals, senior citizens, the handicapped—and important public battles have been won that have loosened the social system. I have even argued that there is a political relevance to experiences of self-discovery that have carried people toward private and inward explorations in the quiet interstices of the world. Unlike many impatient critics and heavy radicals, I would not be quick to condemn these seemingly apolitical interludes as narcissistic or escapist. I recognize their necessity as the seed time of a new culture. And even the loss of allegiance and energy that results from such with-drawal may do more than we realize to weaken the system and slow down its ecocidal dynamism.

But I think not enough—not in itself. That is why, at some point —and I believe the time is at hand—all of us who have been touched by the adventure of self-discovery must face our convivial responsibilities directly and steadily, perhaps even before our personal quest is complete. We must come to see that what we experience in ourselves as the emerging need of the person is the Earth's urgent cry for rescue. Our proper response to that cry is to scale down the structures and institutions which endanger the living variety of the planet: to name their evil, to resist it, to expunge it. Specifically, we must openly declare that there is no place in a world of persons for monopolistic and multinational corporations, for the maniacal middle-class religion of merchandise, for genocidal military establishments, for continued urban expansion, for state socialism, for overbearing public or private bureaucracies, for technocratic politics. The declaration must be true to our style; it must be our original way of being political—perhaps working along the lines of co-operating networks, by way of spontaneous and leaderless consensus, openly, nonviolently, by friendly persuasion and gentle strength, with every intention of winning over rather than trampling down, of recycling our institutional materials rather than simply destroying them. But the declaration must be made. For no one can go on indefinitely hiding from the crushing pressures of the urban-industrial dominance in ashrams or growth centers, lamaseries or rural communes, therapeutic workshops or monastic retreats. Sooner or later, the empire of cities will impinge upon our solitude, break through our defenses, and swallow us alive. There is no wilderness so remote, no corner of the world so private that the Earth will not be able to remind us of her sufferings by the stink in the air we breathe, the poisons in the water we drink, the haze that veils the sun and stars from our eyes—and remind us, too, of all the human miseries such ugliness implies.

As I complete these pages, I sense there are growing numbers who recognize that there must be a politics of the person. In earlier chapters and in the notes that follow, I mention the efforts I have come across that work toward that end with sensitivity and imagination—efforts that range from the French Personalist groups dating back to the 1930s down to the simple living movements in the contemporary American religious community. Beyond what such examples have to teach, I cannot say how the balance is to be struck between the privacy of the personal quest and the clamor of political action. But I know there must be such a balance. Simultaneously or sequentially, as part of some graceful pattern of life or rhythm of energies, there must be a reaching out as well as a delving within, social engagement as well as contemplative exploration. Only in this way do we lend our personhood its necessary convivial dimension and follow the adventure of self-discovery through to its planet-saving purpose.

Notes

Introduction: *Things Fall Apart*

pages xxii–xxiii

Daniel Yankelovich, *The New Morality: A Profile of American Youth in the 70s* (New York: McGraw-Hill, 1974), pp. 11, 23. Yankelovich's surveys bridge the period 1969 to 1973; his general conclusion is that "virtually every aspect of the New Values have deeply penetrated noncollege youth."

pages xxiii–xxiv

Hans Peter Dreitzel, "On the Political Meaning of Culture," in Norman Birnbaum, ed., *Beyond the Crisis* (New York: Oxford University Press, 1977), pp. 98–99.

Chapter 1: *The Rights of the Person*

page 5

Daniel Bell, *The Cultural Contradictions of Capitalism* (New York: Basic Books, 1976). See especially Chapters 1, 2, 3. I will deal further with Bell and other recent critics of the personalist ethos in Chapter 3.

pages 7–8

The sheer quantity and the tone of inquisitive maturity that characterize the growing literature on death and dying in itself indicates a remarkable shift in the public perception of human identity, one that is intimately related to the appetite for self-discovery. The change can be sampled in works like Leonard Pearson, ed., *Death and Dying: Current Issues in the Treatment of the Dying Person* (Cleveland: Case Western Reserve University, 1969); Stanislav Grof and Joan Halifax, *The Human Encounter with Death* (New York: Dutton, 1977); and in the highly popular books by Elisabeth Kübler-Ross, *On Death and Dying* (New York: Macmillan, 1970) and *Death: The Final Stage of Growth* (Englewood Cliffs, N.J.: Prentice-Hall, 1975). Also see the new journals *Death Education* and *Omega, Journal of Dying and Death. The Literature of Death and*

Dying is an annotated bibliography of works on the subject available from the Arno Press.

pages 12–13

Situational groups are best located through local resource guides like the *People's Yellow Pages,* directories which have appeared at one time or another in a number of cities, large and small: New York, San Francisco, Cambridge, New Haven, Atlanta, Phoenix, Seattle, Cleveland, Minneapolis, Durham, etc. A typical example can be ordered from the People's Yellow Pages Collective, Box 31291, San Francisco, Calif. 94131.

page 15

Russell Jacoby, *Social Amnesia* (Boston: Beacon Press, 1975), pp. 116–117.

page 16

The Association for Humanistic Psychology and its quarterly journal are reliable guides to the new therapies. The AHP can also provide an international guide to growth centers. There are a number of ready-reference handbooks: Katinka Matson, *The Psychology Today Omnibook of Personal Development* (New York: William Morrow, 1977); C. William Henderson, *Awakening: Ways of Psycho-spiritual Growth* (Englewood Cliffs, N.J.: Prentice-Hall, 1975); Nathaniel Lande, *Mindstyles/Lifestyles* (Los Angeles, Price-Stern-Sloan, 1976).

page 16

On Radical Therapy, see Jerome Agel, *The Radical Therapist* (New York: Ballantine Books, 1971), and the journal *Issues in Radical Therapy,* available from the Radical Therapy Institute, 2901 Piedmont, Berkeley, Calif. 94705.

page 20

On the helping professions, see Carl Rogers, *On Personal Power: Inner Growth and Its Revolutionary Impact* (New York: Delacorte, 1977). Also, Ray Bailey, ed., *Radical Social Work* (New York: Pantheon, 1976), which treats the various human services from a highly critical perspective.

pages 28–29

"Self beyond culture": The phrase is from Lionel Trilling's perceptive essay "Freud: Within and Beyond Culture," in *Beyond Culture*
(New York: Viking, 1965).

Chapter 2: *The Rights of the Planet*

page 37

The Club of Rome: Its major publications include D. H. Meadows
et al., *The Limits of Growth* (New York: Universe Books, 1972),
and Mihajlo Mesarovic, *Mankind at the Turning Point* (New
York: Dutton, 1974). Alvin Toffler's proposals can be found in *The
Eco-Spasm Report* (New York: Bantam Books, 1975). Buckminster Fuller's world planning efforts are headquartered at the
World Resources Inventory, Southern Illinois University, Carbon-
dale, Illinois.

page 38

For the Gaia hypothesis, see James Lovelock and Sidney Epton,
"The Quest for Gaia," *New Scientist* (London), February 6,
1975; Lynn Margulis and James Lovelock, "The Atmosphere as
Circulatory System of the Biosphere–The Gaia Hypothesis," *Co-
evolution Quarterly*, Summer 1975; and by the same authors, "Is
Mars a Spaceship, Too?" in *Natural History*, June 1976. The quota-
tions in this chapter are from the article in *New Scientist*.

page 40

The summer solstice ritual appears in Anne Kent Rush, *Moon,
Moon* (San Francisco: Moon Books, 1976), p. 384, an excellent
introduction to the Wiccan revival and feminist spirituality generally.

pages 40–41

Margot Adler, *Drawing Down the Moon: The Resurgence of Paganism in America*, to be published in 1979. This is by far
the best and most comprehensive study of neopaganism I have
seen. Two other recent works–Hans Holzer, *The New Pagans*
(Garden City, N.Y.: Doubleday, 1972), and Nat Freedland, *The
Occult Explosion* (New York: G. P. Putnam's Sons, 1972)–are
lightweight, journalistic reports. There have been a number of

ephemeral neopagan periodicals of very uneven quality, the best perhaps being the now defunct *Green Egg,* published in St. Louis by the Church of All Worlds, which described itself as "a Neopagan Earth Religion dedicated to the celebration of Life, the maximal actualization of human potential, and the realization of ultimate individual freedom and personal responsibility in harmonious, ecopsychic relationship with the total Biosphere of Holy Mother Earth." Also see the monthly journal *Gnostica,* published in St. Paul, Minnesota, and *Crystal Well,* published in Los Angeles.

page 42

William C. Gray, "Patterns of Western Magic: A Psychological Appreciation," in Charles Tart, ed., *Transpersonal Psychologies* (New York: Harper & Row, 1975), p. 436. Also well worth attention as an effort to preserve the paganism of the native American tribes is the periodical *Techqua Ikachi: Land and Life–The Traditional Viewpoint,* published by the Hopi Independent Nation, Box 174, Hotevilla, Ariz. 86030.

page 43

On feminist spirituality, see Mary Daly, *Beyond God the Father* (Boston: Beacon Press, 1973); Rosemary Radford Ruether, *New Woman/New Earth: Sexist Ideologies and Human Liberation* (New York: Seabury Press, 1975); Merlin Stone, *When God was a Woman* (New York: Dial Press, 1976); Adrienne Rich, *Of Woman Born* (New York: Norton, 1976), Chapters 1 and 2. Also see the journals *Womanspirit* (Box 263, Wolf Creek, Ore. 97497) and *Quest* (1909 Q St., Washington, D.C. 20009). Materials quoted here from the 1976 Boston festival appear in *Womanspirit,* Summer 1976. There are some critically well-balanced chapters on feminism and the Wiccan revival in Margot Adler's *Drawing Down the Moon.* One sign of the growing interest in feminist spirituality was the conference (titled "The Great Goddess Re-emerging") held at the University of California at Santa Cruz, March 31–April 2, 1978. There have long been a number of pagan and druidical sects in Great Britain; groups of a distinctly feminist type have only recently appeared, such as the women who publish the London journal *Goddess/Shrew* and the clandestine Madrian religion, which claims a few thousand members with communities in France and

Australia. On Madrianism, see the report "When Women Ruled the World" in *Isis* (Oxford), March 2, 1978.

page 43

Barbara Starret's keynote address can be found in *I Dream in Female* (Cambridge, Mass.: Cassandra Publications, 1976).

page 44

"The Dynamo and the Virgin" is Chapter 25 of Adams' autobiography *The Education of Henry Adams*. Also see Lewis Mumford's essay "Apology to Henry Adams," in Mumford's *Interpretations and Forecasts: 1922–1972* (New York: Harcourt Brace Jovanovich, 1976).

pages 44–45

". . . the spirit of the Earth . . ." The quotation is from *Womanspirit,* Summer 1976, p. 36.

page 48

Birkby and Weisman quoted in Anne Kent Rush, *Moon, Moon,* p. 340.

pages 50–53

What follows are only a few representative works in each of the categories of scientific and philosophical thought I mention. Many of these contain extensive bibliographies for further reading.

1. *Psychological-metaphysical critics:* Abraham Maslow, *The Psychology of Science* (New York: Harper & Row, 1966); Michael Polanyi, *Personal Knowledge* (University of Chicago, 1959); Arthur Koestler and J. R. Smythies, eds., *Beyond Reductionism* (London: Hutchinson, 1969), a collection of papers presented at a 1968 symposium at Alpbach, many of them by leading scientists; Seyyed Hossein Nasr, *The Encounter of Man and Nature* (London: George Allen & Unwin, 1968); Jacob Needleman, *A Sense of the Cosmos* (Garden City, N.Y.: Doubleday, 1975).

2. *Consciousness Research and Parapsychology:* Charles Tart, ed., *Transpersonal Psychologies* (New York: Harper & Row, 1975); Lawrence LeShan, *Alternate Realities* (New York: M. Evans, 1976). Also see the bimonthly *Brain-Mind Bulletin* (Box 42492, Los Angeles, Calif. 90042).

3. *Frontier physics:* The quotation from Whiteman is from John White and Stanley Krippner, eds., *Future Science: Life Energies and the Physics of Paranormal Phenomena* (Garden City, N.Y.: Doubleday, 1977), a good introductory collection that includes a listing of research centers and periodicals specializing in new paradigms and methods of scientific inquiry. Also see Fritjof Capra, *The Tao of Physics* (Berkeley: Shambala, 1975). On the recent work of Heisenberg and of Von Weizsäcker's Research Foundation for Eastern Wisdom and Western Science, see the report in William Irwin Thompson, *Passages About Earth* (New York: Harper & Row, 1974), Chapter 5.

4. *Morphic and systems science:* The term "morphic" comes from L. L. Whyte. See his scandalously neglected final book *Universe of Experience* (New York: Harper & Row, 1974). Also, Marjorie Grene, *Approaches to a Philosophical Biology* (New York: Basic Books, 1965), which contains a good introduction to the work of Adolf Portmann.

5. *Wholistic healing:* Elmer and Alyce Green, *Beyond Biofeedback* (New York: Delacorte, 1977); Kenneth Pelletier, *Mind as Healer, Mind as Slayer* (New York: Delta, 1977). Michael Murphy's Transformation Project is headquartered at 3101 Washington St., San Francisco, Calif. 94115. Also see Murphy's novel *Jacob Atabet* (Millbrae, Calif.: Celestial Arts, 1977).

6. Sir Alister Hardy's research in religious experience is reflected in his book *The Biology of God* (London: Jonathan Cape, 1975). Also see the report on his Religious Experience Research Unit in *New Scientist* (London), May 23, 1974.

7. *Anthropology and environmental science:* Ian McHarg, *Design with Nature* (Garden City, N.Y.: Doubleday, 1969); Stanley Diamond, *In Search of the Primitive* (New York: E. P. Dutton, 1974); Nancy Jack Todd, ed., *The Book of the New Alchemists* (New York: E. P. Dutton, 1977).

8. *Esoteric and occult tradition:* Ernst Lehrs, *Man or Matter* (New York: Harper & Row, 1958); Arthur M. Young, *The Reflexive Universe* (New York: Delacorte, 1976); Owen Barfield, *Saving the Appearances* (London: Faber, 1957).

page 53

Thomas Blackburn, "Sensuous-Intellectual Complementarity in Science," *Science,* June 4, 1971.

page 57

The quotation from Jeans's *The Mysterious Universe* (1930) appears as the epigraph for an intriguing collective effort by a group of scientists and philosophers to develop a mental-psychic image of nature. See E. Lester Smith, ed., *Intelligence Came First* (Wheaton, Ill.: Quest Books, 1975).

Chapter 3: *Innocence and Anarchy: The Ethics of Personhood*

page 69

The Network Against Psychiatric Assault (NAPA) is headquartered at 2150 Market St., San Francisco, Calif. 94114. Its publication is the *Madness Network News*. The Center for Independent Living is the most active and militant organization of handicapped people in the United States. It is located at 2539 Telegraph Ave., Berkeley, Calif. 94704.

page 71

See Alvin Toffler's *Future Shock* (New York: Random House, 1970) for his discussion of "adhocracy".

page 74

Philip Rieff, *The Triumph of the Therapeutic* (New York: Harper & Row, 1966).

page 75

John Passmore, *The Perfectibility of Man* (London: Duckworth, 1970).

page 75

Daniel Bell, *The Cultural Contradictions of Capitalism* (New York: Basic Books, 1976), pp. 13, 143, 245.

page 76

Russell Jacoby, *Social Amnesia* (Boston: Beacon Press, 1975), pp. 103, 105.

page 77

Christopher Lasch's essay "The Narcissist Society" appears in *The New York Review of Books*, September 30, 1976.

page 78
Daniel Bell, *The Cultural Contradictions of Capitalism*, p. 79.

pages 78–79
Robert Nisbet, *The Twilight of Authority* (New York: Oxford University Press, 1975), pp. 52, 144. Other recent works that have taken the new religions and therapies to task for their supposed lack of social relevance include Edwin Schur, *The Awareness Trap: Self-absorption Instead of Social Change* (Chicago: Quadrangle Books, 1976), which writes off the human potential movement as "a retreat into privatism" and a "new opiate of the people"; and Harvey Cox, *Turning East: The Promise and the Peril of the New Orientalism* (New York: Simon & Schuster, 1977). Cox, unlike the other critics mentioned here, has at least done his opposition the courtesy of personally sampling its techniques and teachings, rather than working from hearsay or journalistic reports. He nonetheless concludes that " 'the quest for identity' is the current code phrase for the search for self. It is still a symptom of narcissism. . . ." There is also Bryan Wilson's *Contemporary Transformations of Religion* (New York: Oxford University Press, 1976), which deals mainly with new religious movements, interpreting them one and all (on the basis of what seems to be no personal research at all) as "random anti-cultural assertions" and "a diverse set of options out."

page 79
Tom Wolfe, "The Me Decade and the Third Great Awakening," *New York*, August 23, 1976; "Getting Your Head Together," *Newsweek*, September 6, 1976.

page 80
Peter Marin, "The New Narcissism," *Harper's*, October 1975. R. D. Rosen, *Psychobabble* (New York: Atheneum, 1978). And yet, when Werner Erhard of est sought to give his organization greater social relevance by announcing a campaign against world hunger, there were radical critics who met the effort with even greater ridicule as a "dreadful joke." See the report by Alexander Cockburn and James Ridgeway in *The Village Voice*, October 10, 1977.

page 81
Also see George Leonard's reply to Gilbert's article, "Human Po-

tential and the Failure of Nerve," in the *AHP Newsletter,* August 1977.

pages 83–84
Irving Howe, "What's the Trouble?" *Dissent,* October 1971.

page 84
Emmanuel Mounier, *Be Not Afraid,* trans. Cynthia Rowland (London: Rockliff, 1951), p. 138.

pages 90–91
Lionel Trilling, "Authenticity and the Modern Unconscious," *Commentary,* September 1971.

page 92
Sigmund Freud, *Character and Culture* (New York: Collier Books, 1963), p. 303.

page 93
Abraham Maslow, *Toward a Psychology of Being,* 2nd ed. (Princeton, N.J.: D. Van Nostrand Co., 1968), p. 4.

page 94
Alan L. Mintz, "Encounter Groups and Other Panaceas," *Commentary,* July 1973. For another, even stronger critical blast at the new therapies, see Sigmund Koch, "The Image of Man in Encounter Groups," *The American Scholar,* Autumn 1973, which portrays the entire human potential movement as "a threat to human dignity" that "challenges any conception of the person that would make life worth living, in a degree far in excess of behaviorism." Oddly enough, Koch's main criticism is that the new therapies are not private *enough;* that is, instead of taking place in a private office before one professional practitioner, they make use of groups and (as Koch sees it) force an unbecoming social openness upon their members. He seems not to recognize that, in theory, the supportive group is there to invite and approve self-revelation, and so to help break through those forms of reticence that are born of guilty self-censorship. Of course, this theoretical objective can be mishandled: No therapy can guarantee wisdom or superlative ethical conduct. What are we to make of the recent revelations to the effect that a

remarkable number of male psychoanalysts use the privacy of their offices to seduce their female patients? In any case, since group therapies are sought out voluntarily and can be broken off at any point along the way, Koch leaves unanswered the obvious question: Why have they become so popular? What does that fact tell us about the needs of the times? Moreover, like many other critics, Koch creates the impression that the human potential movement is a finished and permanent body of theory and practice closed to criticism and change. Which is exactly wrong. If anything, this so-called movement is still so fluid, innovative, and effervescent as to be nearly shapeless—and it remains far more susceptible to criticism and internal reformation than any other therapeutic style. It is wholly without orthodoxies and has resisted any kind of professional policing. It should be noted that Koch's attack was, in its original form, carried in the *Journal of Humanistic Psychology*.

page 98
Mary Daly, *Beyond God the Father: Toward a Philosophy of Women's Liberation* (Boston: Beacon Press, 1973), p. 24.

Chapter 4: *The Third Tradition*

page 102
The Chinese student song appears in *Resurgence* (London), July–August 1974, p. 9.

page 107
George Leonard, *The Ultimate Athlete* (New York: Viking, 1975), is the best introduction to noncompetitive, contemplative athletics and exercise. Also see Andrew Fluegelman, ed., *The New Games: Play Hard, Play Fair, Nobody Hurt* (Garden City, N.Y.: Doubleday-Dolphin, 1976).

page 110
Robert Heilbroner, *Business Civilization in Decline* (New York: W. W. Norton, 1976), pp. 122–24.

page 111
Marshall Berman, *The Politics of Authenticity: Radical Individu-*

alism and the Emergence of Modern Society (New York: Atheneum, 1970), p. x.

page 123

Nietzsche quoted in Walter Kaufmann, *Nietzsche* (New York: Meridian Books, 1956), p. 149.

page 124

Mounier's writing can be sampled in three English translations: *Be Not Afraid: Studies in Personalist Sociology* (London: Rockliff, 1951), *The Character of Man* (London: Rockliff, 1956), both translated by Cynthia Rowland, and *Personalism*, trans. Philip Mairet (New York: Grove Press, 1952). For a general survey of personalist thought, see J. B. Coates, *The Crisis of the Human Person* (London: Longmans, Green & Co., 1949). Other works that serve as helpful introductions to personalist philosophy and politics are Martin Buber, *Paths in Utopia* (Boston: Beacon Press, 1958); almost anything by Lewis Mumford, but especially his *Conduct of Life* (New York: Harvest Books, 1951); David L. Norton, *Personal Destinies: A Philosophy of Ethical Individualism* (Princeton: Princeton University Press, 1976); and Marshall Berman's study, mentioned above.

Chapter 6: *Home: In Search of a Practical Sacrament*

The books I have found useful as background reading on marriage, divorce, and family are Edward Shorter, *The Making of the Modern Family* (New York: Basic Books, 1975); Philip Slater, *Footholds: Understanding the Shifting Sexual and Family Tension in Our Culture* (New York: Dutton, 1977); Louise Kapp Howe, ed., *The Future of the Family* (New York: Simon & Schuster, 1972); Hyman Rodman, ed., *Marriage, Family, and Society* (New York: Random House, 1967). The biweekly newsletter *Marriage and Divorce Today* surveys current literature, gives statistics, and provides facts and ideas for counselors.

page 141

Among the book titles I have come across that seem to promise bright possibilities for the divorced are *Creative Divorce; Divorce:*

Chance of a New Lifetime; Divorce: The Gateway to Self-realization; Divorce: The New Freedom.

page 143

On the impact of industrialism on the family, see Shorter, *The Making of the Modern Family*, and David Levine, *Family Formation in an Age of Nascent Capitalism* (New York: Academic Press, 1977).

page 145

Kirk Jeffrey, "The Family as Utopian Retreat from the City," in Sallie Teselle, ed., *The Family, Communes, and Utopian Societies* (New York: Harper Torchbooks, 1972).

page 148

For a perceptive analysis of Victorian family life, see Ronald Sampson, *The Psychology of Power* (New York: Vintage Books, 1968).

pages 149–50

Laing, "The Mystification of Experience," in *The Politics of Experience* (London: Penguin Books, 1967), p. 55. Also see his *Politics of the Family* (New York: Pantheon, 1971), and the work of Laing's colleague David Cooper, *The Death of the Family* (New York: Vintage Books, 1971). Cooper describes the "normal" middle-class family as "the ultimate and most lethal gas chamber in our society."

page 152

Shulamith Firestone, *The Dialectic of Sex* (New York: Bantam Books, 1970).

page 152

On communitarian experiments of the sixties and seventies, see Rosabeth Kanter, *Communes* (New York: Harper & Row, 1973); Laurence Veysey, *The Communal Experience* (New York: Harper & Row, 1973); Judson Jerome, *Families of Eden* (New York: Seabury Press, 1974).

page 155

On Delancey Street, see Charles Hampden-Turner, *Sane Asylum* (San Francisco: San Francisco Book Company, 1976). On Synanon, see Lewis Yablonsky, *Synanon: The Tunnel Back* (New York: Macmillan, 1965). More recent materials on Synanon (articles, statistics, research) are available from Box 786, Tomales Bay, Marshall, Calif. 94940.

page 157

On recent religious communities, see Robert Ellwood, *One Way: The Jesus Movement and Its Meaning* (Englewood Cliffs, N.J.: Prentice-Hall, 1973); Stillson Judah, *Hare Krishna and the Counter Culture* (New York: Wiley, 1974). There are articles on 3HO and the Hare Krishna movement in Charles Glock and Robert Bellah, eds., *The New Religious Consciousness* (Berkeley: University of California Press, 1976). Information on the large and highly successful commune Sunburst Farm is available from 808 East Cota St., Santa Barbara, Calif. 93103.

page 160

On Lanza del Vasto's work, see *Return to the Source* (New York: Schocken, 1972). The Community of the Ark has a discontinuous history dating back to 1948. It now numbers fewer than two hundred people living on some two thousand acres near Montpelier, France. The political arm of the Community is *Action Civique Non-violente,* the major Gandhian pacifist organization in Western Europe. Koinonia has also always been a small community, often numbering fewer than fifty people, but its influence and good works (especially in race relations) have spread far and have allowed it to survive and (within recent years) to prosper. It now administers a Fund for Humanity, financed from contributions and from the profits drawn from its fourteen-hundred-acre farm, which distributes grants to poor communities in America and overseas. See Dallas Lee, *The Cotton Patch Evidence* (New York: Harper & Row, 1971), which takes the story of Koinonia up to the death of Clarence Jordan; and "Koinonia Updated," *The Christian Century,* October 13, 1976.

page 160

On Steven Gaskin's Farm, see John Rothchild, "American Communes: Voluntary Maoism," *The Washington Monthly,* June 1975. Other materials are available from Plenty, Box 156, Summertown, Tenn. 38483. On the Bruderhof, see Benjamin Zablocki, *The Joyful*

Community (Baltimore: Pelican Books, 1971). Bruderhof information and publications are available from The Plough Publishing House, Rifton, N.Y. 12471. Information about Auroville can be obtained from the Sri Aurobindo Center at Matagiri, Mt. Tremper, N.Y. 12457.

page 168
R. D. Laing, *Knots* (New York: Pantheon, 1970).

pages 174–75
Ralph Borsodi, *Flight from the City: An Experiment in Creative Living on the Land* (New York: Harper Colophon Books, 1972), p. 17.

Chapter 7: *School: Letting Go, Letting Grow*

Most of the authors I have drawn upon here are mentioned in the chapter; their writing is readily available. Other books I have found helpful are: Michael Rossman, *On Learning and Social Change* (New York: Random House, 1972); John L. Hodge et al., *The Cultural Bases of Racism and Group Oppression* (Berkeley: Two Riders Press, 1975); Colin Greer, *The Great School Legend* (New York: Viking Compass Books, 1972); Joel Spring, *A Primer of Libertarian Education* (New York: Free Life Editions, 1975). A good periodical dealing with free schooling and deschooling is the *New School of Education Journal,* published by the New School of Education at the University of California, Berkeley. The National Humanistic Education Center, 110 Spring St., Saratoga Springs, N.Y. 12866, is a helpful source of information.

page 190
Ivan Illich, *De-schooling Society* (New York: Harper & Row, 1972). John Holt's latest book is *Instead of Education* (New York: Dutton, 1976). Also see his new journal *Growing Without Schooling,* published by Holt Associates, 308 Boylston St., Boston, Mass. 02116.

page 191
Paolo Freire, *Pedagogy of the Oppressed* (New York: Herder and Herder, 1970); Jonathan Kozol, *Death at an Early Age* (Boston:

Houghton Mifflin, 1967), and *Free Schools* (Boston: Houghton Mifflin, 1972).

page 192

"The right to return to one's education" was a major recommendation of the National Commission on the Reform of Secondary Education in its Kettering Foundation Report in 1974. The report referred to this as "recurrent education" which, it suggested, should follow a compulsory period limited to the first eight years of school.

page 193

As I draw up this list, it occurs to me that there seem to be very few women among the free-schoolers and experimental educators. Or at least there are very few of them (beyond Maria Montessori) who have written books or given their names to the cause. Yet, the classrooms of the world have long been one of women's major professional provinces. What explains their absence among the voices of radical discontent?

page 194

Tolstoi, *Tolstoy on Education,* trans. Leo Wiener (Chicago: University of Chicago Press, 1967), pp. 111, 114. An excellent collection of essays.

page 195

George Leonard, *Education and Ecstasy* (New York: Delacorte, 1968); George Isaac Brown, ed., *The Live Class Room: Innovation Through Confluent Education and Gestalt* (New York: Viking, 1975).

Chapter 8: *Work: The Right to Right Livelihood*

The books I have drawn upon in preparing this chapter include the following: Folkert Wilken, *The Liberation of Work* (London: Routledge & Kegan Paul, 1969), and David Jenkins, *Job Power* (Garden City, N.Y.: Doubleday, 1973), which survey experiments in workers' control in America and Europe. Laile Bartlett, *New Work/New Life* (New York: Harper & Row, 1976), reports on new forms of self-management in the United States and offers a helpful resource kit of "networks" dealing in work reform. Fred Blum, *Work and Community* (London: Routledge & Kegan Paul, 1968), is a study of the Scott-Bader Commonwealth, one of the long-standing British experiments in industrial democracy. Clare Huchet Bishop, *All Things Common* (New York: Harper & Row, 1950), deals with the postwar French communities of work, especially Boimondau. David and Elena French, *Working Communally* (New York: Russell Sage Foundation, 1975), is a perceptive critique of contemporary collectives and communes, especially with respect to their need to create viable, communal workplaces. I have also found the following helpful: Ivan Illich, *Tools for Conviviality* (New York: Harper & Row, 1973); Studs Terkel, *Working* (New York: Pantheon, 1974); Stanley Aronowitz, *False Promises: The Shaping of the American Working-class Consciousness* (New York: McGraw-Hill, 1973), the last for its shrewd criticism of organized labor's failure to take industrial democracy as a serious social goal. Louis Davis et al., eds., *The Quality of Working Life* (New York: Free Press, 1974), is a good introductory collection of papers dealing with contemporary reforms of work.

page 212

Among the major centers of job-enrichment research are the Center for the Quality of Working Life at the Institute for Industrial Relations, University of California at Los Angeles, the Quality of Work Program at the University of Michigan, and the Work in America Institute in New York City. The Tavistock Institute of Human Relations in London has also issued a large body of literature dealing with the reform of working life. The Ford Foundation has financed a deal of job-enrichment programs. See its *Newsletter* for September 1, 1975.

page 213

Marx, from the *Economic and Philosophical Manuscripts,* in Karl Marx, *Early Writings,* trans. and ed. T. B. Bottomore (New York: McGraw-Hill, 1964), pp. 124–25.

page 217

The declining morale of the American work force, as measured by absenteeism, unruliness in the workplace, and high rates of job turnover, has become an especially urgent problem among young workers who took jobs during the late sixties and early seventies. For example, absenteeism in the auto industry rose 100 per cent from 1962 to 1972, mainly due to discontent among workers under thirty years old, and primarily among those with some college education. See Neal Q. Herrick, "Who's Unhappy at Work and Why," *Manpower,* January 1972, pp. 3–7. Among steelworkers, "disciplines" issued for absenteeism and general recalcitrance on the job rose from a few hundred in 1965 to 3,400 in the early seventies, again, mainly due to "the rebellion of young workers." See Bill Smoot, "Life on the Job," *The Nation,* July 23, 1977. Some rebel on the assembly line; others simply drop out of the work force. *Business Week* (November 14, 1977, pp. 156–66) reports a dramatic increase in nonworking males from 1966 to 1976, largely made up of young men who will not accept boring work, but prefer to live on welfare or their wives' earnings. One aspect of the problem is the increased number of college graduates in the United States. The Department of Labor estimates that there are 18 million graduates in the country, as of the mid-seventies, but only 14 million jobs that require a college education.

page 218
Daniel Yankelovich, *The New Morality: A Profile of American Youth in the Seventies* (New York: McGraw-Hill, 1974), p. 29.

pages 226–27
Blake, "Jerusalem," in *Complete Writings,* ed. Geoffrey Keynes (New York: Oxford University Press, 1969), p. 700.

page 228
For a persuasive revision of the standard interpretation of the Luddites, see E. P. Thompson, *The Making of the English Working Class* (New York: Vintage Books, 1966). Far from regarding Luddism as a riotous outburst of machine-wrecking, Thompson argues that the movement was a well-conceived and disciplined demand for an industrial democracy that would respect traditional patterns of working-class life and culture, a goal that was never fully integrated into the program of organized trade-unionism. This failure of the unions is a central concern of Herbert Gutman in his study *Work, Culture and Society in Industrializing America* (New York: Alfred A. Knopf, 1977).

page 240

The following are resource groups that can provide useful information on self-management and libertarian work forms: People for Self-management, Box 802, Ithaca, N.Y. 14850; Community Service, Inc., Box 243, Yellow Springs, Ohio 45387; International Group Plans, Suite 607, 2100 M St. N.W., Washington, D.C. 20063, a crusading experiment in workers' control; Vocations for Social Change, 5951 Canning, Oakland, Calif. 94609; Vocations for Social Change, 353 Broadway, Cambridge, Mass. 02139; Center for Community Economic Development, 1878 Massachusetts Ave., Cambridge, Mass. 02140. Jeremy Rifkin, *Own Your Own Job* (New York: Bantam Books, 1977), is a good handbook on "economic democracy for working Americans."

Chapter 9: *In the Empire of Cities*

More than from any other single source, this chapter draws its values from Lewis Mumford's many writings on the history and culture of cities. I also lean heavily on Murray Bookchin's excellent little book *The Limits of the City* (New York: Harper Colophon Books, 1974), a work that is required reading for anyone dealing with urban problems.

page 247

C. A. Doxiadis, *The Great Urban Crimes We Permit by Law* (Athens, Greece: Lycabuttus Press, 1973), p. 24. Also see his *Ekistics: An Introduction to the Science of Human Settlements* (New York: Oxford University Press, 1968).

page 248

James Sundquist, *Dispersing Population: What America Can Learn from Europe* (Washington, D.C.: Brookings Institute, 1975). Typically, there is no mention in this study of the possibility of diminishing the urban population by allowing people to return to rural or small-town communities. The only option Sundquist believes "America can learn from Europe" seems to be that of rearranging urban people in more industrially efficient agglomerations.

pages 248–49

For a critical approach to the financial, political, and psychic liabilities of hyper-urbanization, see E. F. Schumacher, "No Future for Megalopolis" and "City Patterns" in *Resurgence* (London), January–February 1975 and May–June 1977 respectively; Ursula Hicks, *The Large City: A World Problem* (London: Macmillan, 1974); Kenneth E. F. Watt, "The Costs of Urbanization," *The Ecologist* (London), February 1972; Kingsley Davis, "Urbanization of the Human Population," in *Cities* (A Scientific American Book, 1965). There are two good chapters on "the external diseconomies of built-up areas" in E. J. Mishan, *The Costs of Economic Growth* (London: Pelican Books, 1967). Also see Arthur Morgan, "The Birth and Death of Human Cultures," *Manas*, March 12 and 19, 1975.

page 256
The FCEQ poll is reported in the New York *Times*, February 26, 1974, p. 17.

page 257
On the negative social and economic effects of intensive urbanization in underdeveloped countries, see Richard Critchfield, "Explosive Third World Cities," *The Nation*, June 26, 1976.

page 257
Colin Norman, *Soft Technologies, Hard Choices,* a report issued by the Worldwatch Institute, Washington, D.C., 1978.

page 259
Paolo Soleri, *Arcology: The City in the Image of Man* (Cambridge, Mass.: Massachusetts Institute of Technology Press, 1969). Gerard O'Neill's proposals for space colonization can be found in his interview with the *Co-evolution Quarterly* for Spring 1976 and in his book *The High Frontier: Human Colonies in Space* (New York: William Morrow, 1976). Nigel Calder's prospect of iceberg cities is reported in the *Herald-Tribune* (International Edition) for August 11, 1970.

page 261
The statistics on urbanization are from Charles Abrams, "The Uses of Land in Cities," *Scientific American*, September 1965. The statistics for landownership are from the useful pamphlet by Peter

Barnes and Larry Casalino, "Who Owns the Land?" published by
the Center for Rural Studies in San Francisco. Also see Barnes' book
The People's Land (Emmaus, Pa.: Rodale, 1975).

page 263

For a survey of the effects of urban expansion upon land use, see
David Pimental et al., "Land Degradation: Effects on Food and Energy Resources," *Science,* October 8, 1976.

page 264

On the intensive use of petrochemical fertilizers in American farm-
ing, see Barry Commoner, *The Closing Circle* (New York: Alfred
A. Knopf, 1971), especially Chapter 9. Also see L. S. Stavrianos,
The Promise of the Coming Dark Age (San Francisco: W. H.
Freeman, 1976), pp. 33–41.

page 264

On the detrimental social effects of "Green Revolution" agricultural
technology and on the politics underlying the adoption of superscale
farming, see Frances Moore Lappé and Joseph Collins, *Food First:
Beyond the Myth of Scarcity* (Boston: Houghton Mifflin, 1977).
The authors' argument is that large-scale landholding keeps arable
land out of cultivation for selfish, speculative purposes, or uses the
land to raise wasteful exports for the benefit of affluent nations. For
some facts and figures that show how large-scale landownership
works to sabotage agricultural productivity in America, see Ronald
Taylor, "The Tax-Shelter Farmers," *The Nation,* May 14, 1977.

pages 265–66

The Civic Trust of Great Britain has issued an appeal to the government to bring this derelict land under cultivation as a prime means
of urban revitalization. See *The Times* (London), June 21, 1978,
p. 1.

page 266

The statistics on wartime victory gardening are from the annual reports of the U. S. Department of Agriculture for the war years. Also
see *Business Week,* May 24, 1947, p. 21.

page 270

For information regarding the new land reform movement, contact the National Coalition for Land Reform, 345 Franklin St., San Francisco, Calif. 94102, or the Center for Rural Studies, 1095 Market St., San Francisco, Calif. 94103. The Institute for Community Economics, 639 Massachusetts Ave., Cambridge, Mass. 02139, provides materials on land trusting, a means of withdrawing land from the real estate market for small-scale agricultural use. (Prior to 1968, ICE was known as the International Independence Institute.)

page 270

Since 1975, Senator James Abourezk has had a land reform bill bottled up in committee in the U. S. Senate. It is S. 840, "The Family Farm Antitrust Bill." It would forbid any person or corporation holding nonfarming assets in excess of $3 million to engage in farming. This would require all land held by agrindustrial combines and conglomerates to be sold off to small farmers through the Farmers Home Administration. The bill could serve as a focus for the land reform campaign.

page 270

For materials on urban farming, contact the Institute for Local Self-reliance, 1717 Eighteenth St. N.W., Washington, D.C. 20009, and the Farallones Institute, 1516 Fifth St., Berkeley, Calif. 94701. Also see the article by Roger Williams, "The New Urban Pioneers: Homesteading in the Slums," *Saturday Review*, July 23, 1977. Efforts of this kind at do-it-yourself urban rehabilitation could easily be designed to include extensive horticulture and husbandry. Another approach to acquainting urbanites with the skills of farming is that of the London-based organization Working Weekends on Organic Farms. WWOOF organizes weekend outings for city dwellers at its two-hundred-acre biodynamic farm outside the city. Contact WWOOF, 143 Sabine Rd., London S.W. 11.

pages 276–77

Eric R. Wolf, *Peasant Wars of the Twentieth Century* (New York: Harper & Row, 1969), pp. 294–95. Wolf agrees with the standard Marxist contention that "peasants without outside leadership cannot make a revolution." The reason for this is that they stop short of the cities and "lack acquaintance with the operation of the state as a complex machinery, experiencing it only as a 'cold monster.' " In short, it would seem that their values are too revolutionary to make any revolutionary difference. Another study of peasant revolutions (which, again, sees them as "archaic forms of social movement") is E. J. Hobsbawm, *Primitive Rebels* (New York: W. W. Norton, 1965).

Chapter 10: *When Empires Fall*

pages 293–94

Mumford, *The Pentagon of Power* (New York: Harcourt Brace Jovanovich, 1970), p. 138. On the monastic work ethic and its contribution to Western economic history, see Mumford, *The City in History* (New York: Harcourt, Brace & World, 1961), pp. 243–48, 253–61, and *The Myth of the Machine* (New York: Harcourt, Brace & World, 1967), Chapter 12.

page 294

E. F. Schumacher, "Peace and Permanence," in *Small Is Beautiful* (New York: Harper & Row, 1973).

pages 297–98

Thomas Merton, "Rain and the Rhinoceros," in *Raids on the Unspeakable* (New York: New Directions, 1965). For a perceptive study of Merton's Christian personalism, see Raymond Bailey, *Thomas Merton on Mysticism* (Garden City, N.Y.: Doubleday, 1975). Henri J. M. Nouwen, *The Genesee Diary* (Garden City, N.Y.: Doubleday, 1976), offers a day-by-day account of life in a Trappist monastery.

page 299

Taking Charge (New York: Bantam Books, 1977) is made up of study and discussion papers assembled by the Simple Living Collective of the American Friends Service Committee in San Francisco.

page 299

On the Movement for a New Society, see Susanne Gowan et al., *Moving Toward a New Society* (Philadelphia: New Society Press,

4722 Baltimore Ave., Philadelphia, Pa. 19143). The Shakertown Pledge and a program developed from its principles can be found in Adam D. Finnerty, *No More Plastic Jesus* (New York: Dutton, 1978). The Shakertown Pledge Group publishes the newsletter *Creative Simplicity,* available from West Forty-fourth and York South, Minneapolis, Minn. 55410.

On the New Evangelicals, see James Wallace, *Agenda for Biblical People* (New York: Harper & Row, 1976); Wallace is editor of *Sojourners.* Also, Richard Quebedeaux, *The Worldly Evangelicals* (New York: Harper & Row, 1978).

page 300

On the Petersham conference, see Basil Pennington, "Spirituality for a World Culture," *America,* September 3, 1977, and Brother David Steindl-Rast and Ram Dass, "On Lay Monasticism," *Journal of Transpersonal Psychology,* Vol. 9, No. 2 (1977). The most penetrating discussion of monasticism in our time I have come upon is Thomas Merton, *Contemplation in a World of Action* (Garden City, N.Y.: Doubleday, 1971).

page 300

For the Stanford Research Institute report on voluntary simplicity, see *Co-evolution Quarterly,* Summer 1977, pp. 4–19. Also see the useful handbook by the Simple Lifestyle Team of the Center for Science in the Public Interest, *99 Ways to a Simple Lifestyle* (Garden City, N.Y.: Doubleday, 1977).

page 302

The Interpersonal Support Network describes itself as "a rapidly expanding global community of self-governing intentional families creating a continuing, supportive environment within which human beings can experience friendship, joy, and personal growth." For information, contact ISN, Box 2731, San Francisco, Calif. 94126.

Chapter 11: *The Size of Our Lives: On the General Problem of Scale*

page 307

E. F. Schumacher, "On the Critical Question of Size," *Resurgence* (London), May–June 1975.

page 309

Schumacher's other main essays on the problem of scale appear in *Small Is Beautiful:* "A Question of Size" and "Towards a Theory of Large-scale Organization."

page 314

Herbert Marcuse, *Eros and Civilization* (New York: Vintage Books, 1962), p. 149.

The notes for previous chapters mention several organizations that are paying significant attention to problems of scale: Community Service, Inc.; People for Self-management; Center for Community Economic Development; Institute for Local Self-reliance; the Farallones Institute; Institute for Community Economics; The Shakertown Pledge Group; Movement for a New Society. (Addresses are given above.) All these seem to be working resourcefully toward a new quality of life that is personal and democratic. To their number, I would add: The New Alchemy Institute, Box 432, Woods Hole, Mass. 02543 (see the recent publication *The Book of the New Alchemists* [New York: Dutton, 1977], which is a handy compendium of the institute's ecological innovations); the Briarpatch Network, 540 Santa Cruz Ave., Menlo Park, Calif. 94025; the National Center for Appropriate Technology, Box 3838, Butte, Mont. 59701; the Intermediate Technology Development Group Ltd., 9 King St., London, WC2, England; Centre for Alternative Technology, Powys, Wales; the Office of Appropriate Technology of the State of California, 1530 Tenth St., Sacramento, Calif. 95814; The School for Living and the True Price Collective, Box 3233, York, Penn. 17402; the Aquarian Research Foundation, 5620 Morton St., Philadelphia, Penn. 19144; Intermediate Technology, 556 Santa Cruz Ave., Menlo Park, Calif. 94025; Institute for Food and Development Policy, 2588 Mission St., San Francisco, Calif. 94110; the Human Dimensions Center, Rensselaer Polytechnic Institute, Rensselaerville, N.Y. 12147, which publishes the journal *Alternative Futures*.

One of the most imaginative efforts to give mainstream political organization to the personalist and ecological values with which this book has been concerned is Self-Determination: A Personal-Political Network in Northern California, Box 126, Santa Clara, Calif. 95052. The Network was launched in 1974 largely through the efforts of Assemblyman John Vasconcellos with a view to applying the best insights of humanistic and human potential therapies to public policy.

The publications I have found most useful in my thinking about scaling down, decentralizing, and personalizing the urban-industrial leviathan include: *Co-evolution Quarterly, The Mother Earth News, Green Revolution, Working Papers, Manas* (Box 32112, El Sereno Station, Los Angeles, Calif. 90032), *Rain* (2270 N.W. Irving, Portland, Ore. 97210), *The North Country Star* (Box 24081, Oakland, Calif. 94623), *The Environmental Action Reprint Service* (2239 E. Colfax, Denver, Colo. 80206), *Simple Living* (514 Bryant St., Palo Alto, Calif. 94302). *The Ecologist, Mazingira* (put out by the United Nations Environment Program), *Natural Energy and Living,* and, especially, *Resurgence,* all published in England, are also excellent.

ABOUT THE AUTHOR

THEODORE ROSZAK was born in 1933 in Chicago. He graduated from UCLA and received his Ph.D. in history from Princeton. He is Professor of History and Chairman of General Studies at California State University, Hayward. He has twice been nominated for the National Book Award (for *The Making of a Counter Culture* and *Where the Wasteland Ends*) and was a Guggenheim Fellow in 1971–72.